FRENCH FOOD

FRENCH FOOD

ON THE TABLE, ON THE PAGE,

AND IN FRENCH CULTURE

EDITED BY

LAWRENCE R. SCHEHR

AND

ALLEN S. WEISS

ROUTLEDGE

NEW YORK   LONDON

Published in 2001 by
Routledge
29 West 35th Street
New York, New York 10001

Published in Great Britain by
Routledge
11 New Fetter Lane
London EC4P 4EE

Routledge is an imprint of the Taylor & Francis Group.

Printed in the United States of America on acid-free paper.

10 9 8 7 6 5 4 3 2 1

Priscilla P. Ferguson, "A Cultural Field in the Making: Gastronomy in Nineteenth-Century France"
originally appeared in *American Journal of Sociology* 104:3 (1998): 597–641. Permission from the
University of Chicago Press to reprint is gratefully acknowledged.

Library of Congress Cataloging-in-Publication Data

French food: on the table, on the page, and in French culture / edited by Lawrence R. Schehr and
Allen S. Weiss.
    p. cm.
  Includes bibliographical references and index.
  ISBN 0–415–93627–6 — ISBN 0–415–93628–4 (pbk.)
   1. Gastronomy. 2. Cookery, French. I. Schehr, Lawrence R. II. Weiss, Allen S., 1953–
TX637.F69 2001
  641'.01'3—dc21

00–068434

CONTENTS

INTRODUCTION
Hors d'Oeuvres

LAWRENCE R. SCHEHR AND ALLEN S. WEISS

Eating a French meal implies much more than filling a physical need. It partakes of a logic and order considered to be typically French. It implicates the eater in a set of intersecting histories—culinary, local, national, intercultural, symbolic—that mark a dish and a series of dishes, be it a wonderful three-star meal or a modest hamburger and French fries bought on the run between a purchase at the FNAC and a rendezvous in a café. The modest potato was discovered, as we all know, in the new world, imported through an economy of empire-building and colonialism, and eventually integrated into French cooking. It was then adapted by the Americans as their own, only to be shipped back to France in the expansion of the United States's own empire-building and techno-ideological colonialism in the falsely innocuous form of fast food.

Consider a fancier dinner. In the codification of classic French cuisine, each dish has a formal name, with a set group of garnishes and the right sauce encrypted in the name of the dish. A formal dinner or a classic menu is both a parade of dishes and an instantiation of a culinary theory, each of which has historical connotations, be it the name of the garnish or the historic reference to its creation. Somewhere in between, in the cooking of the various regions and in *la cuisine bourgeoise*, dishes have long-standing traditions, rooted in country and city, anchored by the past, by folklore, by generations of women passing along women's knowledge, outside the official encyclopedic routes of men, yet somehow still related to official discourse.

Cuisine is grounded in a primal act of sustenance, and culinary style is based on certain basic foodstuffs and ingredients that make up a palette of

1

"Frenchness" for all to taste. For the author of one international cookbook, the French palette includes butter, thyme, tarragon, cheeses, and so forth. And then there is wine. Whether it is the *gros rouge qui tache*, *piquette*, a vintage Bordeaux, or an effervescent Champagne, when French food speaks, it is rounded out, complemented, and mysteriously ennobled by the wine that accompanies it. To write about French food means engaging wine as well, in a discourse that is equally complicated, and that has to correspond to what our sensory system feels but for which it has no names.

Today, the cross-cultural aspects of French food are even more apparent in the wake of the *nouvelle cuisine*, the introduction of fusion cuisine (though not under that name), the ethnic restaurants in every neighborhood, and especially the changing demographics of mainland France. Whereas fifty years ago, the Hexagon could claim—albeit falsely—a population of Gallo-Celto-Roman origin, things have certainly changed in the past half century: large groups of born and bred French citizens have parents or grandparents from the Maghreb, from sub-Saharan Africa, from the Antilles. Groups of people from other parts of Europe have made France their home and have brought their food with them. Indeed, if the introduction to a culture usually first occurs through its cuisine, the increasing complexity of contemporary French civilization is not belied by its rapidly changing food. Whence the necessity of considering cuisine in any model of cultural studies.

The new millenium arrives with great changes in the French gastronomic field. What can it mean that an upscale brasserie in midtown Manhattan advertises on its awning: "BRASSERIE / SUSHI / BRASSERIE"? What does the revival of the extensive use of exotic spices in several of the great French restaurants suggest? What is the significance of the fact that in 1998 the French art journal *Beaux Arts* inaugurated a column on art and cuisine? These events, of relatively little import themselves, are symptomatic of a larger and longstanding discursive history. The decentralizing tendencies of the post-postmodern tradition have finally begun to nudge the rather insular French cuisine toward many foreign influences, inaugurating a global culinary fusion, for better or worse. Furthermore, for the last half millenium, especially in France, the presence of food *among* the fine arts, as well as its existence *as* a fine art, has been the subject of a continually changing history and endlessly revised debates. Within the broadening aesthetic realm, these issues take on new significance.

All this to say that we see the topic of French food crossed by several axes: a *historical axis* that is in a moment of rapid transformation; a *cultural axis* that at every point has symbolic echoes in other spheres, relating food matters to history, sociology, psychology; an *aesthetic axis* intertwined with the history of the fine arts; and an innately *gastronomic axis* with its own rules, paradigms, history, and rhetoric.

In *French Food*, we have chosen a variety of works relating to food, gastronomy, culinary journalism, and the art and literature of food. The reader will find articles about the origin of modern French gastronomy, the role of food in literature and film, and public and private meals at the end of the nineteenth century. The twentieth-century texts explore food in a variety of modern literary works, as well as the multicultural exchanges that occur throughout the century. Several of the articles take a personal point of view, with explorations of French wine, French food, and the French culinary industry. Read and eat well!

1. A Cultural Field in the Making: Gastronomy in Nineteenth-Century France

PRISCILLA PARKHURST FERGUSON

INTRODUCTION—CULTURAL FIELDS

Although it has been applied to many enterprises, the concept of "field" has proved especially fruitful for the analysis of intellectual and cultural activities. Elaborated in its specifically sociological usage by Pierre Bourdieu (Bourdieu, "Intellectual"), "field" designates the state of a cultural enterprise when the relevant productive and consumption activities achieve a certain (always relative) degree of independence from direct external constraints (i.e., those of State and Church for the arts in premodern Europe). As a "particular social universe endowed with particular institutions and obeying specific laws," a field translates external economic or political phenomena into its own terms for its own use, or, rather, for the use of its occupants (Bourdieu, *Field* 162–63). To the extent that the norms governing conduct, the values inducing behavior, and the rewards determining production operate according to field-specific standards, a field is self-regulating, self-validating, and self-perpetuating.

Thinking in terms of cultural fields modifies our understanding of cultural enterprises. Against the functional divisions that tend to be drawn for such activity, a field constructs a social universe in which all participants are at once producers and consumers caught in a complex web of social, political, economic, and cultural relations that they themselves have in part woven and continue to weave. Against unilinear, univocal approaches that focus on discrete structures, historical incident, or individual producers and products, the complex, dynamic configuration of social and cultural relations proposed by a cultural field offers a model that can do justice to the many and diverse modes of cultural participation on the part of a broad range of individuals, institutions, and ideas. The foundations of the cultural field are laid by neither the singular cultural product nor the producer, but by a spectrum of products and practices that displays the workings of the field as a whole.

Cultural fields have an advantage over encompassing sectors like politics or the economy in that they focus our attention on tangible products and identifiable pursuits. A sustained concentration on cultural fields— their internal disposition as well as their external relations—stocks the sociological arsenal with the kind of controlled studies that integrate empirical, historical evidence into a conceptual framework. The more circumscribed the field, the more solid the ground for sociological scrutiny. It is not surprising, then, to find that the most successful studies work with the specifics of a given sphere of cultural production: the "literary field" proposes a delimited space for investigation; a vast, necessarily imprecise construct like the "field of power" invites speculation.[1] The more limited focus facilitates situating the field as a historical entity as well as a sociological concept. The analysis below also demonstrates that this particularity of focus also furnishes useful analytical distinctions between related but distinct notions such as "field," "culture," and "world"—all of which have been invoked in contemporary sociological discussions, particularly, although not exclusively, for the arts.

A sharper use of the concept of "cultural field" and the power to focus inquiry go far to account for the specifically sociological interest of gastronomy in nineteenth-century France. As a relatively delimited cultural enterprise, the pursuit of culinary excellence that we call gastronomy enables us to address a number of problems that plague discussions of cultural fields. Most notably, it speaks to the sticky issue of antecedents. For, however good an idea we may have about how certain fields operate, we know rather less about how they got to be fields.[2] It is true that any search for "causes" or even "origins" is doomed to fail. Yet the question must be put: At what point do structures and sensibilities, institutions and ideologies, practices and practitioners cohere to "make" the configuration that we designate a cultural field? To this question gastronomy proposes some answers. For, although the culinary arts in the West can be traced to the Greeks and especially the Romans, gastronomy as a modern social phenomenon is instituted in early-nineteenth-century France. It is then, I shall argue, that the culinary arts moved into public space and acquired a public consciousness that justifies identification as a "gastronomic field."

Gastronomy turns out to be a happy choice. On the one hand, it speaks to the broad controversy over the meanings of modernity, and, on the other, it addresses an issue that is unavoidable in almost any discussion of nineteenth-century French society, namely, the real or supposed effect of the Revolution of 1789. In what sense can a given cultural venture be considered "modern"? If debates over modernity and modernization, as well as assertions about cultural fields, tend to assume that the visibly changed and changing society of the nineteenth century favored the separation of cultural enterprises into relatively distinct and autonomous domains, it is not at all clear how this transformation occurred. To evoke literature for a moment, in what ways does the Republic of Letters—a term that recurs regularly in eighteenth-century French intellectual life as a designation for networks of writers and thinkers—differ from the literary field of the nineteenth? For the culinary arts, how is nineteenth-century gastronomy "modern," or distinct from elite culinary practices in the seventeenth and eighteenth centuries?

If the paradox of eating, as Simmel pointed out in a quirky but suggestive piece, is that this physiological activity shared by every human being should give rise to such extraordinary social differentiation, it is clear that modern gastronomy enriched the social order by exacerbating those distinctions. Gastronomy constructed its modernity through an expansive culinary discourse, and, more specifically, through texts. Gastronomic texts were key agents in the socialization of individual desire and the redefinition of appetite in collective terms. The "second-order" culinary consumption of textual appreciation was as crucial for the construction of the gastronomic field as it was (and is) for its operation. Such writings extended the gastronomic public or "taste community" well beyond immediate producers and consumers. Diners, thus converted into readers, became full-fledged participants in the gastronomic field. The public sustained the gastronomic field and the field determined the public. As with the performing arts, writing about food presupposes a different order of consumption inasmuch as the cultural product in question is at one remove from the base product—the work performed, seen or heard, and, in this instance, the food prepared and consumed. These culinary texts of indirection were indispensable for the gastronomic field because they stabilized the ephemeral culinary product within a network of nonculinary

discourse and because they redefined the culinary as broadly cultural production. Texts, both instrumental and intellectual, are therefore critical in
making food what Mauss (1) identified as a "total social phenomenon"—an
activity so pervasive in society that, directly or indirectly, it points to and
derives from every kind of social institution (religious, legal, and moral)
and every type of social phenomenon (political, economic, and aesthetic).
That food so penetrates the social fabric is the work of many factors, but
pride of place surely goes to these texts and writings. To turn singular food
events into a veritable cultural configuration, to transform a physiological
need into an intellectual phenomenon, dictates powerful vehicles of formalization and diffusion. The gastronomic writings that proliferated over
the nineteenth century supplied the mechanisms that brought the culinary
arts into modern times.

In France, reflections on modernity further necessitate coming to terms
with the Revolution. What responsibility for the institution of a recognizably modern social and cultural order can be ascribed to the many and
varied phenomena associated with the Revolution and its immediate consequences?—the abolition of the monarchy, the elimination of traditional
economic constraints on commerce, the foreign wars and domestic political turmoil, to list only the most obvious elements.[3] Given that the
theoretical model of the cultural field in no way demands that all fields
have the same degree of coherence or follow the same logic, the connections of cultural fields to both modernity and the Revolution argue for
comparative analysis, across fields as across societies. The sociological issue
then becomes the identification of those factors that distinguish gastronomy in France—as a historical phenomenon and as a cultural practice. To
what degree is this field anchored in, and therefore definable in terms of,
distinctive cultural traditions and particular historical circumstances?

The gastronomic field took shape in two major phases: emergence over
the first half of the nineteenth century, consolidation thereafter. The resulting cultural formation carried "French cuisine" well beyond a
circumscribed repertoire of culinary products to comprehend the practices
and products, values and behavior, rules and norms, institutions and ideas
that are attendant upon the preparation and consumption of food in this
particular social setting. The gastronomic field turned a culinary product
into a cultural one. This cuisine became "French" as it had not been in the
seventeenth and eighteenth centuries when the culinary arts were associated with the court and the aristocracy, not the nation. Nineteenth-century

culinary institutions and texts effectively transformed the patently class-based culinary product and practices of the ancien régime into a prime touchstone of national identity.[4] The consequent identificatory power of cuisine as a fundamental attribute of "Frenchness" and the high rank of the gastronomic field in the hierarchy of cultural fields in France are a function of the strength, the extent, and the multiple and prestigious associations of the gastronomic field, notably, its many and varied affiliations with the literary field.

Five structural factors signal the transformation of gastronomy into the gastronomic field. First, new social and cultural conditions stimulated production, sustained broad social participation, and encouraged a general cultural enthusiasm for the product in question. Second, specific sites came to be dedicated to cultural production and consumption. Third, the institution of standards and models of authority ensured an acute critical consciousness that focused and checked, yet also legitimated the expressions of cultural excitement. Fourth, subfields generated by continued expansion of the field assured the simultaneous concord and conflict of the parties involved, the consonance and dissonance of new positions and alliances. The resulting interlocking networks of individuals and institutions forged links with adjacent fields, and it is these linkages that were largely responsible for the social prestige of gastronomy.

As the formulation of these field qualities suggests, I conceive of gastronomy in nineteenth-century France as something of a template for the analysis of cultural fields more generally. Its lessons reach well beyond the kitchen and the dining table. Certainly, to appreciate a cultural field in the making is to grasp the concept and its use in a more rigorous way, but to do so raises an intriguing problem. To actually see a cultural field in the making requires a delicate conjunction of historical and sociological recognition. The emerging historical phenomenon and social structure must be apprehended, in a word, simultaneously.

The discussion below begins by locating the foundations of the gastronomic field in France in the complexity and the confluence of institutions, traditions, attitudes, events, and ideas. A second section then deals with the articulation of these phenomena in what I have termed culinary discourse. Without such a discouse, I argue, there can be no cultural field. The sociologist must, then, pay careful attention to the specific terms of the discourse. A third section and conclusion assess the validity of the gastronomic field as an analytic category by considering it against other, related cultural fields. We shall find here that the vitality of this particular cultural field depends absolutely on its relations to other fields.

I. Foundations of the Gastronomic Field

Taken as the systematic, socially valorized pursuit of culinary creativity, gastronomy began with the nineteenth century and it began in France. The very term came into public view in 1801,[5] followed by *gastronome* two years later to designate a new social status of the consumer of elaborately prepared fine food.[6] Like any new social practice gastronomy drew on a nexus of social, economic, and cultural conditions. It shaped to its own ends the standard exemplar of cultural communication linking supplies, producers, and consumers in a set of common understandings. For gastronomy, this model translates into: first, abundant, various, and readily available food stuffs; second, a cadre of experienced producers (chefs) in a culturally specific site (the restaurant), both of which are supported by knowledgeable, affluent consumers (diners); and third, a secular cultural (culinary) tradition.[7] All of these elements—the food, the people and places, the attitudes and ideas—came together in early-nineteenth-century France with a force hitherto unknown and, indeed, unsuspected.

Foods

Paris has long been known for its profusion of foodstuffs and range of food providers—from butchers and caterers to pastry makers and cabaret owners—all of which prompted an appreciative Venetian ambassador in 1577 to report that "Paris has in abundance everything that can be desired." With food coming "from every country . . . everything seems to fall from heaven" (qtd. in Revel, *Festin* 150–51). Two centuries later the great urban ethnographer Louis-Sébastien Mercier showed a city even more intensely involved in satisfying the gustatory needs and desires of its inhabitants with an estimated 1,200 cooks at diners' beck and call (1:1011). Even so, the gastronomic level of nineteenth-century Paris was unmistakably of a different order, fueled, as it was, by more and more wealthy people as well as more and more varied foods brought faster from further away.

In Europe as a whole the eighteenth century saw the end of the cyclical famines that had regularly ravaged the continent for centuries and had been such a part of everyday life. In response to demographic pressures, production increased as the expansion of the transportation system transformed agriculture from a subsistence to a commercial enterprise geared to an increasingly broad market (Teuteberg and Flandrin, "Transformations" 725–26). Specifically for France, with the end of the food shortages of the immediate Revolutionary period, and despite the British naval blockade, the early century proved a period of alimentary abundance, certainly for the urban elites responsible for making gastronomy a distinctive social practice. The great chef Antonin Carême was especially sensitive to the deleterious effects of the "great revolutionary torment" on the "progress of our [culinary] art" for ten years or so, and breathed an audible sigh of relief over the far more favorable conditions in the following years (*Pâtissier*, 1: xxxii). As observers of the urban scene never tired of pointing out, every country now had its national foods in Paris, with the result that the adventurous diner could take a trip around the world without leaving the table (Briffault 180–81). When Brillat-Savarin observed with evident pride that a Parisian meal could easily be a "cosmopolitan whole" ([1839] 329), this acute observer of culinary mores meant what he said. In support of the claim that foods came from all over, the sixteenth-century visitor to Paris gave a list of the French provinces; nineteenth-century claimants were talking instead about Europe, Africa, America, and Asia.

Restaurants: Producers and Consumers in Public Space

The haute cuisine of the ancien régime served the court and the Parisian aristocracy, but modern culinary creativity centered in the restaurant. Although the restaurant antedated 1789—the first urban establishment by that name dates from 1765—the Revolution set the restaurant on its modern course of development. By doing away with all restrictions on which establishments could serve what foods in what form, the abolition of the guilds spurred culinary competition and prompted a number of former chefs to the now exiled members of the aristocracy to put their culinary talents in the service of a general elite public (as opposed to a private patron). The restaurants they opened became a notable feature of the urban landscape. Finally, the demise of the monarchy and the court ended the partition of political, commercial, and cultural life between Versailles and Paris, which was henceforth concentrated entirely in the capital. Politicians and businessmen, journalists, writers, and artists flocked to the city and to its restaurants. It was not simply the dramatic increase in population—Paris doubled in size between 1800 and 1850—that was so important a condition for the gastronomic field. The fluid population of largely middle-class transients moving in and out and around the city stimulated the development of eating establishments of many sorts; the hundred or so restaurants found in Paris in the late eighteenth century increased by a factor of six during the Empire, and by the 1820s numbered over three thousand (Pitte, "Naissance" 773). As Brillat-Savarin recognized at the time, competition became intense once it became clear that "a single well prepared stew could make its inventor's fortune." As a result self-interest "fired every imagination and set every cook to work" (Brillat-Savarin, *Physiologie* 1839, 324).

That competition was vertical as well as horizontal; the range of restaurants—the consequent economic, social, and culinary stratification that they solidified—was as important a factor in setting up the gastronomic field as the production of haute cuisine in a select few of them. For the observer who regarded gastronomy as the one social force left untouched by "successive upheavals of civilization" (*Code gourmand* 1827, preface), there were several others who were clear that it was part and parcel of a new regime—political, social, and economic. Gourmandise, like elections, had moved from the "summits" of society to its "lowest classes," with the result that the social division that really counted in contemporary France was the one drawn between cooks and diners (Périgord, *Almanach* 12). The restaurateurs who made their market niche further down the culinary scale may not have been numbered among the "artists" and the "heroes of gastronomy," but their contribution to the social order was seen as every bit as important (Brillat-Savarin, *Physiologie* 1839, 324–26).[8]

The diners who rushed to the Parisian "temples of gastronomy" in the new century were certainly as affluent as the aristocrats who had sustained the haute cuisine of the ancien régime. But the gastronomic elite of the early nineteenth century was socially far more mixed than their predecessors, and, to judge by the directives of the nascent culinary journalism, markedly more insecure. Like the renowned connoisseur and consummate courtier-politician Talleyrand, some carried over their *savoir-vivre* from the old to the new regime;[9] others, no doubt the majority, had the wealth but sorely lacked the savoir-faire. These were the opulent arrivistes addressed by the culinary journalist Alexandre Balthazar Laurent Grimod de la Reynière, whose detailed instructions in how to be a proper guest as well as a correct host aimed at translating the aristocratic culinary culture of the ancien régime for the use of a new public (Grimod, *Manuel*). However, the public restaurant, not the private gathering, was the primary vehicle institutionalizing gastronomy as a social and cultural practice in early-nineteenth-century France. Even the eating societies that served as important points of culinary encounter met in restaurants where gastronomy was not simply on view but open to all comers. By relocating culinary creativity and fine dining from private homes into public space, the restaurant offered an ideal, semipublic venue for the display and affirmation of status in a bounded space that simultaneously defined nondiners as nonelite and marked all diners as members of the elite.[10] In this manner, competition among diners drove the competition among restaurants.

The participatory disposition of the restaurant contrasted sharply with the imposing banquet spectacles of the ancien régime where the king dined alone in full view of the court. The differences between these two culinary modes are by no means trivial. Whereas the banquet makes use of elaborate, often multitiered culinary creations to manipulate space in the service of a communal spectacle, the restaurant regulates time to effect intimacy. The individual dish offers little scope for the spectacular creation, but it favors the singularization of presentation. The public setting depended upon not only new culinary standards but also a different conception of the meal. Courses were no longer served French style, *à la française*—where many different dishes for a single course are laid out on the table at the same time—but in the simpler, modern style, *à la russe* (it was the supposed innovation of the Russian ambassador during the 1810–11 season)—where a single dish is served for each course to all diners. Against the dramatic display of the traditional French service that so clearly suited the hierarchical arrangement of the ancien régime banquet—where one's place at table largely determined which dish one actually ate—its adaptability to variable numbers of individual diners made service à la russe a perfect system for the restaurant. Despite the persistence of elaborate banquets for ceremonial occasions like the paradigmatically extravagant dinner in 1900 for more than 22,000 French mayors (over twice the number of soldiers served by Carême at a similar occasion during the Restoration), the select restaurant gradually relegated the banquet to an even more exceptional, and evidently ceremonial, occurrence. By virtue of this placement of gastronomy in the public sphere, the restaurant anchored the gastronomic field in a fixed institutional basis.

A Secular Culinary Tradition

The final piece in the foundation of the gastronomic field was a secular culinary tradition that offered both institutions and individuals a common intellectual base. Culinary conceptual autonomy presupposed the consideration of food for its own sake and the ideological subordination of religious, symbolic, or medical concerns to the gustatory, however imperfect the separation of the culinary from the symbolic and the medicinal might actually be (Flandrin, "Diététique"). For even though religious interdictions and directives are fundamental to a great many cuisines, they do not in themselves constitute a cuisine. There is no Jewish or Christian or Muslim cuisine; there are, instead, many culinary traditions that negotiate dietary restrictions, ambient cultures, and agricultures to construct a given set of culinary practices. For the largely Catholic consumers in France, the process of liberation from the extraterrestrial and the extragustatory entailed diverting attention from the negative associations of gustatory pleasure. First among these was gluttony (*gourmandise*), classified by the Church as one of the seven deadly sins.[11] Criticism from secular quarters invoked sobriety as well as the physical and moral health of both individuals and the social order. In eighteenth-century France the *Encyclopedia ou Dictionnaire raisonné des sciences des arts et des métiers* joined gluttony to a second deadly sin in its definition of *cuisine* as "the lust for good food" (*Encyclopédie* 4:537) and *gourmandise* as the "refined and disordered love of good food" (*Encyclopédie* 7:754). Such "experiments in sensuality" denature food, which is transformed into "flattering poisons" that "destroy one's constitution and shorten life" (*Encyclopédie* 4:537–39). Following a tradition found in writings as divergent as the Old Testament, Plato, and Herodotus, the authors of the *Encyclopédie* articles conjured up lurid descriptions of the excesses of the late Greeks and decadent Romans to make the point that any thing or practice that reaches beyond nature is not only useless but noxious, as destructive of political character as of individual integrity. Gourmandise, it ruled, is considered a merit in countries "where luxury and vanity reign [and] . . . vices are elevated as virtues" (*Encyclopédie* 7:753–54). From an individual sin, gourmandise became a social vice, its spread in society a conspicuous sign of the flagrant corruption of the body politic.

Fortunately for the development of French cuisine, these negative judgments of delectable pleasures were offset by strong countervailing pressures from the monarchy and the court, and it was these pressures that set the course of fine French cooking. In France, as at many other European courts, public dining rituals elaborated spectacular displays of status and power that reinforced attachment to ruler and court through the manipulation of social distance and spatial proximity (Elias, *Court*, ch. 3;

Wheaton, ch. 7). When Voltaire equated superfluity with necessity in his poem "Le Mondain" [The Man of the World, 1736], and defined excess as utility ["anything superfluous—a real necessity"], he spoke to and for this elite around the court, which indulged in phenomenal luxuriance in many domains—precisely the milieux against which the *Encyclopédie* inveighed so zealously. Even cookbooks joined these culinary polemics. In 1739 the *Lettre d'un pâtissier anglois au Nouveau Cuisinier François* [Letter of an English pastry-maker to the New French Cook] took a stand against the arid intellectualism and the frenetic luxury that took food and consumers away from the primal simplicity of the past. The very next year saw the response: *L'Apologie des Modernes ou réponses du Cuisinier François, . . . à un pâtissier anglois* [Defense of the Moderns or responses of the French Cook], which applies to cuisine the Enlightenment discourse on science (Girard, "Triomphe," 519; Flandrin, Hyman and Hyman, "Colportage"; Hyman and Hyman, "Imprimer").

This discord between indulgence and restraint had not been resolved a century later. However, the terms of the debate had altered considerably, and they had done so because gastronomy had changed the rules of the game. For a privileged witness, we may take the monumental dictionary-encyclopedia of Pierre Larousse (1866–79): *gourmand* and *gourmandise* received two columns of discussion; *gastronomie* was allotted more than four. More significant still was the moral positioning of gastronomy. Next to *gastrolâtrie* ("the passion for good food pushed to a sort of cult . . . incompatible with generosity" [*Larousse* 8:1065]) and *gastromanie* ("love of good food pushed to excess" [*Larousse* 8:1066–67]), *gastronomie* came across as a model of discipline, control, and moderation. Even though *gourmand* retained many of its pejorative implications, designating an individual "who eats eagerly and to excess," there were no negative connotations for the gastronome, who "loves, [and] . . . knows how to appreciate good food." Consequently, "No one blushes to be a gastronome any more," Larousse declared with his habitual assurance, "but at no price would one want to pass for a gourmand or a drunk" (*Larousse* 8:1397). Because gastronomy was both a science and an art, the gastronome could even be considered something of a philosopher-diner, the antithesis, in any case, of the unreflective eater whose lack of self-control led to the gluttony reproved by the Church and castigated by the *Encyclopédie*: "The gourmand only knows how to ingest; the gastronome moves from effects to causes, analyzes, discusses, searches, pursues the useful and the agreeable, the beautiful and the good." This modern construction of culinary fervor sloughed off negative connotations onto the gourmand, the glutton (*glouton* or *goinfre*), or the *gastrolâtre* (someone who "makes a god of his stomach"), thereby securing for the gastronome the lofty position of high priest for this new cult.[12] It is important to recognize that this new distinction between the gourmand and the gastronome, the glutton and the connoisseur, had everything to do with an articulated knowledge that every keen observer would recognize. But such powers of observation could be sharpened only through close acquaintance with the emerging body of culinary texts.

The encyclopedia commentary of Larousse suggests the sea change in attitudes about culinary consumption that made it possible to assume, rather than argue, the social significance of gastronomy, an assumption that was itself a prime indicator of "field effects"—the behavioral and expressive repercussions of a cultural practice that had achieved the independence imputable to a field. Yet neither the social and cultural conditions that generated the new institutions and beliefs, nor the new actors and sites devoted to the culinary arts sufficed to create a cultural field. The endogenous standards and models of authority that allow social reproduction, the multiplying subfields and interlocking networks that define the positions and determine what is at stake in the field, the social presence that originates in links to other cultural fields—these field characteristics assume and depend upon a different kind of support.

To move cuisine out of the kitchen and off the dining table—that is, to carry culinary practices from the sphere of immediate material production and consumption into the broader cultural arena—compelled diffusion, and diffusion demanded a cultural product of a different order. The inherently ephemeral, irremediably private nature of the material culinary product places severe limits on the cultural currency of the culinary arts; food, after all, must be destroyed to be consumed, and, in purely alimentary terms, consumption is strictly individual. Because the material product itself cannot be diffused, culinary practices and products must have an intellectual form that can be put into general cultural circulation. To the extent that cuisine depends on oral transmission its status as a general cultural artifact and practice remains precarious. The words and texts of an expansive culinary discourse, not the dishes and meals of a circumscribed and confined culinary practice, fixed the culinary product and gave it an existence beyond the sphere of immediate culinary production.

Accordingly, the gastronomic field is structured by the distinction between the material product—the foodstuff, the dish or the meal—and the critical, intellectual, or aesthetic by-products that discuss, review, and debate the original product.[13] The relentless intellectuality of the one is as necessary to the gastronomic field as the insistent materiality of the other. In a paradigm of what cooking is all about, culinary discourse transformed the material into the intellectual, the imaginative, the symbolic, and the aesthetic. The cultural construct that we know today as French cuisine was largely the accomplishment of this discourse, and it was this discourse, secured in texts, that consolidated the gastronomic field.

II. Culinary Discourse

Culinary discourse did not, of course, originate either in the nineteenth century or in France. Western Europe can boast of cookbooks from the fourteenth century, as well as all kinds of writings concerned with food— literary works, scientific and medical treatises to ethnographic observations and scholarly ventures, such as the translations in both 1680 and 1789 of the mammoth work by the Greek culinary reporter-sage Athenaeus (1557 and 1612 into Latin; 1680 and 1789 into French). In culinary affairs as in so many others the seventeenth century is the turning point. Although France earlier lagged behind other European countries in the production of cookbooks, beginning in the mid-seventeenth century a spate of cookbooks thrust cuisine into the public arena and set off the first episode in the debate replayed by every generation since over the merits of "old" (in this instance, largely medieval culinary practices) versus the "new" and "modern."

   Clearly, the nineteenth century built upon the legacy of the ancien régime. Just as clearly, it was a new era. The new element in early-nineteenth-century France was the particular configuration of culinary discourse, the multiplication of culinary genres, and the sheer volume of apposite writing, the whole very much a function of the rapidly expanding publishing and journalistic market. The paradigmatic texts ranged from Grimod de la Reynière's *Almanach des Gourmands* [The Gourmands' Almanach] in 1803 to Carême's summum three decades later, *L'Art de la cuisine française au dix-neuvième siècle* [The Art of French Cuisine in the nineteenth century]. Although writing anchors every cultural field, the transitory nature of culinary products renders the gastronomic field absolutely dependent on a textual base. For language allows sharing what

is at once the most assertively individual and yet, arguably, the most dramatically social of our acts—eating. If words turned food into culinary
texts, so these texts inserted gastronomy into a field. They set the culinary
agenda and instituted the cultural debates that defined the gastronomic
field as well as the logic that determined relations within this field.

Five genres of gastronomic writing laid the foundations for the gastronomic field. The "professional" genres that contributed most obviously
and directly to the formation of the gastronomic field were: the gastronomic journalism of Alexandre Balthazar Laurent Grimod de la Reynière
(1758–1838); the culinary treatises of Antonin Carême (1784–1833); and
the cultural commentary and protosociology of Anthelme Brillat-Savarin
(1755–1826). These three authors were witnesses to, even as they were
agents of, the modernizing gastronomic society. Each aimed to system-
atize culinary knowledge; each contributed to the formalization, and,
hence, the very definition of modern French cuisine. But the professionals
did not operate alone. Indeed, it would seem to be characteristic of cultural fields generally, as it certainly is of the gastronomic field in
early-nineteenth-century France, that the larger social impact of the field
is importantly a function of extraprofessional participation and noninstrumental writings. The greater the association of nonspecialists, the more
numerous the connections to other cultural fields and to society at large
and the greater the social impact. It is precisely this kind of indirect participation that points to the fourth and fifth genres of gastronomic
writings, the political philosophy of Charles Fourier (1772–1837) and the
novels of Honoré de Balzac (1799–1850).[14] These five exemplary works,
taken together, hold a key to the understanding of the place occupied by
the gastronomic field among French cultural fields and within French society. Defining gastronomy as a practice and establishing the genres of
culinary writing, professional and nonprofessional writings together established the textual archive of the gastronomic field in France.

Grimod de la Reynière

Grimod de la Reynière was the first gastronomic journalist. Known before
the Revolution for outrageous culinary extravagances, he made use of his
extensive knowledge to enlighten nineteenth-century elites, most of
whom he thought woefully ignorant of the most elementary gastronomic
practices. Grimod put the culinary conscience of the ancien régime at the
service of the new in an era of acute social and culinary change. His assess-

ments of culinary establishments (restaurants, food suppliers, stores, and products) and practices (Grimod, *Almanach* 1984, 8:255) aimed at ordering a culinary world turned topsy-turvy (Grimod, *Manuel*, xxxi; *Écrits*, 311–16). The new gastronome was not to the manners born but a self-made man in need of instruction. It was Grimod who assumed responsibility for the culinary "catechism" (the term he used for his *Manuel des Amphitryons* [Manual for Hosts], 1808). If the fine art of carving had been lost in the "revolutionary torment," Grimod would rectify the situation. He argued that a host who did not know how to carve was every bit as shameful as an owner of a magnificent library who did not know how to read (Grimod, *Manuel* xxxiii–xxxv, 3). In a proposal that would be taken up by many others in various forms and working from the assumption that gastronomic science had advanced by leaps and bounds, Grimod advocated the creation of still more culinary institutions, including professorships in the lycées (*Almanach* 1984, xxxii), various gastronomic societies, and an elaborate system of what he called "legitimations"—whereby product samples were sent for evaluation to "tasting juries" composed of "professors in the art of Gourmandise" (Grimod, *Almanach* 1984, 1:xvii; 2: xix–xx, 3:xxx; 4:vi–vii). Grimod's gastronomic enterprise was an immediate, and enormous success, with 22,000 copies of the *Almanach* sold in several editions over the four years following publication. "Thanks to the progress of knowledge and philosophy," Grimod declared in the *Journal des Gourmands et des Belles* of 1806, undoubtedly thinking of his own contributions, "gourmandise . . . has become an art" (Grimod, *Journal* 1:23).

Carême

Grimod de la Reynière laid down the law for consumers and dealt exclusively with the "theory" of gastronomy—he bragged that he had never put on an apron, and, in any event, only individuals having the misfortune to live outside Paris stood in any need of recipes (Grimod, *Journal* 107). Antonin Carême, on the other hand, legislated for the professional practitioner.[15] Acknowledged by contemporaries and later generations alike as what he proclaimed himself to be, namely, the founder of modern French cuisine, Carême had an immense influence. His systematic examination of the bases of French cuisine, first, of pastry in all its permutations (which covered savories along with sweets), and then all of French cuisine, from soups to sauces via fish, stuffings, bouillons, roasts, and game, provided the methodological basis for the subsequent expansion of the profession later in the century. Unlike Grimod de la Reynière, who overtly took his cues from an ancien régime that he viewed with considerable nostalgia, Carême disdainfully dismissed the old cuisine in favor of the new—"nineteenth-century French cuisine will remain the model for culinary art" (Carême, *Art* 2:413). All extant cookbooks and treatises on cooking—"these sorry books" (Carême, *Maître* 1:5)—were to be jettisoned in favor of his totally original synthesis: his was "the honor and the merit" of giving "our great cuisine" the treatment that it deserved, and what's more, he had not "borrowed anything from anybody" (Carême, *Cuisinier* 20). Cuisine aspired to the status of both a science and an art, and Carême's goal was to turn those gastronomic aspirations into culinary practice.[16]

Carême very explicitly addressed a modern, newly expanded public, which his works were designed to expand further still. He rested his case for the general utility of his work on the fact that even women could profit by the volumes to instruct their cooks at home (the directive gives an idea of the bourgeois nature of that public). Accordingly, he simplified the meal—four courses for a formal dinner instead of the usual eight—and he pared down the banquets from those of his ancien régime predecessors, giving more space per person and placing fewer and smaller serving platters on the table, and so on (cf. the foldouts of table set-ups; Carême, *Maître*, vol. 2). Ever mindful of expense for this broader audience, Carême defended himself against accusations of excess, coming back again and again to the practicality of his cuisine. Even the early works on pastry made a great point that these semiarchitectural confections were "easy to make," however implausible it may seem to any nonprofessional reader. His great valedictory treatise began with a discussion of the humble beef stew (*pot au feu*), disdained by eighteenth-century and modern authors alike even though, as Carême carefully pointed out, it furnished the principal source of nutriments for the working classes. The *pot au feu* is, moreover, where the sauces, and therefore modern French cuisine, begin. It was this "nineteenth-century spirit of analysis" (Carême, *Art*, 1:lxvi) that led him to a chemical analysis of what actually happens when the housewife puts the stew pot on the fire (Carême, *Art* 2:3–4).

Yet Carême also harked back to an earlier era. He made his reputation working in the houses of the great, not in restaurants, and was very proud of his relationships with his illustrious patrons (notably, Talleyrand, Tsar Alexander I of Russia, the Prince Regent of Britain, and Baron Rothschild), which earned him the sobriquet "the chef of kings, and the king of chefs"). For Carême as for Grimod de la Reynière, the ideal gastronomic couple was the gastronome and the chef: "The man born to wealth lives to eat, and supports the art of the chef." Correspondingly, he had only contempt for the "rich miser [who] eats to live" (Carême, *Art* 2:v, vi–vii). The great era of gastronomy was not the period he was writing for in the 1820s, but the Empire in the first decade of the century, with its great patrons and its opulent "extras"—extraordinary, spectacular banquets, including one for ten thousand soldiers under tents along the Champs-Elysées—the menus of which he gives in nostalgic detail (Carême, *Maître*, ch. 13). Not surprisingly, he was highly critical of the modern service à la russe that works so well in restaurants and is so ill-suited to banquets: "our French service is more elegant and more sumptuous . . . the very model of culinary art" (Carême, *Maître* 2:151).

Carême's dual culinary allegiance meant, first of all, that he had an extraordinarily sharp sense of his own worth, in the kitchen and on the printed page. He went on at length about the long nights spent experimenting with different dishes, the hours in the Royal (then Imperial, then Royal) Library in research on culinary achievements from earlier eras, the killing hours buried in coal-burning kitchens to the great detriment of his health, the expenditure of his own moneys in the service of gastronomy, the lack of culinary appreciation on the part of the French in contrast to foreigners, and so on. Many of these statements sound like nothing so much as the ideal-typical Romantic creator lamenting his sacrifices in the name of art or science. Yet this exalted sense of self went along with, and was set against, an equally strong sense of placement vis-à-vis the culinary past, its present, and its future. A prodigious knowledge of culinary traditions grounded Carême's insistence on his place as the creator of modern French cuisine. Virtually all of his works contain more or less extensive comparisons between traditional and modern culinary methods, and one even presents a "Philosophical History of Cuisine" (1833). All the works explicitly addressed his *confrères*, his practicing culinary contemporaries, of whom three receive book dedications.[17] Carême was ever mindful of training subsequent generations of chefs: in the work that was the culmination of his career, *L'Art de la cuisine française au dix-neuvième siècle*, a section of "Remarks and Observations about the Young" advised young chefs who must make their reputations in culinarily less favored times than the glory days of the Empire.

Carême envisaged a systematically organized profession, with "cookoffs" and examinations for the best chef, the best dish, and so forth. Here again, Carême bridged the old system and the new. These culinary competitions were aimed at regulating market competition. First, the imposition of professional standards adapted to market conditions the guarantee of artisanal quality once afforded by the strict regulations of the guilds. Further, by publicizing both professional standards and the winning professionals, these instances of culinary certification made a strong bid to control the market. As any winner of such an award today will testify, this kind of highly public professional certification possesses significant market value. With such institutional mechanisms connecting practitioners around a common set of experiences, techniques, and values and to the public, Carême's contribution was essential to the formation of the gastronomic field. The subsequent development of professional cooking in the latter half of the nineteenth century would not have been possible without his example and his works, the rules he laid down, the techniques he explicated, and the ideal of the creative chef that he embodied.

Brillat-Savarin

From Grimod de la Reynière and Carême to Brillat-Savarin gastronomy was converted from a practice and a technique to a topic of general discussion and analysis beyond those directly concerned with material production and consumption. For although Brillat-Savarin wrote about food, it was, precisely, all the talk about food by a wonderful witty conversationalist that immediately made his *Physiology of Taste* (1826) the totemic gastronomic text that it remains today. To the culinary paradigm of chef-diner, Brillat-Savarin added the reader, the consumer for whom the cultural, rather than the material product, is the primary concern. Unlike the journalist, who addresses customers, clients, and diners, or the chef, who targets practitioners of the culinary arts, the commentator-analyst reaches to these indirect consumers—the readers whose culinary consumption is indirect because it is noninstrumental.[18] The kind of culinary commentary practiced by Brillat-Savarin and generations of his disciples places gastronomy within the larger intellectual and social universe. For Grimod de la Reynière and Carême, the culinary text was chiefly instrumental, a means to the primary end of producing or consuming what anthropologists term the "food event," that is, the dish or the meal. For Brillat-Savarin, the text was its own end, a status hardly altered by the few recipes included in the work. The often noted stylistic qualities of the *Physiology of Taste*—the anecdotal mode, the witty tone, the language play—give this work an almost palpable literary aura. Even so, and however important this style for the immediate and continuing success of this work, the decisive literary connections were determined less by individual achievement than the nature of the work, which places the *Physiology of Taste* with more clearly literary-intellectual genres within the larger culinary discourse.

More decidedly than Grimod de la Reynière or even Carême, Brillat-Savarin conceived of gastronomy as a distinctly modern social practice. His admission that a fear of falling behind the times had prompted him to undertake the study illustrates the degree to which he equated gastronomy with modernity, an intellectual enterprise representative of a contemporary body of knowledge and a nontraditional, analytical attitude toward food. The many anecdotes and the witticisms should not obscure the claims this work made to theoretical, historical, and even scientific understanding. The subtitle—*Meditations on Transcendent Gastronomy—An Up-To-Date Theoretical and Historical Work*—confirms that these bonds were not incidental and singular, but structural and generic. Brillat-Savarin's assertion was doubly encyclopedic since gastronomy is both comprehensive and foundational, drawing as it does on the natural sciences—physics, chemistry, physiology—and on learning of every sort, including cuisine, commerce, political economy, and medicine. The youngest science was born when the chemist, the scholar, and the political economist took cuisine out of the kitchen into the laboratory and the library. Never again could food be confused with either a sin or a mere bodily function. Like Grimod de la Reynière and Carême, Brillat-Savarin took considerable pains to distinguish gourmandise from gluttony. Gourmandise was "the passionate, reasoned and habitual preference for objects that flatter taste," just as gastronomy was "the reasoned knowledge of everything that concerns man and nourishment." A mental activity dealing with the senses, gastronomy relied on refined sensuality but even more on intelligence: "Animals fill themselves; man eats; the intelligent man alone knows how to eat" (Brillat-Savarin, *Physiologie* 1839, 63, 317, 65).

The second component of Brillat-Savarin's analysis is properly sociological. In effect the *Physiology of Taste* suggested a model for a sociology of taste as this eighteenth-century philosophe metamorphosed into a sociologist, subjecting the "pleasure of the table" to its ever changing social contexts.[19] Brillat-Savarin elevated gastronomy to the rank of a science and justified what he called "social gourmandise" by its exceptional social utility. The *Physiology of Taste* offers a few menus from sumptuous and more modest meals, describes some dishes, and even gives some recipes. But Brillat-Savarin indulged comparatively little in the vice that plagues food writing of every era, namely, the rehashing of gustatory memories. It was not simply the variety of French cuisine that marked the *Physiology of Taste* as a sociological enterprise but the correlations that Brillat-Savarin established between the social and culinary attributes of taste. Gastronomy, as Brillat-Savarin argued the case, was the science that explored those relations. Clearly, as well, it was a social science that examined even as it joined a more general discourse on class and class distinctions. Taste taken in this very specific sense became another powerful marker of class as gastronomy came to define individual appetite in collective terms.

The science of gastronomy had such a formidable task because the social diffusion of gourmandise did not eliminate so much as it complicated the gastronomic hierarchy. If there are individuals whom nature has "predestined" to be gourmands and whose very physiognomy betrays their predilection, more interesting to Brillat-Savarin are those figures destined to assess social positions and professions in terms of their penchant for gourmandise: financiers, doctors, men of letters, and the pious (*les dévots*) head the list (Brillat-Savarin, *Physiologie* 1839, 176–85). Brillat-Savarin further devised a series of "gastronomic tests" calibrated to income with menus ranging from five courses for a 5,000-franc income, six courses including truffled turkey for diners in the 15,000-franc income bracket, to the nine courses of extravagant, complex dishes appropriate for those with an income of 30,000 francs and over (Brillat-Savarin, *Physiologie* 1839, 188–89). A necessary but not sufficient factor, money could not be construed as in any way a cause of taste preferences. It was, rather, an indicator of "gastronomic class," which intersected with social class, to be sure, although not nearly so neatly as it had under the ancien régime. Brillat-Savarin prudently avoided ranking the financier's fare "better." In keeping with the neutralizing language of science, the evaluations of the *Physiology of Taste* were those of the "dynamometer," which registered increasing force as one ascended the social ladder. The dishes able to test the gastronomic faculties of the stolid bourgeois rentier would not be regarded as worthy of examination by the "select few" invited by a banker or governmental minister. With its own hierarchy and its variable standards, the world of gastronomy reproduced the contradictions and the ambiguities of postrevolutionary society—Brillat-Savarin noted a dinner that assembled gourmands of the fourth (the highest) class (Brillat-Savarin, *Physiologie* 1839, 193).

To be sure, the *Physiology of Taste* did not take full account of that public world. Brillat-Savarin found the restaurant, which his "philosophical" history of cuisine placed among the "latest refinements," so new in the 1820s and so different an institution that no one had thought about it enough. With only one "Meditation" devoted to "Restaurateurs," Brillat-Savarin did not really take up the challenge. Yet he was both disconcerted and intrigued. On the one hand, the restaurant was an element of democratization; on the other, restaurants catering to solitary diners fostered an excessive individualism possibly destructive of the social fabric (Brillat-Savarin, *Physiologie* 1839, 318–24). In any event, and however significant a social phenomenon the restaurant might be, the private gathering supplied the model of sociability for the *Physiology of Taste*. Grimod de la Reynière's work had already made it clear that this world too had been greatly altered by the increased circulation of individuals and their culinary habits, the availability of goods and services, and the culinary pluralism that the restaurant represents. By virtue of its interpretation of cuisine as a collective enterprise, defined by the consumers rather than the producers and governed by the social as opposed to the alimentary situation, the *Physiology of Taste* placed cuisine squarely in the public domain. In Brillat-Savarin's work, the science of human nourishment—gastronomy—became something more—a science of society.

The Nationalization of French Cuisine

The texts of this gastronomy also served as a vehicle for a distinctively French culinary nationalism. If French and foreigner alike have long considered cuisine quintessentially French, the explanation lies importantly in an expansionist culinary discourse that relentlessly associates (good) food and France, and has done so for some three or four centuries. From the sixteenth century onward European cuisines generally were moving in their separate directions, away from the commonalities of earlier culinary modes (Flandrin, "Choix"). The Venetian ambassador in 1577 was not alone in remarking on the singularity of French foodways. Then too, many of the cookbooks that began to appear in the mid-seventeenth century made a point of the "Frenchness" of their cuisine. But in virtually all of these instances "French" was not a geographical but a social reference, and French cuisine was French by virtue of the court and the aristocracy. Cookbook writers invariably vaunted their elite connections—in titles like *Les Soupers de la cour* (Suppers at Court; 1755) and in flowery dedications to noble patrons. Works expressly destined for the bourgeoisie, like the *Cuisinier royal et bourgeois* (The Royal and Bourgeois Cook; 1691) or the phenomenally successful *La Cuisinière bourgeoise* (The [female] Bourgeois Cook; 1746), proposed simplifications of the courtly models (Mennell, *Manners*, 80–83), but those models remained in force. This aristocratic model also supplied the basis for the first truly international cuisine, carried by French chefs and cookbooks to court kitchens throughout Europe. Just as European aristocracy in the seventeenth and eighteenth centuries spoke and wrote French, so too it "ate French" and relegated native culinary traditions to the status of poor relations.[20] The culinary writers of nineteenth-century France found themselves in the enviable, and unique, position of working within a celebrated indigenous culinary tradition. The increasing centralization of French society and the attendant concentration of French cultural institutions—conditions matched nowhere else in Europe—further reinforced these associations between the nation and elite cuisine. Of course, France also had nonelite, regional cuisines, but other countries had only such cuisines (which is why Carême, like many of his ancien régime predecessors, was called to cook abroad).

Like the other nationalisms that flourished in the nineteenth century, French culinary nationalism drew on texts. That "French cuisine" was itself the product of texts has led some to deny the very possibility of a national cuisine. Because, for these critics, a cuisine is product based, it can only be local (Mintz, *Tasting*, ch. 7), which makes "French cuisine" little more than an intellectualized Parisian artifice totally dependent upon "true," regional cuisines.[21] Such statements tend to confuse the plurality of culinary practices with the critical coherence of a culinary tradition. As a formalized set of culinary practices, any cuisine is necessarily the product of a culinary discourse, and, to reach beyond the confines of the originating group, that discourse needs texts. Even regional cuisines relied on texts to be constituted as such: as self-consciously formulated culinary codes, regional cuisines in France were themselves products of culinary writings as early as *Le Cuisinier gascon* (The Gascony Cook; 1740) but diffused more widely beginning, once again, in the nineteenth century (Csergo, "Émergence"). The textual reliance of a national French cuisine finds confirmation in the rise of national cuisines in late-nineteenth-century Italy (Camporesi, *Harvest*) and twentieth-century India (Appadurai, "National"), where the absence of a prestigious indigenous culinary model ensured the dominance of regional or foreign identifications until countered by a significant text or set of texts.[22]

The gastronomical writings of Grimod de la Reynière, Câreme, and Brillat-Savarin, along with those of their many critics and disciples, gave the requisite textual basis to a specific set of culinary practices. These writings became, as they had not been theretofore, identified with the country as a whole. The generalization of interest in gastronomy, attested in many quarters and acknowledged by all three authors, supplied a public eager for such materials. These three "professionals"—the journalist, the chef, the sociologist—invested cuisine in France with a force, a value, and a presence that have long been considered characteristic of French foodways. In effect, the culinary discourse in which they engaged "nationalized" French cuisine, and it did so by imposing the standards and arrogating the authority that would henceforth define positions in the gastronomic field.

The authoritative tone of so many of these writers has much to do with the continual jockeying for position in the emergent gastronomic field. Culinary discourse, in fact, offers a perfect illustration of symbolic violence, and nowhere more vividly or with greater impact than in France. The very term "gastronomy"—from *gastro* (stomach) and *nomos* (law)—signaled the importance of rules and regulations in this culinary construction. (Câreme made much of standardizing the orthography for menus [Câreme, *Pâtissier* lvii–lxxxix].) For Grimod de la Reynière or Câreme or any number of their epigones, there was no brooking dissent. To be sure, recipes, most particularly written ones, must be authoritative; at the very least every recipe implies a culinary authority. But recipes were not alone in adopting a legislative mode. Other components of French culinary discourse had just as many, if different, pretensions to authority. Witness the great proliferation of texts that supplied the codes by which gastronomy was regulated, and lived. *The Code Gourmand* of 1827 trumpeted itself as a *Complete Manual of Gastronomy, containing the laws, rules, applications and examples of the art of living well*; it was followed by *The French Gastronome, or the art of living well*, written by "the former Authors of the *Journal des Gourmands*" (among whom was Grimod de la Reynière). This work was in turn succeeded by the *Perpetual Almanach of Gourmands*, containing *Le Code gourmand* with its applications, rules, and meditations of transcendent gastronomy (the reprise of Brillat's subtitle making its particular bid for the authority of the work).

The consciously authoritative tone of such works is as unmistakable as it is significant. Although Brillat-Savarin published the *Physiology of Taste* anonymously, the title page proclaims the author's status as a "Professor" and "Member of several learned societies." Analysis in this work is inextricably tied to prescription. The offhand, humorous tone of the work belies the imperious manner of the precepts and principles. The dichotomy was intentional: the use of "I" and "me," Brillat-Savarin explained, supposes a "confabulation" with the reader, who is free to "examine, discuss, and even laugh." But when he comes armed with the "redoubtable *we*," it is a lecture, and the reader must submit. "I am, Sir, oracle," the authorial persona warned, citing *The Merchant of Venice* in a comical yet firm directive. "And, when I open my lips, let no dog bark!" (Brillat-Savarin, *Physiologie* 36). So too Carême passed over no opportunity to cite his right to readers' consideration, the many and spectacular successes, the eminent personages for whom he had worked, the breadth of his experience and extent of his research, and the utility of his innovations and method.[23]

All commentators agreed that the culinary arts were French, so much so that it is not too much to speak of a culinary nationalism. Grimod de la Reynière announced that he would not regret all the care (and heartburn) that went into the *Almanach des Gourmands* if "the national glory in all aspects of alimentary art" progressed because of it (Grimod, *Almanach* 1984, 2:xx–xxi). Carême simply pronounced France "the motherland of anyone who entertains guests; its cuisine and wines are the triumph of gastronomy and it is the only country for good food" (Carême, *Cuisinier* i; Carême, *Art* 2:i). In an earlier work, he boasted that "this absolutely new Treatise . . . will give new luster to our national cuisine" (Carême, *Pâtissier*, dedication), and in another, he boldly asserted that he had already refuted all the "ridiculous books that are a disgrace to our great national cuisine" (Carême, *Maître* 1:5). The work he had in mind, quite unfairly given the date of its publication, was the cookbook that first associated France with a cuisine—*Le Cuisinier françois* of 1651. The oxymoronic pretensions of a contemporary's cookbook entitled the *Universal English Chef* had Carême so beside himself that he proposed a cook-off, it being a foregone conclusion that French chefs would win any culinary contest (Carême, *Pâtissier* xvi).

Not that French cuisine lived in splendid isolation. Indeed, its "genius" lay in the strength of its capacity to assimilate foreign elements. Although French cuisine was "indisputably the first in the world," as Grimod de la Reynière recalled in 1806, it could become richer still by drawing on foreign foods. But appropriation also meant transformation, which is to say, "Frenchification." French cuisine would incorporate exotic foods "by perfecting them" (Grimod, *Almanach* 1984, 3:295, n.1). Some twenty years later Brillat-Savarin had recourse to this same notion of acclimation to illustrate the relationship of French cuisine to foods, seasonings, and drinks "of foreign preparation" (Brillat-Savarin, *Physiologie* 1839, 316–17). For many, "French" was equated with "classic." The publication of English and German cookbooks in the 1820s sent a conservative culinary critic into great (mock) diatribes against the "Romantic" cuisine that paid no attention to the rules of culinary Classicism. The vogue for English literature was one thing in this period of dramatic clashes between Romantics and Classics in print and on the stage, but, for the author of the *New Almanach for Gourmands*, food was a truly serious affair. Protesting vehemently against the wholesale importation of dishes that "at great expense produce a dubious taste and nausea," this commentator enjoined the French to make judicious choices in English cuisine no less than in English literature. If roast beef and boiled potatoes did no harm to (French) gastronomic sensibilities, plum pudding, salt beef, and mutton soups—"bizarre preparations unsuitable for either our health or our climate"—should be left to those whose "iron-clad palates" were accustomed to such fare, just as all the garlic-laden dishes from the south of France should remain where they belonged (Périgord, *Almanach* 104–8).

Reminiscent of the "theory" of climates traceable to Montesquieu and, in literary studies, to Mme de Staël, this understanding of cuisine in terms of national tradition and temperamental suitability asserts what was implied in the more serious, more "professional" works by the founding fathers of the gastronomic field: the culinary nationalism, even chauvinism, that would become inextricably allied with French cuisine. The constitution of a gastronomic field depended upon a redefinition of haute cuisine as a national cuisine. To be sure, the haute or grande cuisine of the ancien régime had been considered "French"—witness the claims, which Carême felt obliged to refute, of the seventeenth-century cookbook *The French Chef*. Moreover, any number of commentators from the seventeenth century onward affirmed the intrinsic, virtually "natural" affinities between France and fine food. But the "nationalization" of this cuisine occurred in the nineteenth century when an overtly class culinary model turned into a national cultural phenomenon. Although the resulting culinary product was still class based, the class had shifted to include an extended gastronomic elite for the consumption of the material product and a still larger gastronomic public for reading culinary texts.

Nowhere were the rules of culinary conduct more highly and more authoritatively codified than in nineteenth-century France, inspired at

least in part by dismay over evident social change. It is hardly surprising
that foreign models of cooking should have aroused anxiety about culinary
disorder. "Soon," one writer intoned after reporting a spate of works pur-
porting to introduce English and German cooking to the French, "all the
aberrations of an art which has no limits and acknowledges no rule will be
transplanted here" (Périgord, *Almanach* 106). Just so, the author of the
Code Gourmand called for a "fixed and immutable code" to contain the
excesses of the almost libidinous Gastronomy, "the queen of the world"
(*Code Gourmand*, Prologue). Another critic asserted that "cooking, like
drama . . . ought to follow Aristotle's rules" (*Almanach perpétuel des Gourmands contenant Le Code Gourmand, et des applications, règles et méditations de
gastronomie transcendante* 1830, 106). On the other hand, the assimilationist
"genius" ascribed ever more emphatically to French cuisine not only legitimated, it virtually demanded a broad spectrum of sources to enrich native
components. However, borrowing would take place strictly on French
terms and in accordance with preexisting national norms and precepts.

In this manner, culinary discourse constructed a paradigm for the culti-
vation of a self-consciously national identity, a wonderful illustration of the
cultural work of nation building so characteristic of nineteenth-century
Europe. French cuisine was one more "invented tradition" (Hobsbawm
1983) that shored up a national identity. Cuisine and gastronomy were
part of a more general process of cultural nationalization through the
imposition on the periphery of the values, the norms, and even the language of the center (Weber, *Peasants*), an ideal choice for a new and
somewhat shaky republican regime seeking to elide political conflict by
promoting emblems to unify the country rather than divide it (Nora,
Realms). Assimilationist by nature, French cuisine subsumed all the others
in a perfect synecdoche of France. If regional products and dishes continued to play a vital role in national culinary construction, they did so as
subordinate parts of an incomparably greater whole.[24]

The vehicle of this synecdoche, the link between part and whole,
between region and country, is found in the expansive culinary discourse
of the nineteenth century. This connection explains why the ties between
the literary and the gastronomical are not accidental but a constitutive
feature of the gastronomic field. Cuisine in France became fully French
by virtue of the discourse that incorporated food practices into a socioculinary tradition and a gastronomic code. The culinary discourse
elaborated in early-nineteenth-century France created a substantially new,

and almost infinitely extendible, set of gastronomic consumers-readers. The French cuisine secured in these many gastronomical writings could be consumed far more readily on the page than at table. Because capacities for intellectual ingestion far exceed the physiological capacities of the most voracious appetite and most determined glutton, the public for culinary texts is potentially immense. It was this public, which overlapped to a variable degree with actual diners, that provided the most solid foundation for the gastronomic field, determined the positions staked out in that field, and permitted, even demanded, discussion, commentary, and criticism. By allowing repeated "consumption" of the same meal or food, writing and reading neutralize the orality of food. Just as writing fixes speech, so too it stabilizes food. Culinary discourse controls consumption, which it transforms into an intellectual activity. Virtually all the many definitions of gastronomy stress this intellectual displacement, often citing Brillat-Savarin's definition of gastronomy as the "reasoned knowledge" of everything to do with what we eat (Brillat-Savarin, *Physiologie* 1839, 65).

Fourier

Culinary discourse also explains the gastronomic associations specific to a modernizing French society. Beyond the texts directly concerned with the culinary production and consumption—the works of Grimod de la Reynière, Carême, and Brillat-Savarin—are those that analyze and dramatize food as a total social phenomenon. The philosophical writings of Fourier and the novels of Balzac offer excellent examples. More emphatically than any other text at the time, and by its very utopianism, the social order imagined by the utopian philosopher Charles Fourier (1772–1837) demonstrates how food works as a total social phenomenon to mold institutions no less than individual behavior.[25] Fourier based his philosophical system on the social utility of pleasure, specifically, the principle of attraction, the two most powerful principles of which are sex and food, or in his terms, love and gourmandise. No more than sex was gourmandise an individual matter. Fourier constructed an entire social system to turn these individual pleasures to social account.[26]

Yet even as Fourier set his work apart from the ambient gastronomic discourse, he invoked many of the same themes and principles—the scientific nature of gastronomy, the importance of culinary judges and juries, the crucial distinction between gastronomy and gluttony, the social utility of gastronomy in a time of rising economic prosperity. In every case, Fourier took the precept outside the contemporary social order (which he derisively referred to as "Civilization," in contradistinction to the projected social order that he called "Harmony"). Gastronomes, writers as well as practitioners, and even the best among them like Grimod, produced nothing better than "gastro-asininities" (*gastro-âneries*) (*Oeuvres* 6:255, n. 1). Even Fourier's cousin Brillat-Savarin was no better than any other so-called gastronome ignorant of the higher or combined gastronomy, which Fourier baptized *gastrosophy* (*Oeuvres* 8:283) and in which he found "a profound and sublime theory of social equilibrium" (*Oeuvres* 4:130), "the principle mechanism of the equilibrium of the passions" (*Oeuvres* 6:258), and one of the two primary bases of the new social order. The higher gastronomy occupied such an important place in Harmony because it presided over the development of the senses rather than their repression. Fourier premised his entire system on material abundance, which alone could guarantee spiritual abundance (e.g., happiness) (*Oeuvres* 1:77). Contemporary society was based on differential scarcity whereas the increased production of Harmony would spread abundance throughout society. (Fourier broke fractiously with Saint-Simon on just this issue.) The emphasis on plenty led Fourier to define his new culinary order against gastronomy as Civilization understood the practice. The moderation preached in nineteenth-century gastronomic circles was anathema: "A hundred thousand philosophers eat only to keep their passions under control." His view that moderation is a "travesty of nature" (*Oeuvres* 6:255–56) led him to place all activities in Harmony under the twin signs of profusion and the absence of moderation: prodigious appetites will necessitate five meals plus two snacks a day, men will be seven feet tall, easy digestion will make children strong, and life expectancy will be 144 (*Oeuvres* 1:180, n. 1).

Seldom have the culinary and the social order been more explicitly or more visibly tied, and of greater moment than in Fourier's vision. Like Grimod, Brillat, and Carême, Fourier worked to transcend the gross materiality of food, and like them too, he was maniacally concerned with detail. But where they defined gastronomy in terms of art and science, he made it the stuff of economics, philosophy, and politics. His gastronomical political economy endowed the proverbial land of milk and honey with an elaborate, complex social organization grounded in a visionary social science. What makes this culinary utopia more than a curiosity is what it reveals about the emergent gastronomic field in nineteenth-century France. More than any other culinary text, Fourier's writings intellectualized gastronomy, and they did so by making connections to established intellectual enterprises of unimpeachable legitimacy—philosophy and political science, or what in nineteenth–century France were called the "moral and political sciences." Today, we would certainly add sociology, like gastronomy an intellectual innovation of the early nineteenth century.

Balzac

As Fourier carved out a place for philosophy and the social sciences in the gastronomic field, Honoré de Balzac (1799–1850) set up the literary relations.[27] Balzac built on a long tradition of literary culinary commentary which, in French literature alone, dated from at least Rabelais and Montaigne in the sixteenth century. The undoing by unbridled appetite(s) had been standard comic fare from the Greeks (cf. Atheneaeus, *Deipnosophists*). Balzac's perspective differed from that of his predecessors because it was resolutely and self-consciously modern. He boasted of being the "Secretary" to French society (*Oeuvres* 1:11), and certainly one of the striking contributions of Balzac's novels—one greatly appreciated by Marx and lavishly praised by Engels—is the dramatic ethnography of the nascent industrial capitalism of postrevolutionary France. Balzac used the realist novel to define contemporary French society, and in that definition food and feeding loomed large. Balzac's characters eat a good deal, and, more important still, Balzac attaches great significance to the consumption of food as a social and psychological indicator. What visitor to Paris does not identify with Lucien de Rubempré when he decides to "initiate himself in the pleasures of Paris" at a restaurant where a single dinner eats up the fifty francs that would have lasted him a month at home in the provinces. Small wonder that the impecunious young man soon finds his way to the Latin Quarter and a menu at eighteen sous (*Oeuvres* 5:271, 292, 294–5). Balzac understood as Grimod, Carême, and Brillat-Savarin did not, the significance of the restaurant as a privileged location of gastronomic and other modernity—a semipublic, semiprivate urban space, of dubious moral and variable culinary quality. He also showed the degree to which the restaurant acted as something of a safety valve for the increasingly regulated mores of bourgeois society (Aron, *Art*).

Dinners and diners turn up all over Balzac's work. But cuisine is more than a strong marker of distinction. In Balzac's last, and darkest, novel,

Cousin Pons (1846), gastronomy became the stuff of tragedy, a "bourgeois tragedy," as Balzac called the genre in another setting, "with neither poison or dagger or blood but . . . crueler than all the calamities in the house of Atreus" (*Oeuvres* 3:1148). This novel made gastronomy an actor like money, an agent of the dramas, particularly of the tragedies, on which Balzac constructed his modern society. Gastrolatry is the good-hearted, hapless Pons's tragic flaw, his sin gourmandise. Balzac modernized that sin and brought the punishment up to date. Pons is not the target of divine retribution but of identifiable social forces, specifically, avaricious relatives who defraud him of an incomparable collection of antiques. Like the fine collection of antiques that he has amassed with such loving care, Pons's worship of fine food expresses his fine artistic nature and offers compensation for personal disappointments.[28]

In giving gourmandise tragic dimensions Balzac broke with a philosophical tradition that restricted expression of the baser senses—touch, smell, and especially taste—to base-born characters and to the baser genre of comedy. Balzac's reinterpretation of the literary mode for such expression expanded and strengthened the connections between literature and gastronomy and, hence, between the gastronomic and the literary fields. Even as Balzac was positioning himself and his work in the emerging literary field, he was also, if less obviously and less consciously, defining a position in the nascent gastronomic field. The same work addressed both fields, albeit differently. In the one—the literary field toward which Balzac directed his strategies—the literary work supplied the primary cultural product, and reading that work constituted the primary cultural consumption. In the other—the gastronomic field—those same novels were part of a second-order consumption. Reading is an indirect culinary practice, and reading literary or intellectual works is the most indirect of all, furthest on the continuum from the instrumentality of cookbooks and similarly directive texts.

Straddling Fields

Such intersections between continuously shifting cultural fields are not only possible, they are all but inevitable. A given individual may be central to one field, peripheral to another, may change subjective stance toward and objective position in one but not the other, and so on. Other things being equal, the more fields in which an individual occupies a position, and the more central those positions, the more symbolic power or capital at that person's disposal. A "cultural career" is made of the trajectories followed over a lifetime. Exploiting the opportunities offered by this sort of "cultural mobility" is what Balzac did so magnificently. The literary field was not simply the sociological context in which he occupied a position and in which he maneuvered. It also furnished him with a subject: Balzac was not only an actor in the nascent literary field of nineteenth-century France; this author was also, and in some of his greatest works, an ethnographer of that field.

However, as the metaphor implies, straddling fields is possible only to the degree that the fields themselves intersect. Balzac's position in, and analysis of, the gastronomic field, was a function of just such a field intersection. Although it is possible to occupy positions in noncontiguous, even unconnected fields, a high degree of intersection tends to be characteristic of cultural fields. Such convergence is especially notable in modern French society, where the long-term concentration of cultural institutions and activities in Paris favors the intersection of cultural fields as well as the interaction of individuals. Field intersection more generally is promoted by the common educational training received in the elite secondary school, which is another factor behind the conspicuous ties between the literary and political fields in France (Clark, "Literary").

The associations between the gastronomic field and the literary field are vital to the situation of cuisine among French cultural products and to the position of the gastronomic field in the hierarchy of cultural fields. Although the second-order consumption of this "literary gastronomy" places it on the outer reaches of the gastronomic field, this textual consumption is a crucial element in the diffusion of the values and the traditions that govern the field. The literary work effects the ultimate transcendence of the material and transformation of the sensual. This work of transformation points to the decisive distinction between cuisine and gastronomy and their respective functions in the gastronomic field. Cuisine, or culinary codes, concerns production; its injunctions are largely instrumental, its practice more or less site-specific. Gastronomy, on the other hand, is a code that pertains to consumption; it is grounded in primarily gratuitous, that is, noninstrumental, discourse. Each of these cultural products operates within the gastronomic field; each is a necessary component of the cultural consciousness characteristic of that field. For the gastronomic field to come into existence, cuisine had to connect with gastronomy, and culinary production had to be linked to culinary diffusion. It did so through texts that also made connections to other cultural fields—literature especially prominent among them.

III. Other Cultures, Other Fields

Considering gastronomy as a cultural field brings a number of long-standing questions into sharper focus. The development of the gastronomic field from the mid-nineteenth century in France points to the processes that moved the field from beginnings to consolidation. The subsequent professionalization of cooking beginning in the 1880s worked off the continued expansion of restaurants, particularly in the great hotels catering to the nascent tourist industry that acted as important training grounds for cadres of French chefs; at the end of a long career that began in the 1870s, the highly influential Auguste Escoffier boasted that he had sent some two thousand French chefs from his kitchens all over the world (193). The automobile turned increasing numbers of diners into culinary tourists, and, beginning in the 1920s, the Michelin restaurant ratings established a national geography that was at the same time a hierarchy of French cuisine. Professionalization brought further proliferation of texts, specialized journals, newspapers, and reviews that address the domestic cook, the professional chef, and also, increasingly, readers for whom cooking is akin to a spectator sport. New media such as radio and television (and latterly the Internet) are today integral parts of, and active actors in, the gastronomic field.

The evolution of the gastronomic field in France impels us to reconsider the supposed disappearance of cultural singularity in an increasingly global economy. For foodways in France, the "McDonaldization" of food production (by no means entirely imputable to American corporations) and the continuing changes effected by the European Economic Community have raised fears of a possible loss, or at the very least a significant weakening, of distinctive cultural identities. Such fears are by no means new—witness the negative reception given German and English cookbooks in the 1820s or a 1924 warning that "France would no longer be France" when a French meal was no different from repasts elsewhere (Rouff, *Dodin-Bouffant* 1994, 13).[29] But the extent and strength of the field, with its extensive organization, its range of institutions, the values and beliefs those institutions perpetuate, and the self-consciousness that characterizes the field as a whole, lead us to posit the cultural field as a site of resistance to the (real or perceived) eradication of cultural difference.

The more tightly organized the field and the greater its reach, the greater its autonomy and ability to perpetuate its core values. At the same time, the broader cultural resonance of the field, and therefore its capacity for cultural resistance, is importantly dependent upon connections to other cultural fields and other institutions. In other words, a cultural field owes its singular position to a particular configuration relating the part to the whole, the field to the larger society, in which the larger social ties both temper and enhance the autonomy of the field. Complete independence of a field from its larger context can make no sense; it would be the cultural equivalent of solitary confinement. Isolation would nullify any larger impact as surely and as effectively as direct control by institutions.

Besides the great advantage of locating French culinary practices in a specific socioculinary setting, taking gastronomy as a field makes it possible to identify what is French about food in France. Although it may be commonly agreed, and not by the French alone, that gastronomy is somehow "innately" French, only in the nineteenth century, however important the ancien régime contribution, can one identify anything resembling a national culinary discourse. Of course, assigning gastronomy to the French "character" or unique geography or exceptional climate begs the question, all the more so since most of the institutions, ideologies, and practices that express these character traits originated, again, only in the nineteenth century. For, if culinary creativity in France was highly visible in the ancien régime and elite consumption singularly conspicuous, the gastronomic field, like a number of other cultural fields, arose in postrevolutionary France. These fields defined and were defined by publics that were larger, more expansive, and more heterogeneous than their prerevolutionary counterparts. In fixing these culinary practices in a circumscribed space, the gastronomic field allows us to distinguish between what is distinctively French and what is more generally modern about these culinary practices, what French cuisine and French culinary practices share with other cuisines as well as the elements that set French foodways apart.

The concept of the gastronomic field allows us, for example, to make better sense of the connections between French and Chinese cuisine. The high degree of codification of the rules governing both culinary production and consumption clarifies, and justifies, the comparison and sets both against the regional cuisines in each country. Chinese and French elite cuisines built on strong, prestigious elite culinary traditions originally tied to a central government and an urban elite. Both, as well, were sustained by a significant textuality (Freeman, "Sung"), and, in China as in France, visible cultural enthusiasm is tempered, channeled, and contained by authoritative culinary and gastronomic codes. Aside from the actual techniques of preparation and cooking (which are, indeed, very different), Chinese cuisine differs most importantly from the French in its evident philosophical overlay (Chang, "Introduction"). By contrast, French cuisine emerged out of a resolutely "secular" environment. In more recent times, against the continued support of the French government for various culinary initiatives—the Chambre syndicale de la haute cuisine française, the École nationale and Centre national des arts culinaires founded in 1985, the web pages, the classes that teach very young school children how to taste, the culinary competitions such as the Meilleur Ouvrier de France for different categories of cuisine, the commercial manifestations such as the Salon du chocolat, and so on—the policies of the Communist regime that did so much to destroy elite institutions in China greatly affected culinary practices by interrupting the course of culinary tradition and thwarting the practice of gastronomy (cf. Wenfu 1988). Such close, direct political control, even if less stringent than in the recent past, makes it unlikely that a gastronomic field in the full sense of the term could be identified in present-day China.

Gastronomic Fields, Culinary Cultures, and Restaurant Worlds

If China is often compared to France for the refinement and complexity of its cuisine, the United States is more likely to be invoked as its polar opposite. And, although culinary America is a very different and substantially more sophisticated place than it was only a few decades ago, it does not offer the culinary unity or authority requisite for a gastronomic field. There is, in the first place, no cultural product on which to base a field because there is no American cuisine, that is, no culinary configuration identified with the country as a whole.[30] The foodways of colonial America were either unwritten (Native American), foreign (Dutch, English, or Spanish, depending on settlement patterns) or both (divers African). Strong regional identities yield more or less local, product-based regional cuisines—New England, Tex-Mex, Southern, Cajun. Because these cuisines tend to be identified by dishes (North Carolina versus Texas barbecue, New England versus Manhattan clam chowder), they are susceptible to great variation (chowders alone would take us on a tour around the country). More recently, this distinctive American pluralism has come to include the foodways of newer immigrant groups, a number of which fast-food chains have made an integral part of the American diet (Belasco; Mintz, *Tasting*): in Pizza Hut and Taco Bell, McDonald's, Burger King, and Kentucky Fried Chicken, foreigners (Fantasia) as well as Americans find the most visible common element of American foodways. Whatever other culinary unity Americans may have comes not from food but a food event: Thanksgiving. The United States may well be the only nation that harks to a meal as foundational event, that is, one of the founding, and perduring, myths of a singular American destiny (Ferguson, "Cuisine"). Yet, here too, the legendary meal of turkey, pumpkin, and cranberry gives rise to innumerable variations fixed in regional or ethnic custom (sweet potato casserole with marshmallow topping; spaghetti or chili as a side dish), family tradition (mince pie instead of pumpkin), or idiosyncratic modifications.[31] In other words, pluralism wins out even for a food event that is insistently constructed as a defining national occasion.

This cultural pluralism supports, as it is supported by, a relative lack of cultural authority. None of the various national tourist guides (Mobil, AAA) approaches the authority of the Michelin guide whose annual restaurant ratings in France arouse such great expectation and anxiety on the part of diners and restaurateurs alike. It is symptomatic, and emblematic of American foodways, that the well-received Zagat restaurant guides for a number of cities and regions in the United States (and now, Paris) rely on self-selected informants rather than experts. Similarly, in the case of literature, no literary prize awarded in the United States, not the National Book Award, not the Pulitzer, enjoys the authority and the consequent impact on sales of the top literary prizes in France, most notably the Prix Goncourt (Clark "Literary"; *Literary*, ch. 1).

Yet, of course, even a society without a cuisine has characteristic foodways, which is to say that it has a culinary culture—a set of identifiable values and representations that have shaped and continue to inform those foodways. A certain degree of (self-)consciousness characterizes contemporary culinary cultures, which is why it can be argued that a French culinary culture emerges prior to the nineteenth century (Revel, *Festin*; Mennell, *Manners*, ch. 4). What the nineteenth century added with the establishment of the gastronomic field is the acute consciousness of positions and possibilities for social mobility in a circumscribed social space.

Given that every society has a culinary culture, it falls to the ethnographer to chart that culture and track down indigenous foodways. A culinary culture is more comprehensive, less concentrated, less necessarily conflictual than a gastronomic field. It is also not centered on a specific cultural product. French culinary culture includes but reaches well beyond French (haute) cuisine and the gastronomic field. Similarly, American culinary culture comprehends much more than the fast food eateries that are so salient a feature of the American landscape. And where texts are essential to the intellectualization of food and therefore the constitution of the gastronomic field, a culinary culture incorporates a wide range of representations, most of which will not be intellectualized, or even written, sayings ("Show me a soldier plate"), anecdotes (George Bush's avowed distaste for broccoli), advertising slogans ("Where's the beef?"), and images from radio, cinema, and television: Popeye's association with spinach is indelibly inscribed in the culinary memories of generations of moviegoing Americans.[32] French culinary culture, too, has been shaped by popular sayings ("Dans le cochon, tout est bon" [Everything in the pig is good to eat]) as well as media representations (François Mitterrand's obituaries made much of the president's food and dining preferences). Whereas visual images lend important support to the gastronomic field, they are absolutely central to the formation of a culinary culture. By the same token, the texts that play the major role for a gastronomic field are less salient in the more broadly based, less focused, more loosely participatory culinary culture.

If the gastronomic field does not make sense either of or for American culinary culture, what account can be made of the America that dines out more and more, not at McDonald's but in restaurants situated at the antipodes of industrialized fast food? The America that reminds one suspiciously of France, with its adulation of avant-garde chefs and taste for culinary adventure both close to home and in far-flung places? How do we discuss the urban America in which restaurants have been so signal a factor in the reconfiguration of the cityscape and the practices it generates (Zukin, *Landscapes*, ch. 7)? A production of culture perspective suggests *restaurant world* as an appropriate model, that is, to adapt the technical definition of *art world*, "the network of people whose cooperative activity . . . produces the kind of [culinary] works that [restaurant] world is noted for" (Becker, *Art* x). Such cooperative networks can exist only in fairly circumscribed social or geographical settings endowed with mechanisms that promote connection. The sheer size of the United States, the ambient cultural pluralism, the conflicting occupational identifications of chefs and cooks (Fine, *Kitchens*) dictate that restaurant worlds in the technical, sociological sense are the exception rather than the rule.[33] This restaurant world is structured by a network of high-end restaurants run by self-consciously innovative chef-entrepreneurs. General professional support comes from a number of organizations and periodicals (Dorenburg and Page 298–304; Cooper 281–88), but more important for these elite chefs are the elite media representations that diffuse critiques and praise of given restaurants as well as anecdotes about star chefs, who, television at the ready, are likely to turn into media personalities in their own right. Centrifugal economic factors (each restaurant produces a singular cultural product and competes with others in the same market niche) are countered by centripetal social forces generated by close personal and professional connections (Ferguson and Zukin).[34] While the density of these elite restaurants is highest in New York City, the network of chefs is nationwide and, not infrequently, international as well.

Each of these models fits with a larger paradigm of assumptions concerning the relationship of food and society. The *restaurant world* focuses on production of a more or less well defined culinary product—which, in the case of the fin-de-siècle American restaurant world, can be characterized as avant-garde, eclectic cuisine. A restaurant world coheres through networks of individuals whereas a *culinary culture* fixed in practices and values is above all a model of culinary reception or consumption. Finally, a *gastronomic field* is structured importantly by a largely textual discourse that continually (re)negotiates the systemic tensions between production and consumption. The model chosen will depend on the theoretical and intellectual agenda. Culinary culture and the restaurant world take us to food; the gastronomic field points us toward other cultural fields and particularly toward the arts.

CONCLUSION

The sociological import of gastronomy or cuisine extends well beyond the particular cultural product. Taking gastronomy as a field refines our understanding of cultural fields as such, their characteristics and their character, how they operate and evolve, the respects in which they are similar and those where they differ, their connections to the larger field of cultural production and the larger society. From the outset, it has been apparent that the nature, or medium, of the cultural product is a fundamental determinant of the structure of both the field and the relations between production and consumption. Unlike the literary field, where the primary and secondary product rely on the same vehicle—writing—but like the musical field, the gastronomic field is structured not simply by the duality of direct production and indirect, critical commentary—the case for any cultural product—but by the radical disjuncture between the material and the intellectual products and the consequent dependence of the field on the written document. The objection is often raised that words "get in the way" of the primary cultural experience (tasting, seeing, reading, listening) (cf. Wolfe, *Painted*), that their intellectualization neutralizes the senses. But, in cultural fields, there is no getting around words. Whatever the deleterious effects on individual appreciation, it is the discourse of criticism and chronicle that must bear most of the weight of the cultural field.

The premium that second-order discourse places on innovation aligns gastronomy with the arts more generally in modern society where the indirect cultural production sustains the more or less stable configuration that renders conflict creative. Wherever one comes down in the debates over cuisine as an aesthetic phenomenon, it is indisputable that cuisine in France warrants classification among the arts by virtue of the attributes shared with other cultural and specifically artistic fields. The simultaneous susceptibility and resistance to change, the drive toward innovation against the force of tradition, aligns gastronomy with other modern arts that occupy fields that are similarly divided, or, more accurately, fragmented among multiple production sites, each of which negotiates invention and convention. Every field will have its distinctive networks and strategies, its bastions of traditionalism along with outposts of innovation. By simultaneously containing and promoting competition, the field generates the inevitable struggles that are the signs of cultural ferment and creativity. For good or for ill, the arts in contemporary society are tightly bound to their apposite cultural fields. Accordingly, the study of culture will do well to look to the concept of the cultural field to elucidate both the mechanics and the range of cultural experience.

The gastronomic field is so useful as a particular example precisely because it enables us to talk more concretely and particularly about cultural experiences that are easily lost to sociological study when language and practice are not aligned in theoretical understanding.

NOTES

1. The difference is evident in Bourdieu's own work. See, in addition to the suggestive discussion of the journalistic field in *On Television*, the extensive empirical examination of *Homo academicus*, and the grounded interpretation in *The Rules*

of Art. Typically, Bourdieu's analyses navigate between more and less closely defined fields (*The Field of Cultural Production* [ch. 5]). Alain Viala's examination of the seventeenth-century literary field in France works so well precisely because it scrupulously centers on readily observable cultural products and practices.

2. Bourdieu's own empirical analyses tend to map the field as constituted. They mostly draw the larger societal and intellectual consequences in order to identify the mechanisms and the logic by which the field reproduces itself. *Homo academicus* begins with the postwar university field and gives relatively little consideration to the conditions out of which the field emerged. Although the subtitle of *The Rules of Art—Genesis and Structure of the Literary Field*—indicates the goal of tracking the emergence of the literary field in mid-nineteenth-century France, the title betrays the theoretical scope. Moreover, the emphasis falls on the structure and logic of the literary field and its evolution in the last half of the century rather than on the conditions out of which the field emerged in the first half.

3. At the very least, nineteenth-century France was the site of considerable turbulence. From 1789 to 1871, there were three monarchies, three republics, and two empires; three revolutions (1789, 1830, 1848), one coup d'état (1851), and one insurrection (the Socialist Commune of 1871). Napoleon I's defeat at Waterloo in 1815 ended almost a quarter century of war and put France under occupation; Napoleon III's devastating defeat by the Prussians in 1870 after a mere six weeks of military engagement led to a second occupation by enemy troops as well as significant loss of territory (Alsace-Lorraine).

4. Arguably, only the culinary class changed, with the bourgeoisie replacing the aristocracy. But the (self-)identification of the bourgeoisie with the nation in this as in other cultural and political concerns effaced the class connotations of cuisine and implanted patriotic ones through the kinds of discourse discussed below. See Ory (passim, 1992).

5. The standard reference is to a quite dreadful poem of 1801, "La Gastronomie, ou l'Homme des champs à table" (Gastronomy, or the Man of the Fields at Table), by Joseph de Berchoux. But since a term appears in print well after it has been in circulation, Berchoux is undoubtedly more of a scribe than an inventor. What is important is the role that gastronomy and its derivatives came in to play in very short order to designate a practice that was perceived as new. Following Elias (*Civilizing*, part 1) in taking words as sociocultural indicators and seeing dictionaries as repositories of convention, I note that although the French have officially been gourmands since the fourteenth century and modern gourmets since the eighteenth, not until the nineteenth did they became gastronomes. Gastronomie first appeared in French in 1623 as a translation from the Greek of the (lost) poem of the Epicurean philosopher and culinary sage Archestratus (Athenaeus 1:445–47, 2:237). Here as elsewhere all translations are my own unless otherwise indicated.

6. The gastronome was invariably male. Beyond the fact that men held the purse strings and haute cuisine was a very expensive pursuit, the public culinary sphere was inhospitable to women: chefs as well as gastronomes were male. The

host whose duties Grimod de la Reynière spelled out with such care could only be male. Moreover, as with other urban spaces (shops, parks, public transport, and above all, the street), its inherent promiscuity gave the restaurant an uncertain moral status that effectively excluded upper- and middle-class women. At the most extreme, the gastronome dined alone. Certain of these writings are both misanthropic and misogynist. See, for one example, the "Discours d'un vrai gourmand: Avantages de la bonne chère sur les femmes" (Discourse of a True Gourmand: Advantages of Good Food over Women) (Grimod de la Reynière 1984, 2:128–34).

7. Cf. the preconditions identified by Chang and Freeman (passim, 1977) for the appearance of a Chinese cuisine in the twelfth century. Although these analyses are framed in terms of a culinary *product*—Chinese cuisine—like most commentary, they construct "cuisine" comprehensively, as a set of structured culinary *practices* and *texts* uniting producer and consumer, which I term "gastronomy."

8. The connection between gastronomy and suffrage became something of a cliché, both phenomena taken as signs of modern times and of the democratization of French society. It is worth noting that both practices remained confined to elites. At the time these works were written, during the Bourbon Restoration (1815–30), the right to vote was determined by the amount and kind of taxes paid and enfranchised approximately 1 percent of the adult male population. The July Monarchy (1830–48) expanded the voting base to some 8 percent of the population without altering the basic system. But, just as political life actively involved many nonvoters, notably impecunious scholars and intellectuals, so too gastronomy touched a public that did not dine in the great restaurants (see the discussion of Balzac, below). In both cases, the striking development of publishing and journalism was a primary factor in this general cultural diffusion. There were, of course, other populations untouched by either restaurants or the texts that talked about them and about whom few culinary journalists talked. Briffault (1846, ch. 5) stands out with even his minimal attention to hunger and to "People Who Do Not Dine," from unemployed workers to prisoners.

9. The political opportunism of Charles-Maurice de Talleyrand-Périgord (1754–1838) was only slightly more notorious than his love of fine food, allegedly leading a political opponent to remark that the only master Talleyrand never betrayed was Brie cheese (Guy 119). Carême, who was Talleyrand's chef for a time, categorically affirmed his gastronomic supremacy (*L'Art* xiii–xvi).

10. Boundary-setting mechanisms identified by Goblot as defining for the French bourgeoisie include the *baccalauréat* degree and the various means (Latin references, for example) and the sober formal dress for elite men. Dining out in elegant restaurants was another sign with which the elite distinguished itself from non-elites and upheld group solidarity. More generally on culinary stratification, see Bourdieu (*Distinction* 177–99).

11. The other six are avarice, anger, envy, pride, lust, and sloth [*avarice, colère, envie, orgueil, luxure, paresse*]. The seven sins were codified in the sixth century as deadly or, as French has it, "capital" sins, since these dispositions (rather than acts)

were at "the head of," and therefore responsible for, a multiplicity of sinful acts (anger, for example, leading to murder).

12. The paradigmatic recasting of vice as virtue and redefining sin as socially useful comes in a novel by the immensely popular writer Eugène Sue, *Gourmandise*, one in the series of *The Seven Deadly Sins*, which were written before and during the revolution of 1848. Sue's demonstration of the social utility of all the deadly sins accords gluttony [gourmandise] the pivotal role. All eight nephews and nieces of the hero are engaged in food production (pastry maker, fish monger, grocer, bread maker, game supplier, butcher, wine merchant, and captain of a merchant vessel with the emblematic name of *Gastronome* who imports foodstuffs from the colonies). The reformist socialist author set up a profit\-sharing scheme not unlike those proposed in other of his novels, and assembled all the "sinful" and "sinning" protagonists of the first six novels for a joyous repast at the end of *Gourmandise*, conviviality reinforcing the positive functions of this erstwhile social sin.

13. This distinction situates cuisine at the opposite end of the production-criticism continuum from literature—where the original product (the literary work) and the critical interpretation make use of the same vehicle—words. In this respect, cuisine, like music, is a performative art. As such, it depends on words for its social survival—recipes (scores) that make it possible to reproduce the original. (Of course, one can question whether the original product is the recipe on the page or the dish on the table.) On this continuum, the plastic arts lie somewhere between the literary and the performing arts because although there is a disjuncture between the medium of creation-production and the idiom of criticism, there is a tangible, more or less durable product. The overlap of (creative) writers and critics has a good deal to do with the intellectuality possible in writing. From this point of view, cuisine represents the intellectualization of a sensual, material product—food.

14. It is not by chance that gastronomy owes its existence to founding fathers, and this despite the "natural," "logical," and traditionally dominant associations of women with food and feeding. But those associations concern the domestic order, whereas gastronomy occupied the public domain. Furthermore, in statements similar to those made relative to artistic activity, women were deemed incapable of culinary creativity. They were "slaves to routine," as a not atypical remark at the time asserted. If a man "hadn't grabbed a hold of the frying pan, [culinary] art would have stayed where it was, and we would still be eating Esau's lentils and Homer's roast beef" (Périgord 1825, 121). Carême, for his part, characterized modern cuisine as both "virile and elegant" (1841, dedication and xxviii). On the whole, the professionalization of the culinary arts over the nineteenth century excluded women in the most public, upper reaches, an exclusion that is still apparent in upscale French-oriented restaurants today, in France and elsewhere (See Mennell 201–4; Cooper; Ferguson and Zukin).

15. As he repeatedly stressed, Carême's works were not simply collections of recipes but culinary treatises. But they are much more than that, especially as

Carême very much fancied himself a writer, even while lamenting his untutored style (1841, xi). Not only is virtually every recipe preceded and followed by observations, anecdotes, and sundry remarks; each volume also contains inordinately ambitious disquisitions of a more general order, a lengthy "Preliminary Discourse," a "Parallel of Old and Modern Cuisine," a "Philosophical History of Cuisine from the discovery of fire to the present," "Aphorisms, Thoughts, and Maxims," "How Napoleon Ate in Exile on St Helena," "A Critical Review of the Grand Balls of 1811–1812," and similar commentary.

16. Although French cookbooks had for some time urged cooks to forswear the strong spices of medieval cooking (ginger, coriander, cinnamon, allspice) (Flandrin, Hyman, and Hyman 1983), it was Carême who most decisively and emphatically replaced these with herbs (thyme, basil, savory, bay leaf, parsley, chervil, tarragon) and plants (garlic, shallots, onions) (Carême 1833, lxi–lxiv). A description by an English visitor to the Rothschild household where Carême was in charge gives an idea of this new, simplified yet complex, and highly self-consciously modern cuisine as it appeared on the table: "Its character was that it was in season, . . . up to its time, . . . in the spirit of the age, . . . , no trace of the wisdom of our ancestors in a single dish; no high-spiced sauces, no dark brown gravies, no flavour of cayenne and allspice, no tincture of catsup and walnut pickle, no visible agency of those vulgar elements of cooking, of the good old times, fire and water. . . . Every meat presented its own natural aroma, every vegetable its own shade of verdure" (Morgan 2: 415–16).

17. Carême's game was rather more complicated because the chefs and steward (maître d'hôtel) to whom he dedicated his works were carefully situated with respect to their elite employers: M. Mueller (*Le Pâtissier pittoresque*) was the chief steward for the Russian tsar; M. Boucher (*Le Pâtissier royal*), the steward for Talleyrand's household; the Robert brothers (*Le Maître d'hôtel français*), chefs who had worked in the most illustrious houses in Paris and Europe. Not until *L'Art de la cuisine française au dix-neuvième siècle* (1833) did Carême, who remained extremely conscious of his humble origins, feel secure enough to dedicate his work directly to his patron (and even then the dedication was at one remove, since the dedicatee was Madame Rothschild).

18. Instrumentality can be (re)defined by the reader's circumstances. Gillet (1993) argues that cookbooks constitute true gastronomic literature, and that recipes not only can but should be read as an exercise in literary gourmandise. Changes in culinary as well as reading conditions similarly affect instrumentality. Medieval recipes, for example, mean little to us today, even if we could procure the exact ingredients, while, at the other end of the spectrum, the complexity and technicity of the professional cooking Carême initiated make it all but impossible for nonprofessionals to give his recipes anything but a noninstrumental reading. And what reading should we give to a work like *The Alice B. Toklas Cook Book*? Should the celebrated hashish fudge really be attempted?

19. The *Physiology of Taste* seems to have been the first work to exploit physiologie as a sociological as opposed to biological or medical concept. In the decade

that followed, *The Physiologie* came to refer to a short essay of four to ten pages published in a small and usually illustrated volume, which purported to identify the characteristic social types, institutions, or accoutrements and behavior of modern society (Ferguson *Paris* 82 ff.).

20. Mennell (102–33) argues that the distinctive culinary practices of the English gentry and prosperous farmers, which had no equivalent in France, were "decapitated" when the urban aristocracy adopted French culinary models beginning in the late seventeenth century. French professional cuisine developed from this courtly and later urban model; the methods of English professionals, including more women, evolved out of the more domestic culinary practices associated with more modest households and the countryside.

21. Jean-François Revel (1979, ch. 8) similarly denies the possibility of a national cuisine but for different reasons. The opposite of essentially conservative, traditional regional cuisines is an "international" cuisine defined by techniques and methods and rooted in the search for originality. While these categories make sense from a strictly culinary point of view, they elide the culinary nationalism that identifies a particular culinary configuration as "French." On the complex process by which fries ("French fries") became the "alimentary sign of Frenchness" and the sequence that transformed Camembert cheese from a clearly regional product into one recognized by the French themselves as "French," see respectively, Barthes (1972) and Boisard.

22. For Italian cuisine the text was Pellegrino Artusi's *La Scienza in cucina et l'arte di mangiar bene—Manuale pratico per le famiglie* [The Art of Eating Well] (1891), which, in Camporesi's argument (*Magic* 113–52), created a code of national identification that did more for national unification than Manzoni's great epic novel *I promessi sposi* [The Betrothed]. That certain dishes (corn polenta, potato gnocchi, spaghetti with tomato sauce) came to enjoy a national status was due importantly to Artusi's textual promotion.

23. That authority might be contested. The gastronome and the chef were touted as the ideal culinary couple, but the relationship was fraught with tension from competing demands due most particularly to the chef's ambiguous and fairly untenable position as simultaneously an artist and an artisan. Each of these roles assumes a different relationship with a patron/consumer/client. Cf. a contemporary "defense" of gastronomes against the "aberrations of [an innovative artist's] delirious imagination" that railed against the absence of a "culinary law" that could "contain the culinary art within its true boundaries . . . and would put . . . a brake on the propagation of doctrines pernicious to gastronomy" (Périgord 1825, 4).

24. The synecdochal perspective, the perennial dialogue between center and periphery, between haute cuisine and popular cuisines, between intellectualized cuisine and product-based regional cuisines, is revealed with particular clarity in the introduction to a novel that introduced the paradigmatic gastronome, *Dodin-Bouffant* (conceived as an homage to Brillat-Savarin). The author admits hesitating to publish a work on an apparently frivolous topic so soon after the

immense suffering sustained in the Great War of 1914–18. But should he neglect one of the "oldest and most essential of French traditions?" "A quiche lorraine . . . or a Marseillaise bouillabaisse . . . or a potato gratin from Savoy has all the refined richness of France, all its spirit and wit, its gaiety . . . , the seriousness hidden beneath its charm, . . . its malice and its gravity, . . . the full soul of its fertile, cultivated rich earth, of which its aromatic cream sauces, snowy poultry, delicate vegetables, juicy fruits, savory beef and frank, supple and ardent wines, are the blessed manifestations" (Rouff 1994, 12–13). (Rouff also co-authored a massive, multivolume culinary history of the French provinces.) On Proust's hymn to French culinary sensibility in *À la recherche du temps perdu*, see Ferguson (in press).

25. The irregular publishing history of Fourier's work makes his contribution to culinary discourse more conjectural than for the others. Although his first work appeared in 1808 (*Théorie des quatre mouvements et des destinées générales*), his last remained in manuscript until 1967 (*Le Nouveaux monde amoureux*). But Fourier's ideas were known well before the (fragmentary) edition brought out by his disciples in the mid-1840s (Beecher).

26. In the vast majority of gastronomic writing the parallels with sexual activity are irresistible and seldom resisted. It is not by chance that collectivities so assiduously regulate the one and the other to keep the direct sensuality of the individual from disrupting the social order. Second-order consumption also looms large for both. In this as in other domains Fourier's writing is conspicuous for its mixture of tones and genres, all of which add up to what can be fairly characterized as controlled delirium designed to convey the fundamental attraction of a new social order predicated on neither justice or nor equality but happiness: "The events resulting from this Order will give you, not the objects of your desires, but a happiness infinitely superior to all your desires" (1966–68, 1:170).

27. A generation younger than the other founding gastronomic fathers, he knew their work well. His gastronomic credentials include a "Gastronomic Physiology" (1830), the entry on Brillat-Savarin in the *Biographie Michaud* (1835), and the *New Theory of Lunch* (1830) (1938, 2:43–47, 62–63, 671–76).

28. "For him celibacy was less a preference than a necessity. Gourmandise, the sin of virtuous monks, opened her arms to him, and he threw himself into them as he had thrown himself into the adoration of art . . . For him good food and Bric-a-Brac were substitutes for a woman" (1976–81, 7:495). Balzac continues, reproving Brillat-Savarin for not placing enough importance on "the real pleasure" to be had at table. "Digestion, by using human forces, constitutes an inner battle which, for gastrolaters, is the equivalent of the greatest climaxes (*jouissances*) of love." Even more completely than his collection, Pons's gourmandise satisfies the desire for the total merger with the desired object.

29. Fantasia demonstrates that such fears are not without foundation in the France of the late twentieth century, given the inroads of fast food and, more importantly, changes in the eating patterns of the French (fewer women at home to prepare a full-scale lunch, commuting distances that make in-house canteens

more practicable for employee as well as employer, different, "modern" foodways more attuned to culinary pluralism). Perhaps the most striking of his findings is the clear distinction drawn by the adolescents interviewed between fast food and traditional forms of restauration, notably the café, distinctions based on the very different types of sociability appropriate to each: where fast food represents a rejection of the traditional French culinary norms of the adult world and a quick "American" fix, the café remains important as a place to drink and to talk much as it has been for a century and more. Fischler (212–17) places these debates within an international context, noting that loss of cultural identity is a concern in Spain and Italy as well as France.

30. If there is no American cuisine, there is an identifiable American diet (prevalence of fast food eaten out and prepackaged foods eaten at home, high levels of animal protein, salt, fat, and processed sugars and correspondingly low levels of fresh fruit and vegetables, preference for soda over water). See Mintz (117–22) along with the warnings issued with disquieting regularity by various health authorities.

31. The celebrated chef and cookbook writer James Beard, who did so much to promote American foods, nevertheless proposed a heavily gallicized revisionist meal even as he claimed allegiance to the traditional turkey: along with a stern warning against cranberry [it obliterates the taste of the wine], he recommended serving champagne or vodka with a first course of caviar or smoked salmon, followed by a French red wine for the cheese course and another, sweet wine for the pumpkin pie, the whole topped off with kirsch, framboise, or cognac (323). It is not without import for my overall argument that Thanksgiving, as a national food event, is the product of texts, relayed by a panoply of representations: first, the journal of Edward Winslow that recounted the meal of 1621; and subsequently, the proclamation of 1863 by which Abraham Lincoln declared Thanksgiving a national holiday and the annual presidential declarations since.

32. In 1996 the Jewish Museum in New York City presented a wonderful video exhibit of Jewish food on American television from the 1950s to the present. Similar shows could undoubtedly be mounted for other "ethnic" cuisines of long-standing. Movies such as *Eat Drink Man Woman* (Chinese cuisine), *Big Night* (Italian cuisine), and the iconic film of French cuisine, *Babette's Feast*, are important vehicles of diffusion of elite culinary values and practices.

33. Cf. the striking absence of such connection to the larger in the restaurants studied by Gary Fine (*Kitchens* 133–37) in a medium-size urban setting (Minneapolis/St. Paul). Fine relates these thin networks to the fragmented economic organization of the restaurant industry (each restaurant producing its own, singular product) and the structures of restaurant kitchens. That this world of restaurants is far from a restaurant world is clear from the speculation of a reader Fine cites about what would be necessary to turn the world of these restaurants into an art world (264). Zukin (*Cultures* 5) confirms this picture in a study of a range of mid-level restaurants in New York City.

34. As concerns patterns of interaction, a number of New York chefs interviewed (Ferguson and Zukin) mentioned that the irregular hours a chef spends on the job effectively restrict socializing to other chefs, both informally (one chef regularly ended the evening in the kitchen of a competitor-friend two blocks away) and formally, through institutions such as the James Beard Foundation and charitable benefits. Thus, simply in the first week of May 1998 as I was revising this article, four of New York's top chefs prepared a reception to benefit the Frick Collection; the James Beard Awards winners were announced at a benefit dinner; and another dinner to benefit the James Beard Foundation brought together forty-eight chefs from across the country, all of whom had at one time or another cooked in The Quilted Giraffe, the famed restaurant of the 1980s (it closed in 1992).

2. Grimod de la Reynière's *Almanach des gourmands:* Exploring the Gastronomic New World of Postrevolutionary France

MICHAEL GARVAL

Brillat-Savarin, like another Amerigo Vespucci, inherited all the glory that was owed to Grimod de la Reynière.

Charles Monselet

. . . Gourmandise is an enormous book, always open to whoever knows how to read it, and whose pages offer a series of moving tableaux, whose horizon spreads as far as the eye can see.

Grimod de la Reynière

Alexandre Balthazar Laurent Grimod de la Reynière (1758–1838), while nearly forgotten today outside specialist circles, became famous in his day as the author of several pioneering gastronomic works. Within just a few years, he published a short-lived *Journal des gourmands et des belles* (1806), a *Manuel des amphitryons* (1808), and, most importantly, an eight-volume *Almanach des gourmands* (1803–12). This was a transitional period for French society in so many ways, fine dining included. In the wake of the French Revolution, the ancien régime model of elegant meals served exclusively in wealthy, aristocratic households to the privileged few, was giving way to a new order of broader bourgeois consumption. The rising bourgeoisie longed to eat as well as its aristocratic betters had before, and those who once supplied refined fare to the nobility now clamored to meet the needs of a new, untitled clientele. In particular, the restaurant, which had originated in the decades preceding the Revolution, was launched into prominence by talented chefs who, no longer attached to aristocratic households, needed new outlets for their skills.

French food had been renowned for its refinement from at least the mid-seventeenth century onward; however, this sophistication circulated within a rigid, closed system of exchange between aristocratic hosts, their distinguished guests, and an elite food service sector of cooks, serving staff, and specialty food purveyors who catered to their wishes. In contrast, the period in which Grimod wrote his gastronomic works witnessed an incipient democratization of culinary luxury, that would continue throughout the nineteenth century and into the twentieth. As the epigraph from Charles Monselet suggests, there was a gastronomic new world to be explored. Grimod de la Reynière was the first to grasp and begin to exploit its vast potential, inventing a role for himself as an intermediary between the swelling ranks of bourgeois consumers, ever more eager for culinary refinement, and the burgeoning providers of gastronomic pleasure—food shops, wine and spirit merchants, restaurants—vying for their share of a growing market.

Despite his originality, Grimod has been undeservedly overshadowed, indeed nearly eclipsed by his successor, and in many ways imitator, Jean-Anthelme Brillat-Savarin: "Brillat-Savarin is much more widely read and his *Physiology of Taste* is available nowadays in numerous editions. This different treatment is a true historical injustice for . . . Grimod is really the sole founding father of gastronomy in whom all the gastronomes and chroniclers of gastronomy of the nineteenth and twentieth century recognize themselves" (Bonnet 7). Since its publication in 1825, Brillat-Savarin's *Physiologie du goût* has remained easily available and familiar to the general public, if only through its memorable aphorisms. While also popular when first published, none of Grimod's works would be reedited for over a century and a half. Finally, a paperback sampling of Grimod's writings, *Écrits gastronomiques*, published in 1978 and reissued in 1997, included excerpts from the first year of the *Almanach*. A complete edition of the *Manuel des Amphitryons* appeared in 1983. To date, however, the seminal *Almanach des gourmands* has never been reedited in its entirety and little of Grimod has been translated into English.

Scholarship on Grimod's oeuvre has been extremely limited. The most recent bibliography, Ned Rival's *Grimod de la Reynière, Le Gourmand gentilhomme*, dates from 1983. No more than a few pages are devoted to Grimod and his work in most recent historical studies of gastronomy (Aron, Revel, Ory, Pitte). Rebecca Spang gives Grimod fuller treatment in her excellent study *The Invention of the Restaurant*; however, the most extensive critical study of Grimod's work is Jean-Claude Bonnet's introduction to the 1978 *Écrits gastronomiques*. While informative and insightful, Bonnet's essay privileges the philosophical and aesthetic dimensions of Grimod's writing. This elucidates important aspects of Grimod's work, and seems a useful strategy for rehabilitating it in the eyes of a French public that covets the high-culture prestige of gastronomy. Yet Bonnet's approach neglects the broader, more popular thrust of Grimod's work, its fascination with the rich possibilities for commerce, publicity, and celebrity that the terra incognita of gastronomy could offer.

The purpose of this essay is therefore twofold. It offers an introduction to Grimod's important yet unfamiliar oeuvre, particularly to his pivotal *Almanach des gourmands*, which experimented with a dazzlingly rich variety of novel subjects and forms: from consuming summer oysters, to tenderizing meat with electric shocks, to reviving a cook's sense of taste through regular purges; and, from restaurant reviews, to guidebook-type "promenades" and "itineraries" of purveyors and eating establishments, to "correspondance gourmande" with the almanac's readers, to product endorsements based upon "blind" taste tests. On another level, this essay seeks to expand our critical understanding of Grimod's work beyond a strictly high culture perspective, and consider its broader impact, for so much of the massive, later development of popular gastronomic discourse, in journalism, advertising, and tourism, can be traced to Grimod's imaginative explorations in the *Almanach des gourmands*.

THE REVOLUTION AS HORS D'OEUVRE

In a necessary follow-up to the Revolution, a turn-about put fortunes into new hands and the mind of all these *nouveaux riches* turned especially toward purely animal pleasures. It was believed that they would be rendered service by being offered a reliable guide to the most solid part of their dearest pleasures. The heart of most wealthy Parisians had suddenly been transformed into a gullet; their emotions are nothing more than sensations, and their desires, appetites. They are properly served by being given in several pages, in the guise of good food, the means of getting the best for their appetites and money.

Grimod de la Reynière, *Almanach des Gourmands* (1:i–ii)[1]

. . . the result of the changes of gourmandise is much more important to the happiness of man in society than that of social, administrative, or judiciary changes.

Grimod de la Reynière, *Almanach des Gourmands* (7:31)

Son of a wealthy financier, Grimod laments the overall effects of the Revolution. "This revolutionary torrent . . . invaded and ruined everything" (2:61). In particular, life in polite society has suffered; little aristocratic *savoir-vivre* has survived the guillotine. Gone are the charmingly refined suppers of yore (2:61). Women, who had graced these suppers so captivatingly, are less appealing now, for they have become immodest (2:64). The dukes and peers of the monarchy have been supplanted by bankers and entrepreneurs who, while rich, are far less polite (2:63). Alas, money alone cannot make a gracious host (2:30–31, 140). The consummate, old-style Amphitryon, rich yet enlightened, a fount of gustatory wisdom and owner of an enviable wine cellar (4:166), is like an endangered species whose survival must be assured; our pleasure depends on it (2:36).

Yet Grimod acknowledges that, for gourmandise, substantial good has come of the Revolution. Not all of what once distinguished French cuisine has been lost. Thus, the "rolls of the la rue Dauphine" (6:45–49), whose production has recommenced after being interrupted by the Revolution, "unite all the fans of the old and new regimes . . . reconcile all opinions . . . reduce all distances, because they please all tastes" (6:48). In many ways, moreover, the Revolution has improved French cuisine: "if the Revolution was deadly in France for most of the Arts, that of cooking, far from having suffered, owed it rapid progress and moving activity (Grimod and Bonnet, 79). The culinary arts—along with the general public's interest in and appreciation of them—have progressed well beyond where they were before, as pâtisserie demonstrates:

> We must pay homage here to the progress made in the art of baking in France over about a dozen years. . . . This useful revolution was also the work of the public, which supported it as best as it could. The consumption of pastry has more than doubled in Paris. . . . In this area, palates have become more delicate, more demanding, more difficult; and all the artists, attached to the old school, who have remained behind this revolution, have seen their fortunes and businesses rapidly decline and collapse. (2:155–57)

Where gastronomic pleasure is at stake, Grimod prefers a "useful revolution" to an ancien régime of stale routine. Progress occurs when the public—with proper guidance—esteems worthwhile innovations. Grimod's role, his responsibility, is to recognize and praise culinary achievement, and encourage the people to do the same. Indeed, the exhortation to pay homage to progress exemplifies Grimod's understanding of his broader gastronomic *mission civilisatrice*, for his is the royal "we" of a self-appointed public gastronome, at once shepherd and trendsetter, leading the French people along the path of good taste.

In the final volume of his almanac, in "Des progrès dans la Cuisine dans le XIXe siècle," Grimod reviews what has been accomplished since the Revolution. Cuisine is far more varied now than before (8:59). Furthermore, "Amphitryons have made their table something serious" (59); the renaissance of the Amphitryon, for which he hoped earlier, seems now to be occurring. Meanwhile, *cuisiniers* have acquired a new stature: "Having stopped being simple maîtres-queux, in becoming real artists, they have figured out how to be respected and be better paid than the greatest *maîtres d* were formerly" (60). Guests too have evolved: "the taste of guests has been purified; becoming more enlightened, they have also become more difficult" (60). Finally, the table has become "the pivot of all political, literary, financial, and business matters" (61). In all these salutary developments, Grimod boasts, the *Almanach* has served as a beacon: "Since the *Almanach* first appeared in 1803, people have gotten used to studying and widening the great art of the palate [*le grand Art de la gueule*]" (60).

Through the eight volumes of his almanac, Grimod makes his peace with the Revolution. He realizes that it has allowed him to claim his role, in the spotlight, as the arbiter of all things delicious. To use the sort of culinary metaphor dear to Grimod, the Revolution serves as an hors d'oeuvre to the new world of his almanac, separate from yet a necessary preamble to the main work.

A PROTEAN AUTHOR FOR PROTEAN MATERIAL

No rule exists for such compositions; they are at the mercy of the artist's genius.

Grimod de la Reynière, "Des pièces montées,"
Almanach des gourmands (7:6)

Flexible in how he sees his role as author, Grimod is well-suited to the heterogeneous, rapidly evolving field he explores in his almanac. He describes himself as a "professor," a "judge," an "historian of Gourmands" (2:244; 4:140), "the prime minister of the palate [*gueule*]" (6:viii–xiii) and, simply, a "gourmand," a term he defends against the Academy's definition of it as "glutton" or "greedy individual [*goulu*]." While these terms connote intemperance and insatiable greed, "gourmand" has, in recent years, in polite society, taken on a much nobler meaning (3:1). No mindless, gluttonous slob, the *gourmand is* instead a gustatory veteran who, through years of application, has evolved an extraordinarily sensitive, discerning palate (3:2). In short, Grimod elevates gourmand to a "profession" (3:248), though he is careful to distinguish it from that of *cuisinier*. By this he means no disrespect to chefs, whom he praises constantly as "artistes," even "génies." Rather, he thus acknowledges a necessary division of labor between practitioner and theoretician, as illustrated by his idea for a "History of French Cooking" in which "a talented cook would have to write everything related to practice, while a knowledgeable gourmet would write the historical and theoretical part" (3:273–74). Similarly, he refuses to provide recipes, for "the Almanac of Gourmands is not a cookbook; our obligation is to try to stimulate our readers' appetites; it is up to artists alone to satisfy them" (5:7–8).

According to the liminal "Bookseller's Notice," the purpose of the rapidly written first volume is to "gauge the public's taste through an essay." As a free-ranging expository form, and an attempt or trial, "essay" suggests both compositional openness, and a spirit of experimentation. Were this "bagatelle" to please the public, then "we would promise it a more complete and even more polished edition the following year." In other words, it is at once a first volume, and market research for the second. Similarly, while the material considered here is "quite vast . . . for a simple Almanac, . . . [t]his useful and portable form . . . [is] to many readers' tastes" (1:v–vi). From the outset then, Grimod is keenly aware of the wealth of his subject, eager to experiment with it, and willing to adapt to the public's wishes. By volume 6, he looks back on its evolution and observes that he has consistently found more to say: "The field [*carrière*] has gotten bigger in front of us, as we have tried go through it" (6:viii–ix).[2]

In this work in progress, Grimod tries different ideas, topics, and formats, retaining some and discarding or modifying others. Even the original "almanac" concept would soon fade, as Grimod evolved his project in other directions. The first volume opens with a "Calendar of nutrition [*Calendrier nutritif*]," a long, month-by-month review of seasonal specialties, and closes with a twelve-page republican calendar. In the second, the republican calendar moves to the beginning while the "Calendrier nutritif" drops out. By the third, both elements disappear entirely. In their place, Grimod develops others: anecdotes, "gourmand poetry," an "eating song," even a "gourmand necrology." In particular, Grimod plans originally for a restaurant and food source guide in alternate volumes, and does leave this out of the second after its debut in the first, but soon finds his readership clamoring for one yearly. By volume four he acknowledges that, among "real Gourmands," this is the most read, reread, food-stained section, and promises to publish it annually (4:38). The "Itinerary of nutrition" in volume one, and the "Gourmand's Walk in Paris" in three, as their titles suggest, are organized geographically, moving clockwise around the center of Paris, mixing categories of establishments: drugstores, pastry shops, restaurants, dinnerware merchants, adjacent on the page, as on the city streets.[3] In volume 4 he proposes to vary this regular feature by changing the form. Instead of ordering by neighborhood, he will do so by category (restaurants, *pâtissiers*, etc.). The new "Petite revue gourmande" will perhaps provide less variety than before, but its organization "will please methodical people more and . . . make research easier" (4:139). Responding to the public's preference for this format, he continues it in the remaining four volumes, commenting frequently on the popularity of this section with a mix of pride and some dismay, for its success had eclipsed his more creative efforts elsewhere in the *Almanach*. As he complains in a letter, this sort of writing is "the most insipid to write and the most difficult to edit"(quoted in Desnoiresterres 296); while promoting the "artists" reviewed, it does little for his renown (8:201).

Grimod strives always to offer something new and better. He constantly tests his abundant ideas, even in his improvements to the almanac's index. In volume 1, the "alphabetic table" is the fourth section from last, whereas from volume 2 on it moves to the end, with articles listed in italics, making it and its contents easier to locate. Grimod also tries to follow the inclinations of his public. In an important note at the end of volume 1's preface, reiterated in later volumes, Grimod solicits "opinions, information, and even *samples*." He thus invites the public to help formulate the almanac, a novel idea that would flourish later on, particularly in the more democratically minded American market, culminating in the Zagat restaurant and food source guides, based entirely upon reader surveys. In Grimod's case, he takes to heart readers' interest in particular topics, publishing the "Revue Gourmande" more frequently than planned, and scrutinizing "la Morale Gourmande," i.e., largely unexplored issues of punctuality, politeness, and mutual responsibility of guest and host: "Gourmand mores [*Morale*] have become . . . an ever more vast and fertile field, that we were offered a sort of virgin land to clear" (5:x). By volume three, Grimod is receiving abundant letters, and food samples ("légitimations"), which must be sent "FRANC DE

PORT" (3:xv) if not to be returned. In the change from the author's initial, wishful solicitation of correspondence and samples, to his inundation by such mail two years later, we see the success of the *Almanach* in general and, in particular, of Grimod's strategy of involving the public. We shall look more closely later at the process he develops for evaluating an ever greater number of food samples.

Constantly experimenting with the form of his composition, and expanding into new territory, Grimod is keenly attuned to analogous innovations by culinary *artistes*. Examples from one volume include: eel pâté from Abbéville (6:34–37), truffle maraschino (6:42–45), Curaçao from Douai (6:62–66), and tricks for creating monstrously large hard-boiled eggs (6:66–70) or dyeing live shrimp red (6:70–74). Other innovations discussed are even stranger, like the fine condiment producer Maille's new vinegar that restores a woman's virginity (2:218), a useful article in an age of female immodesty.[4] Grimod enthuses as well about a new method of food conservation in "Des légumes et fruits en bouteille" (3:138–43), the "founding father of gastronomy" thus praising the forerunner of canned peas. In "De l'électricité dans ses rapports avec la cuisine" (2:210–15), he lauds a new process for killing animals by electric shock, which tenderizes the meat at the same time. There is no more need to age the carcass: just zap, then roast, with equally good results! Grimod also marvels at "Des sachets préservateurs" or "Sachets anti-apoplectiques" which, when hung around the neck, so they rest above the stomach, will protect the *gourmand* from the occupational hazard of overeating-induced apoplexy, for an entire year (5:24–28).

In the final two volumes of the *Almanach*, Grimod distances himself from this fascination with innovation for innovation's sake. In volume 7 he notes that although over two years have passed since the last one, there are few new discoveries,

> which would lead us to believe that the more that the great art of food is ready to reach perfection, the more it has become stationary in some way. This kind of immobility is not a great evil. In this beautiful field [*carrière*], it is better to perfect what one has than to give oneself over to vain aberrations, in order to find something better, which is often the enemy of good. (7:178)

Such futile innovations are "these sad abortions of a clouded, delirious mind [that] have only an ephemeral existence and shine only from a passing burst of light" (7:179). In volume 8, he begins in the same vein, then adopts the opposite viewpoint:

Has then the genius of our great artists of cooking gotten cold? Or are they in the process of proving that this art having reached the pinnacle of its glory, must remain still and has no more conquests to make?

Let them not be mistaken; in this field as in all the other arts, whoever stops falls behind. It is only in flying always toward new discoveries that one can hope to keep a glory that diminishes bit by bit if not added to. (8:156)

Much in these contradictory comments anticipates debate over French Romanticism, two decades later. As the stance adopted in volume 7 suggests, there is the danger of reckless innovation. Phrases like "vain aberrations" and "these sad abortions of a clouded, delirious mind," applied to unhappy culinary inventions, could refer to painter Frenhofer's dubious "masterpiece" in Balzac's "Le Chef d'oeuvre inconnu." Yet, underlying the position defended in volume 8, is an emergent avant-garde imperative in the arts, the idea that a creative artist can only succeed—and secure lasting fame—through constant innovation. Beneath this, we sense Grimod's malaise about his own writing, its reception, even the future of the *Almanach*. By the preface to volume 5, he notes that it is hard to continue writing with "the same dose of engagement and originality that was seen in our first volume. After having plucked the flower of our subject, we have since tried to make use of the fruit, and to instruct Gourmands at least, even if we could not amuse them" (5:ix–x). In the 1812 *Almanach*, Grimod celebrated innovation, while lamenting his own flagging creativity, which helps to explain why this volume would be his last.

GRIMOD AND BRILLAT

Reading Grimod's *Almanach* for the first time, when familiar with Brillat-Savarin's *Physiologie du goût*, one experiences *déjà lu*. So many of the preoccupations and points of view, and even specific formulations and anecdotes thought to exemplify Brillat-Savarin's originality, first appear in Grimod's *Almanach*. This should come as no surprise, for it was precisely when Grimod's work was being published, to considerable public acclaim, that Brillat was embarking on early versions of his *Physiologie du goût*. Brillat's debt was so overwhelming that he dared not avow it. There is not one mention of Grimod in the *Physiologie du goût*. Some of the principal components of Brillat's *Physiologie* that already figure prominently in Grimod's *Almanach* include: a glorification of gourmandise; a preoccupation with the relations between host and guest, with a particular concern for assuring the guest's complete happiness; an overriding concern for careful education of the palate, but also for nutritive and dietary considerations, in short for dining as a total mind and body experience; and a strong sense of food's social, historical, and political contexts. Many specific stories, analyses, and observations in Brillat are reminiscent of ones in Grimod, like Brillat's tale of the Chevalier de Langeac, which recalls Grimod's similar anecdote about a curé.[5] The most damning comparison though is between Brillat's celebrated aphorisms and their prefigurations in Grimod's *Almanach*. To wit:

BRILLAT-SAVARIN	GRIMOD DE LA REYNIÈRE
III. The fate of nations depends on how they are nourished.	How often has the fate of an entire people not depended on the relatively quick or slow digestion of a prime minister? (Grimod 78)
IV. Tell me what you eat; I will tell you what you are.	*Tell me whom you frequent; I will tell you who you are.* In two words that is the secret of braises. (6:136)
X. Those who get indigestion or get drunk do not know how to eat or drink.	A Gourmand must always avoid indigestion. (3:248)
XIV. A dessert without cheese is like a beautiful woman missing an eye.	A great dinner without hors d'oeuvres is as valueless as a woman without rouge. (4:8)
XV. One becomes a cook, but one is born a roaster.	The art of roasting meats precisely is one of the most difficult in the world, where one finds a thousand good cooks for every perfect roaster. (Grimod 89)
	A good Amphitryon is almost as rare as a good roaster. (2:140)
	Good roasters are even more rare than great cooks. (4:16)
XVI. The most indispensable quality in a cook is promptness [*exactitude*]: it must also be that of the diner [*convié*].	A true Gourmand never makes others wait for him. (1:215)
XVII. Waiting too long for a late guest is a lack of respect for those who are present.	

While Brillat's formulations here are generally more elegant, Grimod already expresses the heart of the matter, and these are just some of the more obvious comparisons. Indeed, all the ideas conveyed by Brillat's twenty aphorisms can be found in Grimod's *Almanach*, at least in embryonic form and often developed at length.

Grimod's manic energy, his discoverer's exuberance, lay the foundation for Brillat's greater sobriety, maturity of judgement, and stylistic sophistication. Remarkably, Grimod even anticipated someone succeeding him in this way. In a note to the "Avertissement de l'Éditeur" in volume 1 (unfortunately omitted from Bonnet's edition), Grimod writes,

> The haste in which this little work was conceived, written, edited, and even printed will undoubtedly expose us to many reproaches and reclamations. We shall forestall that with a word: perfection is time's daughter. An absolutely complete collection of this sort is the work of twenty years of care, research, labor, and meditation.

As M. F. K. Fisher notes admiringly in her "Translator's Preface" to the *Physiology of Taste*, Brillat-Savarin indeed "spent perhaps twenty-five or thirty years writing" his magnum opus. With extraordinary prescience, Grimod foresaw how the terrain uncovered in his almanac could be cultivated to more elegant effect by someone of a steadier temperament. Though Brillat did not acknowledge it, he too understood that Grimod's originality, plus his own application, could yield the *Physiology of Taste*.

PARIS, CAPITAL OF GOURMANDISE

For Walter Benjamin, Paris is the capital of the nineteenth century. For Grimod—a proud Parisian, unlike provincial magistrate Brillat—it is the capital of gourmandise. For example, the regrettable dirtiness of the sprawling market at Les Halles is not worthy of this great city, "the Capital of the Gourmand Empire" (6:217). Paris not only has the finest cuisine ("the first in the universe" [3:210]), but also consumes more fine wine than any other city ("there is none where more sophisticated is sold" [4:165]). It is, for a gourmand, "the center of all pleasures" (8:43). Yet why?

The French had long considered Paris the center of most everything, from politics, to commerce, to the arts. But this Paris-centric perspective burgeoned in Grimod's day, as Napoleonic centralization and expansion made Paris ever more central to an ever-larger realm. In addition, as Grimod's work attests, postrevolutionary France was experiencing an unprecedented culinary boom. Before the Revolution, aristocrats had eaten better in Paris than anywhere else. Now, with an increasing democ-ratization of gourmandise, everyone could aspire to eat better here than anywhere else, while waiting for the gospel of fine dining to reach the rest of the planet.

Throughout the *Almanach*, Grimod assumes that Paris, the world's greatest city, has the best food and drink. For example, Parisian cuisine's preference for butter, and sparing use of garlic, proves its incomparable subtlety and, in particular, "its superiority over the cuisines of Languedoc and Provence" (8:15), awash in olive oil and aioli. Elsewhere, while just as chauvinistic, Grimod considers more thoughtfully the reasons for Parisian culinary greatness. Paris, he observes in "Des voyages gourmands," receives the best from around the world:

> The gourmand, and especially the Parisian gourmand, generally travels little. Accustomed to seeing all the provinces bring him the best of their production as tribute, he has no need to seek them at their origin; as long as he has wealth and taste, he enjoys, without moving, all the gourmand riches disseminated on the surface of the four corners of the globe. (8:40)

There is a revealing, "Napoleonic" slippage here from "toutes les Provinces" to "(l)es quatre parties du Globe." From the perspective of a Parisian gourmand under the First Empire (and still today, for that mat-ter) all the world's a province, paying alimentary "tribute" to Paris with its finest offerings. French cuisine—and a fortiori Parisian cuisine, its quintessence—is enhanced by adopting the entire world's best dishes and "discoveries." To a German reader's suggestion that French *cuisiniers* should explore foreign cuisines, Grimod responds, "Although French cuisine is without contest the best in the world, we think it could be enriched with a great number of foreign dishes and appropriate them while perfecting them" (3:295). Similarly, "if France has become the supreme arbiter in the art of taste, it is greatly due to the care it has taken to reject no foreign dis-covery" (4:59). Finally, Grimod notes in the last volume, reviewing France's progress in the culinary arts over the past two decades, "our great artists, not content with national discoveries . . . did not hesitate [*rougi*] to explore foreign lands and to let them offer all the cuisines of the continent; except for rectifying and making conform to our taste, the dishes they have brought back from their travels" (8:59). French cuisine's genius lies in "correcting" and "perfecting" a foreign dish—like *coulibiac*, for example, originally Russian—making it France's own, gallicizing its name, giving it a French passport, as it were, to travel back to the four corners of the earth as a French delicacy. Such return trips generally originate in Paris, culinary crucible, transportation hub, and foreign trade fulcrum.

Two interrelated concepts define Paris's role as the world capital of gourmandise: *émulation* (one of Grimod's favorite terms), and *rayonnement* (our term). *Émulation*, for Grimod, means setting a standard of creative achievement that spurs others on to ever-greater progress. In a distinctly modern, avant-gardist view of creation, innovation begets innovation. As Grimod suggests in volume 3, the food critic, like counterparts in non-culinary arts (he had been a theater critic), guides creators through his judgements:

> If in this new picture we more often have recourse to our criticism rather than to our praise, that proves that emulation has made artists of good food make progress, from which the public gets great benefit and to which we would like to believe our Almanac is not a stranger. (3: xii)

By volume 5, he asserts:

> The appearance of the first year's gourmand's Almanac produced on all state of the mouth of the capital effects of which it is almost impossible to form an idea when one has not had the chance to witness it. It has excited an emulation theretofore unknown, by developing the talent, the love of glory, and the thirst for success in most artists; in short time, it has made great strides in the art of the palate. (5:79–80)

Through judicious criticism and praise of culinary *artistes*, Grimod's *Almanach* catalyzes *émulation*. He had hoped his abortive *Journal des Gourmands et des Belles* would do so even better, monthly publication making it more responsive to developments in the culinary arts.[6]

The *Almanach* features many specific examples of *émulation*, like that of Parisian mustard houses Maille and Bordin: "Such success gave birth to emulation and several cities [like Dijon and Meaux] sought to dispute in Paris superiority in the preparation of mustard" (2:90–91). This illustrates the general pattern. Superior culinary achievement begins in Paris, then spreads to the provinces, and eventually to the rest of the world. *Émulation* thus engenders *rayonnement*, or cultural "radiance."

While the term "rayonnement" did not acquire this figurative meaning until 1869 (*Le Petit Robert*), the idea of French civilization as a beacon, radiating out onto heretofore less enlightened parts of the globe, ignited during the revolutionary and Napoleonic periods. *Rayonnement* has since informed much of France's relation to the rest of the world, from early efforts to export the revolution elsewhere in Europe, to French schools in colonial outposts, to international organizations like the Alliance Française and Médecins sans frontières, to Paul Bocuse's branch restaurant in Tokyo.

While waiting for a monthly *Journal* to provide "the surest way of spreading the best food doctrine in France and even part of Europe" (3:162), Grimod uses the *Almanach* toward this end, particularly its "nutritive itinerary" section:

> This itinerary does not only please those who usually live in the capital, but we know, without a doubt, that it has also become the gourmand compass of residents of the provinces and even strangers who make appearances here from time to time. They have hardly returned home that this itinerary still guides them when they want to get alimentary products from Paris. Most of the merchants and producers we celebrate know this well. (4:xiv)

Grimod's mediated Paris, the "ville gourmande" outlined in his itinéraire, serves as the world's "compass" or "guide" for gourmandise. The passage also anticipates such later developments as culinary souvenirs (e.g., Galettes de Pont-Aven from Brittany, Sacher torte from Vienna, Indian River grapefruit from Florida) or mail-order food catalogues that allow gourmands in far-flung places to enjoy delicacies from elite purveyors like Fauchon or Williams-Sonoma. In these ways, as in so many others, Grimod was a visionary.

GRIMOD AS VISIONARY

Grimod's *Almanach* is peppered with promising ideas, many of which would only blossom later. His fertile imagination anticipated so much of subsequent gastronomic writing, and of the whole food industry's later evolution. Experimenting with the form and content of his almanac, Grimod foresaw the advantages of periodical publication. In addition to his short-lived *Journal des Gourmands et des Belles*, he often reflected in his almanac on the potential of a "Journal-Gourmand," imagining much of later culinary journalism, from newspaper restaurant reviews to magazines like *Gourmet* or *Bon Appétit*. In such a publication,

One would put, from birth, everything that the Genius of good food had the pleasure to invent each day; one would signal the progress of artists and their constant efforts to be worthy of public favor; one would give a glimpse of the price of all edible goods, local and exotic; lastly, one would keep a record of all well-known indigestion. (2:229)

A clearing-house for breaking culinary news, market trends, and gastro-nomic gossip, Grimod's hypothetical "Journal-Gourmand" could also become "an easy means for correspondence among the gourmands of all countries . . . [and] between Paris and the provinces" (2:229–30). Demanding but fair in its judgements, the "Journal-Gourmand" would encourage foreign countries to send their best goods to Paris: "each coun-try's glory would profit by sending nothing mediocre to Paris, for the journal would exercise severe but impartial censure on such products" (2:232). Producing a publication like this would be expensive, but the investment worthwhile, both to investors and the public at large, as the journal "would shortly bring about a noticeable improvement in all prod-ucts of our gourmand producers [*nos fabriques gourmandes*]" (2:231). Above all, the speed with which such a publication could disseminate gastro-nomic news would make it so effective: "This prompt publicity given to new processes would stimulate other artists' emulation, would fire up their imagination, and would direct their work toward the goal that every capa-ble man in this field must have: waking our appetite and pleasing our sensuality" (3:160).

This use of *publicité* suggests as well Grimod's interest in advertising food products in publications, like his, targeting gourmands.[7] In his open-ing editorial to the March 1806 *Journal des Gourmands et des Belles*, Grimod imagines that in later issues,

We shall have a separate article of announcements of edibles as soon as the abundance of such matters permits. Thus, gentlemen grocers, bak-ers, distillers of alcohol, you are invited to join *to the sample (which should be sent only to our office)* the exact price of the objects to be listed. (n.p.)

In volume four of the *Almanach*, in the "Marchands de vins" section of the *Petite revue gourmande*, Grimod cautions, "One must be cautious with wine merchants who have announcements every day in the classifieds [*Petites Affiches*]. It is to be surmised that they would not take such care in getting themselves known if they really deserved to be so" (4:168). Beware of where you get your information: trust listings in my

Almanach, rather than paid advertisements. The warning however belies Grimod's awareness of fundamental similarities between his project and food and beverage advertisements. Thus, in the same volume, he comments on his *jury dégustateur* or tasting panel and, specifically, on the commercial impact that publication of the panel's proceedings can have: "the result of these judgments announced the following year becomes for the authors, if not a patent on immortality, at least quite a useful announcement. There is not one who, by the growth in his business, did not feel the full effectiveness" (4:xx).

Grimod's *jury dégustateur* is part of his original system for evaluating food samples, called *légitimations*, an idiosyncratic term first explained in volume 2:

> This word . . . means the action of an artist of good food, who submits samples of his know-how or business to the palate of a professor in the art of gourmandise; and by extension, it was given to the sample itself . . . because it is a kind of letter of credit by which these [artists] are recognized and made legitimate for the jury that weekly decides on their respective talents.
>
> These legitimations are tasted in a large mechanism [*un grand appareil*] and with rigorous fairness; opinions are gathered according to appetites: the whole trial is recorded; and it is when the results are in that the contestants [*prétendans*] get honorable mention in *l'Almanach des Gourmands*. (2:xv–xvii)

In each volume after this, Grimod shares the jury's verdicts, and comments regularly on the process. Volume 3's frontispiece, for example, depicting a "Séance d'un Jury de dégustateurs," is followed by a detailed description of the engraving. The Jury members are sampling a pâté: "on their faces can be read the deep thought that must characterize every Gourmet in the exercise of his functions." The "Secrétaire de la Société," dictating minutes to a scribe, sits opposite the President, who counts votes. Other samples, on a buffet, await tasting. Paintings on the walls depict scenes from culinary history. The bell next to the vice-president summons servants only when needed and "the judges speak without distraction and with full independence." Later, at his readers' request, Grimod elaborates further on the *jury dégustateur*, its origins and procedures. From the outset, he did not want to judge *légitimations* alone "whose results would determine the reputation and fortune of a great number of artists" (5:81). Election to the jury must be unanimous. Between five and twelve members convene Tuesday nights. Women may attend, but cannot vote. Members stay put during sessions lasting at least five hours. "Affaires" are considered one at a time, voted on, the decisions recorded and excerpts thereof sent to the interested parties who, for unfavorable judgments, can correct and resubmit, otherwise the *Almanach* publishes defamatory results as is. Grimod stresses that the jury samples without knowing the producer's name, "so that the merit alone of the products is the determining factor" (6:223–24). Surrounding the *jury dégustateur* with such pomp and circumstance, Grimod seems to appreciate both its exciting novelty, and potential promise. Indeed, his scheme of "professional" tasters passing public judgement has since flourished, from local bake-offs to international culinary competitions, product endorsements to *appellation d'origine contrôlée* regulations, and "Best of . . . " lists to "blind taste tests" in advertising.

Grimod's *itinéraires*, *promenades*, and *revues* also anticipate Baedeker, Michelin, Gault-Millau, and other guides. At times, Grimod's language even approaches that of today's guidebooks. The restaurant Véry "is worth a visit, even as a simple object of curiosity" (3:91–92), a phrase prefiguring Michelin's "mérite un détour" and "vaut le voyage" for two- and three-star attractions. Reflecting further on tourism in "Essai de géographie gourmande" (3:213–26), Grimod foresees rich connections between travel and gourmandise. In a recent play, *L'École des gourmands*, an accomplished gourmand teaches his godson geography "by means of gourmandise"—asking, for example, what town (Strasbourg, of course) is famous for carp, salmon, foie gras, and crayfish (3:214). This method for learning French geography, which should be applied as well to learning European and world geography, would transform our vision of travel:

> With this new method of studying geography, this subject, which was hardly more than a knowledge of names, will become a knowledge of things; those who travel to perfect it, will no longer go to consult the scientists [*savans*] of each country, but will address themselves to the chefs and gourmands. They will visit markets instead of libraries and will be as jealous of bringing back home with them the knowledge of a new dish than they were formerly proud of returning with the drawing of an ancient monument.
>
> We shall leave our readers to meditate on this text, which can give rise [*enfanter*] long commentaries. (3:219)

Grimod's *Almanach* thus anticipates more than just guide books, foreseeing the broader phenomenon of culinary tourism, which would blossom in the late nineteenth and early twentieth centuries, first with the spread of railroads, then, all the more so, with the advent of the automobile (cf. Pitte, 173–81, and Weber, 177–94). Meanwhile though, as Grimod asserts in "Des voyages gourmands" (8:40–43), travel holds little appeal for Parisian gourmands, who enjoy so much of the world's bounty at home.[8]

Such prescient thinking abounds in the *Almanach*. While Grimod generally excludes women from the heights of gourmandise, he does allow that one young girl, now just "friande," shall some day become "a well-known gourmande" (3:237). This lukewarm feminist is however a staunch advocate for the rights of *cuisiniers*: their crucial profession must be pulled from "the oblivion where the indifference and ingratitude of most men seem to have plunged it" (5:64); their work must be properly recognized and rewarded, assuring the best fame and fortune (5:63). Seeming to foresee Escoffier's *Guide Culinaire*, Grimod observes, "A logical nomenclature [*Une nomenclature raisonnée*] of the various sauces known in cooking, would fill more than half a tome" (5:5). Despite his general predilection for novelty, he also seems to anticipate Gault and Millau's fourth nouvelle cuisine commandment, "You will not be systematically a modernist," as he argues for restoring the *garbure*, a venerable peasant dish, to its former glory (7:9).

Probably most innovative though in Grimod's work is his self-appointed role as intermediary between a public hungry for culinary luxury, and a fine food industry eager to please. This role is essentially that of the food critic, though in some respects Grimod already prefigures the food "personality" as well. An erstwhile theater critic, who reveled in fine dining's theatricality (e.g., 3:23), Grimod loved putting himself on stage. Intense, polemical, often embroiled in quarrels or lawsuits, he was a striking presence as well, handsome despite severely deformed hands hidden in white gloves. Between 1783 and 1812, he also acquired a reputation hosting "déjeuners philosophiques" or "dîners du mercredi," often organized around elaborate themes or hoaxes, like the final one on July 7, 1812, for which guests received announcements to his funeral. Arriving for the ceremony, they found a sumptuous banquet, presided by Grimod himself, still very much alive.[9] In the *Almanach*, Grimod alludes to these antics, basking in the notoriety they gave him. Preoccupied with fame, he weighs the advantages and disadvantages of the *Almanach* as a vehicle for both his fame and that of the artistes he praises (e.g., 2:ix; 4:310; 8:201). Above all, Grimod enjoys playing the public tastebud, through the highly visible activities of the *jury dégustateur*, and elaborate mises-en-scène of the *Almanach*'s frontispieces, where he stars, transparently, as "un Gourmand." Jean-François Revel, seemingly resentful of Grimod's ingenuity in procuring free food, condemns "the first organized moocher [*le premier parasite organisé*]" (265). But this takes too narrow and moralistic a view toward a mode of professional gourmandise that has enjoyed such a bright future— exemplified, in France, by Curnonsky, "prince des gastronomes," or Raymond Oliver, the first French television chef; and, in America, by Vincent Price, Julia Child, Graham Kerr, and so many more (cf. Stern and Stern 97–110). Cashing in on the appeal of gastronomy as a new form of entertainment, Grimod was a Galloping Gourmand for a pretelevision age.

Brilliant, weird, and, above all, original, Grimod wrote memorably about the shining new world of gourmandise emerging around him. Somehow, in the interim, we have forgotten. The time has come to rediscover Grimod's extraordinary voyage of exploration, in the lively pages of his *Almanach des Gourmands*.

NOTES

1. Unless otherwise indicated, references to volume 1 of the *Almanach* will be to the 10/18 edition.

2. His choice of the polyvalent term "carrière" is suggestive: it is at once the novel "course" he follows, the bounteous "quarry" he mines, and the "calling" he answers—his self-proclaimed vocation as a professional gourmand—that continue to expand before his eyes, as he writes the *Almanach*.

3. Details given for addresses vary: the exact address is provided, only the street name, or only the establishment's name—generally the case with the best known, i.e., the restaurants Le Rocher de Cancale or Véry, for which Grimod reserves particular praise: "nothing is better . . . than the sumptuousness of M. Véry's rooms, and here the bounty of the cooking responds to the beauty of the locale" (3:91).

4. Cf. above, 5. Maille's new vinegar "returns to ladies what they formerly could lose only once, and . . . consequently allows them to rediscover it in order to lose it anew." He adds that were this not the *Almanach des Gourmands*, he would elaborate.

5. Cf. "Le Piège," in Brillat-Savarin, 326–29 (362–65 in translation) and Grimod de la Reynière, 1:233–34. Both passages occur, moreover, in sections entitled "Variétés." In Grimod's version, two women bent on vengeance invite a curé, renowned for gourmandise, and serve him copiously but plainly. He eats his

fill, while they eat almost nothing. Instead of dessert, an exquisite second dinner is served. The curé tells off his hosts, and storms out. Reappearing, he seems calmed and eats like a horse [*mange comme quatre*]. We assume he has relieved himself in the interim, perhaps vomited. Following the "cheater cheated" pattern of folk tales, medieval farce, and Renaissance novellas, the "mystifiers, mystified in turn" now understand that "one should never attack a real Gourmand on the matter [*chapître*] of good food."

6. Unhappy with the results, Grimod pulled out of the project. He felt the publishers, "have ruined this plan in seeking to perfect it; they stuck *ladies* in who had nothing to do with this journal; they gave couplets preference over gourmand literature, etc. etc." (3:162).

7. Similarly, discussing Grimod's prodigious advertising campaign for his 1781 *Réflexions philosophiques sur le plaisir*, Desnoiresterres notes Grimod's remarkable grasp of advertising's potential: "La Reynière understood advertising brilliantly and . . . if he was not its inventor, he is, in any case, the first to have understood it on such a scale" (94).

8. Grimod acknowledges that some local products do not travel well; however, "all things considered, gourmand travels are not for Parisians, who will only get mediocre benefits; but we invite those who live far from the center of all pleasures not to disdain this method of shaping their taste while satisfying their appetites" (8:43).

9. Similarly, Grimod's inaugural 1783 *souper* appears to have been a funerary "theme" meal. There are divergent accounts, and it is not clear exactly what happened, except that the event made a splash, establishing Grimod's reputation as an eccentric. Both the invitations and the dining table seem to have been decorated with a "catafalque" and candles. Grimod's biographer Desnoiresterres refers us to Bachaumont's *Mémoires secrets*, which holds that the funerary decor was meant in honor of a famous actress who had died recently (*Mémoires secrets*, t. XXII, 94. 13 February 1783, in Desnoiresterres 84–85). While Bonnet finds this plausible, he contends that "the links of orality and funereal seem more secret and deeper in Grimod. . . . This association of bulimia and mourning, of the funereal and the festive is a determining point in the birth of gastronomy, this bloom of bourgeois culture that appears after the Revolution and the great fear it inspired" (15).

3. Culina Mutata:
Carême and *l'ancienne cuisine*

PHILIP HYMAN

One striking aspect of French cooking, at least since the seventeenth century, is its periodic rejuvenation via various forms of "new cooking." Enunciated more often than not by its greatest practitioners, the finest and most renowned French chefs are not those who excel in executing traditional dishes to perfection but, on the contrary, ones who modernize recipes of their predecessors or, better yet, innovate and create new ones. They secure for themselves places in the culinary pantheon, often leaving their mark on a generation of cooks through their writings and/or teachings that expound views counter to those expressed by their predecessors and former masters. In this respect, Antonin Carême was not the first chef to attack the cooking of previous generations, nor would he be the last, but the methods he used to promote "modern" cookery are worth examining not only because of their consequences for the future development of cuisine in nineteenth-century France but of what they teach us about what seems to be a specifically French phenomenon—the periodic renewal of cuisine by chefs who seem to feel the need to reevaluate the state of the art roughly every fifty years.[1]

I. THE VOCABULARY OF THE KITCHEN:
SPICES, GARNISHES, AND SAUCES

To begin, since Carême believed cuisine was constantly advancing, he did not formulate rigid doctrines nor did he consider his cuisine to be the end of an evolution of the culinary arts: "My colleagues can now see undisputed proof of the advances in nineteenth century French cooking for which I have been responsible. I do not claim that this new work should bring an end to further progress in the culinary art: craftsmen who are imbued with the true spirit of science will no doubt produce innovations; but it is my work that will have inspired them"(*L'Art de la cuisine française*). In short, for French chefs, cuisine is by its very nature something one must improve upon (though not everyone is capable of making improvements). The "old" will, in time, cede to the new, but just how did Carême see the "old" cookery that he sought to reform? His position with regard to the great culinary traditions he describes as "old," as well as his attitude toward his own cooking, are the subjects of the following paragraphs.

How, first, is *ancienne cuisine* defined by Carême? On some occasions his response is clear: "I think of *ancienne cuisine* as belonging to the eighteenth century, while the modern springs from the beginning of our notorious and unhappy revolution" (*Maître d'hôtel* 1:3). Although barely fifty years separate him from this *ancienne cuisine*, Carême had a limited knowledge of it; he was born in 1783. So his ideas on the subject are either acquired from books, based on hearsay, or founded on what he thinks he can recognize of it in methods still current in his own time. Nonetheless he presents the reader with what he believes are its most salient features. First and foremost, according to Carême, is its abusive use of spices and seasonings: "Ginger, coriander and cinnamon were frequently used in former cookery, whereas in the modern we use them rarely or, to be more exact, not at all" (*L'Art de la cuisine* 1:lxii).

Carême ascribes this spiced cooking to the celebrated "Italian influence," usually placed at the end of the Renaissance:

> Reading authors on French cookery from the middle of the last century, it is easy to see the extent to which the chefs of this period had retained that Italian taste introduced to the French court by Catherine de Medici. Nonetheless, French cooking made perceptible progress during the reigns of Charles IX and Henry IV, as well as the golden age of Louis XIV. The science made great strides, judging from the authors of *Les Dons de Comus* and *Les Soupers de la Cour* and other books written at about the same time. However, I stress, one realizes how highly seasoned and spiced French cooking was at that time. Italy, beautiful yet excessively hot, gives rise to a strong and aromatic *cuisine* for its inhabitants, if only to act as stomachic tonic. Thus Italian cooking has left us with an overwhelming predilection for spicy foods; . . . with all that results from our favorable climate and the mildness of the fair French air, there is no need to spice our food. Nevertheless, even at the end of the reign of Louis XIV our cookery was still too spicy, as it was, to a certain extent, during that of Louis XV. (*Maître d'hôtel* 1:13)

Indeed, Carême sees spices as the source of a persistent evil and the Italian presence as an obstruction to culinary progress, in contrast to the benefits that most historians attribute to their presence then as now.[2] However that may be, by isolating a specific trait in the cooking of his predecessors and making it a target for reforms he helps define his own cuisine and rallies support to his "cause." He clearly succeeded judging by the remarks of one of his greatest admirers, Lady Morgan, who had the "privilege" of tasting Carême's cookery in 1829; one of its great merits, she noted, was precisely this absence of spices. Even before attending Carême's dinner, she had read his books and thus knew "the merits of the man who had first declared against *la cuisine épicée et aromatisée*" (Suddaly 238). In the description of this same dinner, which she praises, she underlines the fact that:

> it was in season, that it was up to its time, that it was in the spirit of the age, that there was no *perruque* in its composition, no trace of the wisdom of our ancestors in a single dish; no high-spiced sauces, no dark brown gravies, no flavor of cayenne and allspice, tincture of catsup and walnut pickle, no visible agency of those vulgar elements of cooking of the good old times, fire and water. Distillations of the most delicate viands, extracted in "silver dews" with chemical precision, "on tepid clouds of rising steam," formed the *fond* of it all. Every meat presented in its own natural aroma, every vegetable its own shade of verdure. (Suddaly 237)

Although one may object that Lady Morgan is comparing Carême's cooking to that of her native England, spices clearly were for her, and for Carême, archaic elements in cuisine that concealed or destroyed the individual tastes of the food, and one cannot deny her recognition of Carême's role ridding cuisine of their malicious effects. Ironically, despite Carême's complaints, spices had been progressively losing their importance in French cooking from the seventeenth century onward and some of his immediate predecessors had expressed opinions not dissimilar to his own.[3] Without developing here the ideas worked out particularly by Jean-Louis Flandrin, the *moderne* nineteenth-century chef still finds the cooking of the late eighteenth century too spicy for his taste; Carême, perhaps simply to emphasize his "modernity," does not place himself *within* the general movement but considers himself the *first* to break with all past centuries, which he prefers to treat indiscriminately as a group insofar as the use of these "dangerous" condiments are concerned. One might think that herbs fared better than spices in the eyes of Carême. Not so. They were banished, for the most part, from his kitchen. In writing of fish cookery, he says: "I have also removed from my cooking of fish those quantities of aromatics and spices that our forebears were wont to use for seasoning, for it is a strange delusion to believe that fish should taste of thyme, bay, mace, clove or pepper, whereas we have irrefutable evidence every day that fish cooked in salt water alone is excellent" (*L'art de la cuisine* 2:287).

This said, Carême does not abandon the use of pepper, thyme, or bay altogether. Still on the subject of fish, he continues:

> If we have certain sorts of fish needing preparation with a *court-bouillon*, marinade or *mirepoix*, should we not for this very reason, sweeten them with flavorings and spices; using our artistry to render agreeable these different modes of imparting flavor without allowing their comportment parts to intrude on a discriminating palate.
>
> It is for those with such palates that we must make every effort in seasoning; the common cook might then renounce their highly flavored and spiced *ragoûts*. (*L'Art de la cuisine* 2:287)

Noting that those aspects that he finds "excessive" in the old cookery still exist and are associated with "the common cook" (*les cuisiniers vulgaires*), Carême seeks to reform their habits, or banish them all together from French kitchens.

Besides "vulgar" seasonings, Carême emphatically finds fault in some archaic garnishes inherited from the eighteenth century, specifically those that combine fish and meat and which he considers particularly antigastronomic: "If the matter is given a moment's thought you would have to say that the genius of these [past] artists had no notion how ridiculous it was to serve up meat and poultry with fish" (*L'Art de la cuisine* 2:7). This remark applies especially to fish dishes garnished with meat, rather than the other way round. Carême was particularly proud of his revival of an old recipe for carp with the earlier trimmings removed, renaming it *carpe à la Chambord moderne*: "Here, we have no more larding, no pigeons, no sweetbreads, no foie gras, no cockscombs or kidneys, but instead a succulent ragout appropriate to this scale, with accompaniments and clusters of fish and truffles, nothing fatty at all; this vice has been eliminated from French cooking" (2:185).

At the same time, Carême is well aware that contemporaries may need persuading before accepting his reforms, though not for the reasons that might be expected: "I foresee my critics protesting at the cost of my garnishes: my response would be that they cost little more than the original, fatty, ones and, moreover, it is up to us to keep costs down, not spending more than the host can afford" (2:185). In consequence, the new garnishes represent a new luxury. But it was not the quest for luxury that motivated Carême; he felt a real repulsion for these meat/fish combinations. Listen again to his *Traité des grosses pièces de poissons*:

> In the infinite number of whole fish dishes that I have just described, my colleagues should note that I have banished forever from French cookery those tired routines of serving fish *au bleu* with their scales, and again that stupid fad for larding carp and pike when cooked *à la Chambord*, as well as the gothic embellishments of sweetbreads, pigeons, and poultry used for these kinds of fish. I may say that I have long since changed these ridiculous practices, repudiated as they are by sensuous men with discriminating taste. (*L'Art de la cuisine* 2:287)

The fact that Carême calls these meaty garnishes "gothic" suggests an assimilation of the cookery of the Middle Ages with that of his immediate, eighteenth-century, predecessors even though the mixture of flesh [*gras*] and fish [*maigre*] that Carême deplores was as alien to medieval or Renaissance cooks as it was to the cuisine of Carême's time. As with spices, Carême's use of language, and his false gathering of disparate strands persuades the reader that, just as there is only one *cuisine moderne,* there was only one *cuisine ancienne*. His innovative powers seem all the greater faced with this monolithic vision of the past and his most scathing criticism is reserved for remnants of the ancient gastronomy still practiced in his day:

> We shall exclude from this chapter ["Traité des grosses pièces de carpes"] the fish served *au bleu* with a *court-bouillon*: current good taste frowns upon this manner, both ridiculous and pedestrian, of serving the dish thus armor-plated with scales. The old mode is contrary to the spirit both of gastronomy and good cooking practice; it must disappear from French cookery forever. I have long been eager to strike a blow at this ancient and disgusting practice, and if some old diehards were thinking of still serving this gothic repast, they should know how dangerous the practice can be, since the chevalier C***, having swallowed a carp scale, felt searing pains in his gut and would perhaps have perished had it not been for the prompt assistance of a disciple of Aesculapius. (2:295)

Clearly, *ancienne cuisine* is not only "antigastronomic," it is also dangerous.

To pass to sauces; this is one of Carême's most important contributions to the cuisine of his time. His codification of the basic sauces and the instruction he gives as to their uses would influence generations of chefs to come. Up until the sixteenth century, sauces bound with bread were very common, then the flour-based roux and the increasing use of egg yolks as a liaison appeared in the seventeenth century. By contrast, in the *nouvelle cuisine* of the eighteenth century, many sauces are not bound at all, and might be described as infusions rather than emulsions. In the second edition of *Les Dons de Comus*, the presumed author, Marin, writes: "Modern cookery is a sort of Chemistry. The Science of the Chef consists today of breaking down, making digestible and quintessentializing meats, of drawing forth nourishing and light juices, of mixing them together in such a way that no one flavor predominates and yet everything can be tasted" (xiii). Here we find expressed, about a hundred years earlier, one of Carême's preoccupations, a harmony of tastes, yet in a "chemistry" that runs counter to the nineteenth century. Carême does not abandon meat essences; he is simply distinguishes them from sauces and makes the latter the more important:

> I have now come to the chapter ["Traité des Essences en gras et en maigre"] where I must return to laying down first principles, by again shaking up accepted ideas. Authors who, up till now, have written about the culinary art have always dealt with sauces made from reduced, concentrated essences which are not thickened; extract of aspic, for instance, they called aspic sauce. It seems to me that, to constitute a sauce, it is vital that the vehicle of taste should be bound, to obtain a substantial and velvety medium with which to coat our entrées as we obtain with *espagnole*, *velouté*, *allemande* and *béchamel*. (*L'art de la cuisine* 3:246–47)

Even with a liaison, certain eighteenth century sauces would not be considered thickened in Carême's mind. *Les Dons de Comus*, already mentioned, was one of the first treatises of the *nouvelle cuisine* of that period, and its author, Marin, gives a list in the second edition of "the daintiest little sauces according to the modern taste" (133). Of the forty-eight sauces listed, half contain a binding agent, the other half do not, and it is plain that some of the "thickened" sauces are thickened very little at all. In seven, we find the instruction *singer un peu* (add a little flour) and it would appear that the result is not very thick. For example, Marin gives two versions of *sauce à la Hollandaise*—one "clear," the other "thickened." The one described as clear contains flour, but apparently just a little ("*singer un peu*"), whereas for the thickened Hollandaise, the instruction is to add more flour (*singer un peu fort*) and an egg yolk as well (145). Supposing that Carême would have considered only the second version a true sauce, then the number of "unthickened" sauces (thus encompassing those with only a little thickening) becomes greater than one might have thought from Carême's assessment of Marin. This mania for thickened sauces, revived by Carême, has continued, unquestioned, into our own time until the *nouvelle cuisine* chefs of the 1970s reopened the debate, either by refusing to use the master sauces perfected by Carême, or by lightening them.

II. REPRESENTATION: HOW TO SERVE AND WHAT TO CALL A *NOUVELLE CUISINE*

In France, changing the way food *tastes* is just a start; one has to change the way it looks as well. Carême's reforms of cooking took in both the preparation of food and its representation. Obviously, the way food is presented on serving dishes is of great importance. Carême's style was that of the age he lived in and much has been made of the verticality of his famous architectural presentations. On a more subtle plane, he also gave great importance to the serving dishes themselves and even on this level all archaism was to be banished from the "modern" table. His nemesis on this occasion, as on so many others, is Vincent La Chapelle. La Chapelle had included engravings of serving dishes and centerpieces in his famous *Cuisinier Moderne* of 1735 that, in Carême's opinion, were totally unsuited for his new cookery: "I find that round and oval shapes suit the serving of our cooking infinitely better than these square, octagonal or festooned dishes" (*L'art de la cuisine* 2:11–12). Carême proposed redesigning these dishes and even the pots used in the kitchen! But more than the shape of the dishes it was their profusion that provoked Carême's most vehement remarks: "We disapprove of this fashion for serving enormous dishes such as have appeared since the renaissance of the art . . . again we have reformed this usage which came down to us, no doubt from the grotesque manner of serving current at the end of the 18th century" (2:10).[4]

Elsewhere, quoting a recipe of Vincent La Chapelle's, he says: "One is amazed at the prodigious quantity of meats, roots and vegetables which make up his *Oille à l'espagnole* . . . the appearance of this stew must have been repulsive, but at that time cookery was still in its infancy as an art; this ragoût was fashionable and well-thought of" (1:236–37).

According to Carême's account, these "monster" dishes were characteristic both of *cuisine ancienne* and of recent practices that had ironically contributed to the "renaissance" of the art of cookery. In one of his rare critiques of Talleyrand and Laguipierre (the famous chef under whom Carême had worked), he taxes them for serving these gross dishes:

> That *cuisine moderne* should be as elegant and sumptuous as possible is, I am sure, correct. So I have not illustrated in my category of *grosses pièces* any of those gigantic affairs I saw served when the art of modern cookery was in its infancy. At dinners given by Prince Talleyrand, I have seen removes so large that one man could scarcely carry them. I have witnessed Godards and Chambords whose rich garnishes were enough to feed a dozen guests. 1 have seen Laguipierre serve one huge dish that came straight from the 18th century. It was an Olio (this dish alone constitutes and characterizes Spanish cooking) served on the biggest oval platter I have ever seen in my life. The student practitioner, observing so much effort, energy and money expended on these culinary monstrosities, must say to himself: here are reforms to carry out, the time is ripe for the creation of an art at once pure, youthful and brilliant. (3:493)

This "mountain of food" applies to both the dishes themselves and to their arrangement on the table. A hallmark of the *moderne* in contrast to the *ancienne* is "this elegance unknown to our predecessors who overloaded their tables to excess" (*Maître d'hôtel* 1:ii). Several times Carême refers to the drawings of La Chapelle: "What astounds me is the profusion with which he spread the tables of people of good taste at the time; that is not elegance" (*Maître d'hôtel* 1:15). So that his reader may fully appreciate the difference between these two schools, he reproduces the table plan of La Chapelle opposite that of a "modern" table (see illustration).[5]

As with spices, our protagonist exaggerates. Carême takes his place in a movement that began in the seventeenth century targeting the real or imaginary excess of the *anciens* in heaping dishes with food and overloading the table. In 1674, L.S.R. condemns the practices of *his* predecessors in the following manner:

> Nowadays it is not this prodigious overflowing of serving dishes, the abundance of stews and hotch-potch, the extraordinary accumulation of meats that make for a good table, nor the haphazard heap of different sorts of foods, the mountains of roasts, the multiplicity of side dishes, nor *entremets* served so bizarrely as to make it appear that both art and nature have utterly drained their resources to satisfy the senses, that appeal most to the delicacy of our taste, but it is rather the

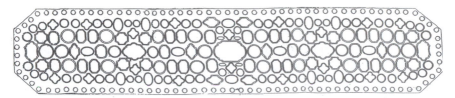

Table set for 100 people by Vincent La Chapelle in his *Cuisinier Moderne*.

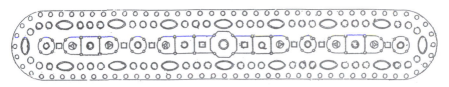

Table set for 80 to 90 by Carême in his *Maître d'hôtel français*.

exquisite choice of meats, their subtle flavors, the correctness and nicety of their presentation, their quantity proportionate to the number of diners and finally the general organization of details which make an essential contribution to the excellence and embellishment of a meal. (1–2)

A hundred years later, in his *Tableau de Paris*, Mercier (5:45) takes up the same theme: "During the last century food was served up in pyramids. Diminutive, yet ten times costlier dishes were not yet known. Only in the last fifty years have we introduced discrimination into eating."

But the quantity of food served, its taste, and its presentation are far from our chef's only concerns. Another topic attracts the wrath of Carême and still is subject of heated debate today: the naming of dishes. We quote but a part of his list of names to be proscribed:

> It is the same with soups *à la jambe de bois {peg-leg}* (rather than saying beef marrow): if we add to that *la culotte de boeuf* [beef panties] , veal *roulé en crotte d'âne* [donkey droppings] taken from *Cuisinier Gascon, culs d'artichauts* [artichoke "ass"], *les pets de nonne glacés* [glazed nun farts], and other entrées and desserts of that ilk; and when at table we ask the waiter the identity of an entrée: Sir, it's peg-leg soup; what an ignoble phrase! it's an entrée of pheasant socks *à la Conti;* or, again, it's beef fillets sautéed in the form of glazed boot heels, and so forth. (*Maître d'hôtel* 1:40–41)

Any pretext, including language, illustrates the absurdities of *ancienne cuisine*. Carême mobilizes every resource to promote his own cooking and bring about the downfall of the cuisine of his rivals. But Carême's was only "moderne" to a limited degree. His highly decorative style of cooking was more in tune with the service *à la française* than the newer service *à la russe* and he would defend the old principles even if it meant looking back rather than forward with a new generation of chefs:

> The Russian style of serving thus differs greatly from our own in that none of the dishes appears on the table. All the entrées are carved, as well as the fish and the roast. As each entrée is served, the maître d'hôtel goes back to the kitchen to fetch the next one to have been made ready. Certainly this method of serving is conducive to good eating; but our service *à la française* is more elegant and lavish. It is the model for artistic cooking; thus in all the courts of Europe, our service *à la française* is still appreciated and followed. Is there anything better than the sight of a table set *à la française* in the modern style? (2:150–51)

To some extent Carême might be seen both as the last great exponent of a disappearing tradition and the first of a new and ascendant vogue.

CONCLUSION

The purpose of this short paper has been to examine some of the ways in which Carême sought to distance himself from his predecessors and to place his discourse in the broader context of a debate between the proponents of *nouvelle* and *ancienne* cuisines starting in the seventeenth century. In order to achieve his goals, Carême criticized specific practices and proposed innovations that would make his "new" cuisine easily recognizable to the gastronomically curious eagerly seeking clues as to what the disgruntled chef is proposing. The new cuisine is placed in a philosophical context that highlights not only its gastronomic superiority to the cuisines of the past but its dietetic, aesthetic, and philosophic advantages as well. In order for Carême's reforms to become reality, they must pass through an "earmarking" stage that enhances the new and stigmatizes the old, characterizing it as "harmful," "ridiculous," and "grotesque." The emphasis on innovation may be found at every level, from the naming of a dish to its seasoning. Though Carême's methods echo those of previous centuries (the wholesale condemnation of "antigastronomic" methods are common in the writings of L.S.R and reoccur in Marin among others), he seems to ignore the fact that many of his reforms are part of a more general historic movement. Because he has no real sense of history, he essentially sees all the

cooking that preceded his own time as one confusing "ancienne cuisine"—
a sort of "dark age" out of which his cooking emerges. Incapable of making
true distinctions between the cuisines of centuries past, Carême had no real
sense of how his own reforms compared to others. He therefore overesti-
mated the importance of his own contribution to French cuisine and
underestimated those of his predecessors.

The case of Carême should be studied in a more general context of what
Magnun G. Ostermann called Culina Mutata, "culinary mutations." It
throws light on the way individuals influence *l'art culinaire*, specifically the
role of the articulate chef, and it also calls attention to the cyclical phenomenon mentioned earlier: the renovation of grand cuisine in France
periodically from the seventeenth century onward. Lastly, the existence of
a "debate" about cookery in print and specifically in cookbooks is, in itself,
particularly interesting. It underlines the role of gastronomic controversies
in defining cuisine and associates the chef not only with manual skills but
with conceptual powers as well. Food, even good food, is not just something one eats: one prefers the old school or the new, one articulates
opinions. In short, in France, what you can *say* about what you eat as
important as how you eat it, and what you *know* about food is as important
as how it tastes.

NOTES

1. The title of this article is the same as that use by Magnus G. Ostermann in
1757 for a piece he wrote in honor of Carl von Linné (Linneaus), the famous
Swedish botanist. It was published with other essays as part of *Amoenitates academ-
icae* in 1760. His purpose, unlike mine, was to call attention to how new foods
changed cusine, but his title sums up in a universally understandable phrase a
problem that is central not only to this article but to my interest over the years.
This article originally appeared in French in the exhibition catalogue *L'Art Culinaire au XIX Siècle: Antonin Carême* (Paris, 1984), 63–70. It was later translated by
Susan Thrippleton, Pat Phillips, and Tom Jaine and published as part of the proceedings of the *Oxford Symposium on Food and Cookery 1984 & 1985: Cookery: Science,
Lore & Books* (Prospect Books Ltd., London), vol.2, 150–51. The Oxford Symposium translation is an entirely new and greatly revised version.

2. The Chevalier de Jaucourt would write in a famous article on "Cuisine" for
the fourth volume of Diderot and D'Alembert's *Encyclopédie* in 1754 that "the Italians were the first to pick up the flame of the ancient Romans and the debris of
their cuisine, and it was they who taught the French good cooking. . . ." Cookbooks repeated this lesson throughout the eighteenth century. One reads in the

"Avertissement" to the famous *Dons de Comus*, for example, that "the Italians civilized all of Europe, & it was they, without any doubt, who taught us how to eat" (Marin xii).

3. The author of *Les Dons de Comus* had written: "Seasoning has been the downfall of many a mediocre cook and it is the part of cooking that requires the greatest attention. Salt, pepper and other spices are ingredients more precious than gold when used properly but true poisons when too employed too freely. They must be used sparingly, like gold, with a light hand, intelligently. Otherwise, there is no salavation, your dishes will be ruined and instead of essences that you have carefully distilled you will have foods that are corrosive to the palate."

4. When Carême talks of the "renaissance of the art," he refers to the renewal of the art of cookery, which he dates to the beginning of the nineteenth century.

5. *Maître d'hôtel* 1, plates 2 and 3. The first figures shows the profusion of dishes that Carême criticizes in his predecessors, while the second shows the barer table proposed by Carême. When we compare the two, it is clear that the "profusion of dishes" is not the only criticism: the angular plates (octagonal, hexagonal, etc.) of La Chapelle give way to round or oval ones with Carême. Even the table, which is octagonal with La Chapelle, has become oval. With Carême the center of the table is uncluttered; there are only small stands to enhance the raised dishes. The two plans are drawn to the same scale, each representing a table about twenty meters long. Not only does Carême anticipate seating 10 to 20 percent fewer people than La Chapelle, thus leaving each guest more room, but the serving dishes are also smaller and more accessible to each person. A less heavily laden table, smaller side dishes, new shapes, and more room for each person: these are the broad outlines of Carême's reform in the serving of dinner. Without going so far as to accept the Russian form of service, he nevertheless seeks to remodel the presentation of food, thereby manifesting one of the concerns of innovative chefs: new recipes alone do not a *nouvelle cuisine* make.

4. Tastes of the Host

MARC SMEETS

 his is how the fin-de-siècle writer Joris-Karl Huysmans summarizes the effect that conversion had on him: "Conversion is a switch, but man is always the same train." Although the train passes a switching, Huysmans still remains the same train as before, running on a continuous track. But what about the effect of this conversion on his literature? Could it, symbolically speaking, be the same "religious" train running on the track, the train that stays the same all the way, never changing? Or does Huysmans's conversion affects his literature, its style, and his choice of topics, so that it is impossible to speak of the same train? In order to try to clear up this issue, we will analyze and compare two passages, one from *A Rebours* (1884) and the other from the 1901 work *Sainte Lydwine de Schiedam*. The switch is situated between these two works, each of which devotes some time to another kind of switch, the transubstantiation of the host, the presence of God in the Eucharistic bread.[1]

Here is the passage in question from *A Rebours*:

> But what was worse was that the two substances that were indispensable for the holy sacrifice, the two substances without which no oblation was possible, had also been adulterated: the wine by repeated diluting and the illicit addition of Pernambuco bark, elder-berries, alcohol, alum, salicylate, and litharge; the bread, that bread of the Eucharist which should be made from the finest of wheats, with bean-flour, potash and pipe-clay! And now they had gone even further; they had had the effrontery to leave out the wheat altogether, and most hosts were made by shameless dealers out of potato-flour! Now God refused to come down to earth in the form of potato-flour. That was an

undeniable, indisputable fact. . . . Because of the easy manipulation of
this flour and the attractive appearance of the wafers made with it,
this outrageous swindle had become so common that the mystery of
transubstantiation scarcely existed any longer and both priests and
faithful communicated, all unwittingly, with neutral species.
(344–45; 216–17)

This passage from chapter XVI of A Rebours deals with Jean Des
Esseintes's complaint about the falsification of sacramental elements.
According to him it is important to avoid denaturalized ingredients and
artificial materials in the manufacture of the host. If the altar bread is prepared with synthetic components, one risks creating a terrestrial body, a
shell unworthy of transformation, at the time of the consecration, into
celestial flesh; God will not descend. The host will stay empty, the spiritual and corporeal marriage will not take place and the infinite powers that
should emanate from the sacrificial loaf will be absent. The consumption of
neutral matter will not have any effect on the believer. Body and soul
merge only under optimum, authentic circumstances. One needs "the
finest of wheats," "a competent substance for the Blessed Sacrament" (345;
216) for God to show Himself to us at the moment of consecration.

For various reasons this is an astonishing passage. The Duc Des
Esseintes idolizes appearances, adores all sorts of falsifications. We recall
his wish to collect "natural flowers that would look like fakes" (187; 97), as
well as the turtle transformed into a strolling piece of jewelry, an amalgam
of "real and artificial stones" (130; 55). A Rebours is the breviary of artifact,
the bible of "anti-nature," in which artificiality has become the way of life.
Nature, writes Huysmans, "has had her day; she has finally and utterly
exhausted the patience of sensitive observers." Let us extol then the artificial, which is "the distinctive mark of human genius" (103; 36).

Still, as we can see, this acclaim is somewhat ambiguous. In spite of
everything, Des Esseintes still feels, as Berg writes (39), "nostalgia for a
preserved, uncontaminated natural state," "a natural, untouchable small
pocket." This would be a pure spot, impervious to contamination. This
nostalgia for nature is connected with the idea of authenticity, of truth, but
also with the quest for God.[2] What a strange paradox, for one has to use
the expedient of "anti-nature" to find God. The artificial hold on the world
tries to regain the authentic nature; "fake eternity" has to be abandoned in
order to reach "holy eternity"(Gaillard 139). The chaotic world, diverse
but reduced by the artifact to a controllable unity, is nothing but a deval-

ued representation of the *"great One"*; therefore "the maniacal attraction for the simulacrum is revealed as a lost, desperate quest for authenticity and the truth" (Gaillard 139). In the end, the cult of the artificial creates its own opposite: the need for the natural and nature as a place where one can meet God. What do denaturalized turtles or fake flowers really matter? Artifact, imitation, is only an intermediate way of attaining the essence of nature: unity, the "unity" called God. The quest for authenticity ultimately becomes the quest for totality, since its creator resides in this universality.[3] Des Esseintes then is already heading for religion and the quest for holy eternity. And in so doing, he is obliged to reject his "cult of the artificial"; he must reject imitation in order to reach nature. Des Esseintes is the man who has two faces, a decadent Doctor Jekyll and Mister Hyde: the idolater of fakes and the doubting Christian.

The singular passage about the host is a magnificent illustration of this duality, since the host eludes artificiality and assures the authenticity that des Esseintes needs so badly. Moreover this authenticity seems to be one of the most important characteristics of the divine food. But in order to understand the weight of the passage in the novel, it is necessary to give a brief historical background about the fascination with the holy wafer.

The transubstantiation of the host, especially in medieval Christianity, was always experienced as an enchantment. In *L'Enfer et le fantasme de l'hostie*, Piero Camporesi quotes many examples concerning the astonishment of the faithful at the moment of Eucharistic consecration: this "incomprehensible enchantment that radically erased the substance of the bread while keeping its appearance" (167; quoted in Buvik 39); the "inanimate" transforms itself into "animate" in order to unleash a vast number of miracles (191). The small piece of bread, "an earthly fragment" is transformed during the communion into "celestial flesh": what is realized is "an intimate fusion between the flesh of man and that of his creator" (168). In his impressive *Histoire du sacrament de l'eucharistie*, Jules Corblet offers numerous examples of written traditions and historical miracles on the subject of the transubstantiation of the altar bread. Besides the many blasphemous acts after which the heretic is converted to Catholicism, there are many examples in which the protagonist walks away fortified, strengthened, and reassured after having seen the host turned into "a beautiful child from whom shone waves of light" (473) or into "the aspect that Jesus Christ had on the cross at the moment of his agony" (478), or after having consumed the miraculous bread in the guise of "a completely bloody bit of flesh" (465). This is what the hero of *A Rebours* eventually dreams of, the ultimate transubstantiation for which he longs. But there is no fortification, no healing possible. While the mystery of transubstantiation still exists, it is no longer a sine qua non because of the use of denaturalized, artificial materials.

In Huysmans's later, postconversion hagiography, *Sainte Lydwine de Schiedam*, the priest of Schiedam tries to fool Saint Lidwina by offering her a fake, unconsecrated host:

> the day before the Nativity of Our Lady, the priest gave the saint confession and promised to bring her the holy Species the next day. She remained sad, for an angel told her right away: "A new storm is brewing; this priest will give you unconsecrated bread. God wants me to warn you so that you not be deceived." Thus he arrived the next day, and in front of a certain number of friends of Lidwina, he raised the host from the custodial and, sacrilegiously, had her worship it. Then he gave communion to the sick woman, who, aghast, rejected the wafer. Don André feigned indignation and yelled, "What, you wretched madwoman, how dare you vomit the body of Our Lord!" "It is easy for me to distinguish the body of Jesus from a simple unleavened bread," replied Lidwina. "If this host had been consecrated, I would have swallowed it without the least bit of difficulty, but that one is not; my entire nature opposes my consuming it, and I must give it up, whether I want to or not."[4] (120–21)

This is an act of sacrilege in which the holy bread is profaned. The priest of Schiedam, anxious to deceive the "fake" saint, offers her an unconsecrated host. Lacking any divine force, the so-called host is rejected by Lidwina. Indeed, it would be blasphemous to consume this *panis mysteriorum*. Consonant with medieval hagiography, there is a reversal of the divine plan: the village priest, who would normally be a God-loving person, is tempted—diabolically—to fool the servant of God.[5]

The power of the Eucharistic bread consists among other things in its ability to appease spiritual and corporeal hunger, provided that the host has been consecrated. The communion of neutral species, of unconsecrated bread, at that time was seen as an impious offense, an act of blasphemy, a diabolical stratagem. For if one can "lock up" God in a small piece of unleavened bread, wouldn't the temptation arise to profane Him? With God within easy reach, there is also "the contamination of the very pure by the very impure" (Camporesi 156). In *Sainte Lydwine de Schiedam*, given the unconsecrated host, the Redeemer is not "hidden behind the appearances" (121); Lidwina is obligated to reject the false body of Christ and refuse what would otherwise be an "admirable marriage" (Camporesi 168). Through the intercession of the angel as messenger from God, Lidwina has the received grace and can distinguish the body of Jesus from a regular piece of unleavened bread. The act is even more extreme: Lidwina depends entirely on the divine powers of nutrition concentrated in the host, for she consumes the holy bread only six times a year (88) and although that is her only food, she experiences no other hunger whatsoever. Fooling the saint with an unconsecrated host would be tantamount to murder, since the divine nourishing powers could not move from the false *panis sanctorum* to appease either her spiritual or corporal hunger. No wonder she has the ability to separate the divine works from diabolical temptations, to separate what is natural from what is artificial.

And that separation returns us to the veritable question of the artifice of the host, for one of the historical epithets of the host is "la sainte artifice" (Camporesi 195): "artificial" here means *arte factum*, made of art. Thus artifact and nature are closer than we thought, since nature, mistress of all art (*natura artis magistra*), implicitly produces "artifice." Considered from this angle there is no schism: nature and artificiality come together rather than diverge.

It is in that light that we return to the question of artificiality in both books. Lover of all that is artificial, of all that is imitation, Des Esseintes seeks the authenticity embodied by God, through or beyond a second nature. Saint Lidwina also strives to find again this original purity, but does so in another context. Des Esseintes is particularly interested in the veracity of the host. The holy bread serves as a specific model for a quest for authenticity that is the reverse of the artificial. Saint Lidwina cannot take communion because the bread has not been consecrated. She is more concerned with the presentation, while Des Esseintes is concerned with the preparation, and only secondarily with the presentation of the host. Moreover, Des Esseintes symbolizes doubt while Lidwina is an incarnation of certainty. Whatever distance may separate the two, whatever the difference in genre may be, and whatever part one is tempted to assign to the author's conversion, the saint and the duke share some characteristics that relate to this matter of nature and artifice. Their fragile health, their solitude, their suffering, their fear of the unknown, even their anchorites' lodgings. Most important for our purposes, given their shared concern about the vacuity of the host, Des Esseintes and Lidwina attach great importance to the sacri-nutritive union and are steadfastly opposed to the corruption of the host. Indeed, we can say that the sybarite and the martyr share the same obsession of eating: eating well, eating in a holy way; all this is still eating. Each is an apostle, not of "la dive bouteille," but of divine food. They try to guard the quality of the celestial bread in order to guarantee its intrinsic value and authenticity. Des Esseintes and Lidwina defend as well as can be expected the sacred image of the host—the duke in the nineteenth century, the saint in the fifteenth. Their common cause is the obsession with a form of purity that they try to achieve, Des Esseintes desperately, Lydwine through suffering, a purity that they call God.

From this point of view, the protagonist of *A Rebours* continues the work of the saint (though before the fact), since he transposes the problem of supra-substantial change to a more delicate and sophisticated, a more "fin de siècle" level, i.e., the preparation of the unleavened bread. But at the same time, conversely, why not see the saint as someone who deepens the work of the duke? If Des Esseintes tackles the problem of the artificial substances, Saint Lidwina gets to the heart of the matter of the Eucharist, which is the transformation of all the substances of the bread into all the substances of the Holy Body. The symbolism of the host assures so to speak the link between the so-called psychological approach in *A Rebours* and the so-called hagiographic approach in *Sainte Lydwine de Schiedam*. This is why Buvik appropriately points out that "*Sainte Lydwine de Schiedam* does not break as cleanly as one often says with Huysmans's earlier texts" (33). Huysmans himself had remarked this in *La Préface écrite vingt ans après le roman*: "I might quite well sign my name at the present moment to the pages of *A Rebours* relating to the church, for they appear in very deed to have been written by a Catholic" (*A Rebours* 60). Further on he says: "this book was priming for my Catholic propaganda which is implicit in it in its entirety, though in embryo" (69). Is it too risky to say that the theme of the falsified bread mentioned in *Sainte Lydwine de Schiedam* appears already in *A Rebours*? Or do we have to maintain the opposite? That the *hapax* of the host which we find in *A Rebours* is picked up again and developed in *Sainte Lydwine de Schiedam*? These two figures, at the level of the quest for sacramental purity, seem almost interchangeable, for we have the impression that Des Esseintes is haunted by the same obsessions as Saint Lidwina and vice versa. And at the same time, one could say the similar things about the texts. Although *A Rebours* is considered by its author as a novel, we cannot help reading it as a sort of fictional hagiography in which the historical and scientific values are put aside. *A Rebours* is the history of a pilgrim seeking sanctification; it is the story of a man who disproves his artificial cult in order to find God. And we can read *Sainte Lydwine de Schiedam* "à rebours," i.e., against the grain, not as a classic example of a hagiography, but as one of Huysmans's novels.[6] So ultimately this literary and religious symbolism, which could be categorized as a "desire for eternity," links two apparently different texts and two apparently different literary points of view. Des Esseintes's quest for authenticity resembles Lidwina's Eucharistic fear, as they both take part in the same literary and religious plan: they are Huysmans's sacrificed pawns on his way to the essence of art, of religion, of life. They are on exactly the same train.

NOTES

1. I would like to thank Lawrence R. Schehr and Jaap van der Bent for their help in translating the original French.

2. As Gaillard notes, "In an eclectic, fleeing world, one must go through the homogenization that is a simulacrum, in order to satisfy a real need for the infinite, for presence, for foundation, for the absolute, in short, to find . . . God; God in his equivalencies, his substitutes, his figures, God, in that complete power of the law of the code that occupies his place, and which is the veritable place holder" (139).

3. As Buvik (39) writes, "What critics have discussed less is that des Esseintes' reflections on food and eating, at first related with his wild cult of the artificial and associated with his existential sadness, are more and more oriented toward Catholicism, as he searches, not for a guarantee of falseness, but, on the contrary, of authenticity."

4. Translation mine.

5. Corblet offers a similar story on the subject of Saint Catherine of Siena (484-85) (which resembles the history of Saint Lidwina of Schiedam in almost every way); Camporesi (180; quoted in Buvik, 47) recounts a story of a peasant woman told by Caesarius of Heisterbach, a Cistercian preacher of the thirteenth century.

6. See, on the novelistic aspects of the hagiography, Vircondelet's preface to the novel.

5. Agape and Anorexia:
Decadent Fast and Democratic Feast

NAOMI SCHOR

One of the most celebrated banquets of the Banquet years was the Republican banquet catered by the maison Potel et Chabot[1] that brought together 11,250 mayors of France and the colonies—a total of 13,456 participants according to Pascal Ory—in the Palais de l'Industrie at the 1889 World's Fair. That banquets were, as Roger Shattuck has demonstrated in his classic work on the "belle époque," *The Banquet Years*, one of the most characteristic and widespread forms of social gathering at the fin de siècle—cutting as they did across various professions and social classes (though the poorest were excluded from the feast)[2]—obscures what makes this celebrated banquet so significant: it brought together bureaucrats, the agents of the Republic, the new class of notables. It is this administrative constituency that characterizes the era: the Belle Époque marked the triumph of the French administration that had initially been put into place by Napoleon. What the mayors were engaged in was not so much alimentary excess as self-congratulation, what they were celebrating was the triumph of an indigenous administrative structure that forged national identity and consolidated an empire.

Against this banquet of the Republic triumphant I would like to set not some sort of banquet of the dispossessed, of the *refusés*, but rather two other digestive rituals, one aristocratic, the other popular, one characteristic of the reign of artifice in fin-de-siècle literature, the other inscribed in a tradition of ritual consumption dating all the way back to early Christianity, not to say late antiquity.

A mere five years before the megabanquet of 1889, which constitutes a benchmark of Belle Époque banquets, *A Rebours* appeared, and *A Rebours* may well be the major work on an eating disorder ever written. Suffering from a sort of existential nausea, unable to digest the copious fare of the Third Republic wealthy class, upon his retreat to Fontenay Des Esseintes reduces his diet to a regular and frugal menu:

> He also regulated the unchangeable hours of the meals; they were, moreover, uncomplicated and very succinct; the weakness of his stomach no longer allowed him to absorb varied or heavy dishes.
>
> At five o'clock in winter, after dusk, he lunched lightly on two soft-boiled eggs, toast, and tea. Then he dined toward eleven o'clock, drank coffee, sometimes tea and wine during the night. He munched on a little snack [*une petite dînette*] at five a.m. before going to bed.[3]

But to no avail: the digestive disorders from which he had suffered return, he becomes bloated and is forced to restrict his diet further, eliminating all stimulants and taking all manner of natural antispasmodics:

> . . . finally his appetite stopped, gassy warm pangs, dried fires rang through his stomach. He swelled, felt stuffed, after each attempt at a meal, could no longer bear a buttoned pants or a tight vest.
>
> He stopped using alcohol, coffee, tea, drank dairy, took cold-water, stuffed himself with asafetida, valerian, and quinine. (131)

His appetite is briefly revived when on his trip to London-on-Seine he enters a tavern near the railroad station and is confronted by the sight of some Englishwomen digging in to some local dishes: "After having lost his appetite so long ago, he showed consternation before these trencher-women [*gaillardes*] whose voracity sharpened his hunger" (172). Stimulated by the sight of others' healthy appetites, Des Esseintes's own appetite returns for a brief moment: he "had hunger pangs at seeing others stuff their faces, he ate some roast beef with potatoes and downed two pints of ale, stimulated with the slightly musky earthy taste that fine, pale beer gives off" (171–72). A similar instance of *mimetic hunger* occurs when Des Esseintes goes out for a walk in his garden and encounters a poor child whose lips are caked with a "white crud from pica cheese crushed on bread and sown with pieces of green onion" (197). Provoked by the sight of the boy's repulsive caked lips, Des Esseintes is overcome with an imperative desire to consume an identical repast; just as the unbecoming sight of the English trencherwomen stuffing their faces unleashes his blocked appetite, it is the crud on the poor boy's lips that provokes his hunger for the humble and foul food. Hunger under the regime of decadence is not an instinctual desire, it is triangulated desire, and moreover a perverse, not to say pathological one. For what sets the neurotic Des Esseintes's juices flowing is not so much the sight of the other's healthy appetite as the dietetics of disgust, a form of what one might call *Eckellust*, or what Huysmans calls a "pica," the Latin word for *pie*, which signifies in medical terms: "morbid taste for inedible substances." In short, that which Des Esseintes wishes to ingest is inedibility itself, what he wishes to consume is the abject: "this unspeakable open sandwich [*tartine*] made his mouth water. It seemed to him that his stomach, which refused all nourishment, would digest this awful dish and that his palate would be excited by it as if it were a feast" (197). Transformed by the effects of mimetic desire the peasant repast appears to Des Esseintes like some prized treat, a tempting morsel. But when his servants bring him a sandwich identical to the adolescent's, in a scene analogous to the one in Baudelaire's *Le Gateau*, which clearly functions here as Huysmans's transparent but unacknowledged intertext, he is repelled by it and throws it to a pack of children to fight over. The fratricidal struggle over the cheese-smeared bread is Huysmans's version of a sort of what we might call *la faim* or *le ventre des pauvres*. Version or perversion? For as Huysmans writes: "Des Esseintes sniffed the air . . . a perversion took him over" (197). If in Baudelaire's prose poem hunger induced by social inequity transforms a mere piece of "almost white bread" into a piece of cake, in Huysmans's novel the mere sight of a plebeian tartine stimulates the appetite of the degenerate aristocrat. Baudelaire's evocation of a beautiful land where malnourished children engage in a violent struggle over a piece of bread allegorizes class struggle and shatters the narrator's Rousseauistic illusions of the conflation of natural sublimity and human goodness, whereas Huysmans's relocating of the scene of fratricidal struggle in his own backyard corresponds to a very different reading of the social text. If the humble sandwich does not succeed in curing Des Esseintes, the spectacle of the poor children fighting over a piece of bread provides him with revivifying food for thought. These are not the thoughts of a disillusioned postrevolutionary narrator, but of a decadent protagonist steeped in the fin de siècle philosophies of Schopenhauer and Darwin. Swept up in the equalizing pessimism of the period, the realities of class struggle are denied; indeed, in this truly perverse analysis of social reality, in a familiar stereotypical myth of the fortunate poor, they are depicted as corporeally if not economically favored. They may be starving but they are endowed with the brute energy necessary to win the struggle for existence:

And the future was, in sum, equal for all, and neither the ones nor the others, had they had a bit of sense, would have been envious. For the rich, it was in a different environment, the same passions, troubles, labors, illnesses; it was also the same mediocre excitements whether it be alcoholic, literary, or carnal. There was even a vague compensation for all these ills, a kind of justice that reestablished the equilibrium of sadness among the classes, dispensing more easily the poor from the physical suffering that more implacably attacked the more weakly and emaciated bodies of the rich. (197–98)

Still suffering from bouts of nausea, Des Esseintes procures a gadget that extracts the juice from the makings of a beef stew, a juicer *avant la lettre*. Subsisting on this quintessence of nourishing foods, Des Esseintes is temporarily cured of his "neurosis." Decadence is then an eating disorder which culminates in the rejection of substantial food and its transubstantiation into artificial substitutes.

But the beneficial effects of this therapy are only temporary and soon Des Esseintes is once again afflicted by his dyspepsia. After progressively substituting a series of excessively disincarnate and artificial foods for a normal diet, Des Esseintes is put on an entirely artificial regimen by his doctor, "a nourishing wash of peptone" (230) to be administered three times a day:

> The operation succeeded and des Esseintes could not but congratulate himself quietly about this event that in a way crowned the existence he had created for himself. His penchant toward the artificial had now, even without him having wanted it, reached the supreme fulfillment; one would go no further; the nourishment thus absorbed was certainly the last deviation that could be committed. (230–31)

What is at stake is orality; in the inverted world of the decadent hero cure can only come from the reversal of the digestive tract. Therein lies the difference between the bourgeois consumption described in bourgeois realist and naturalist literature and decadent aristocratic nourishment. Hence, Anne-Marie Bancquart's observations do not entirely apply in the case of Des Esseintes:

> The literature from the beginning of the Third Republic is marked by fascination with nourishment. Perhaps a substitute for a sexuality that could not be directly described, but surely and more surely a preoccupation of the middle classes (middle-class public and

middle-class writer) who give the act of eating a privileged spot in their lives. Eating is immediately "profitable"; the circuit from absorption to digestion to excretion is satisfying because it is simple. With what one eats, one can know if there is a "deficit," if one has the "wherewithal," and if one has (or not) the taste to save. (13)

Des Esseintes's cure is brought about by nourishment given from below, a series of enemas; anality is converted from the locus of excretion to the locus of absorption. Artifice does not consist merely in the substitution of a series of potions that bear no resemblance to natural food, but also in the perverted form of ingestion. Just as in the case of bourgeois digestion focused on the production of waste, aristocratic ingestion is a displaced form of sexuality, but the sexuality being displaced is in Huysmans's own words, deviant. Or, to put the matter differently, it is not artifice, anti-physis that restores Des Esseintes to health but anality, the displacement of the maternal model of nourishment, by a form of nourishment patterned on homosexual intercourse. In the inverted world of the decadent male, the rectum is not the grave, but rather the source of life, the site of a rebirth.

I want to turn now from the decadent fast to a very different eating ritual. My initial example is drawn from the *Tour de la France par deux enfants*, the best-selling textbook meant to inculcate late-nineteenth-century school children with the ideology of the Third Republic, of a France recovering from the triple traumas of the defeat of 1870, the Commune, and the loss of Alsace-Lorraine: as the two orphaned children's educational tour of France comes to an end, they settle with their refound uncle Frantz on Grand'Lande, the property belonging to his friend, the sea captain le père Guillaume, who had brought them safely to harbor. Joining forces Frantz and his two orphaned nephews and père Guillaume, his wife, and three daughters, enter into an association to reclaim the farm, which was partially demolished during the war. In time the family grows to include the young orphan the two brothers had met during their journey, Jean-Joseph. Finally in the epilogue, set on Christmas Eve 1904, some twenty-five years after the children's arrival on the farm, in the immediate aftermath of the war, the little commune is joined by M. Géral, one of the boys' benefactors and father figures, and his son, freshly back from the colonies. All the members of this commune then sit down to eat, and it is this banquet that I would like to set against both the banquet of the bureaucrats and the solitary repast of the decadent bachelor:

Everyone dines and the long table set with twenty-four places, mixing every age, is a gay spectacle. The youngest are placed by their mothers and elder sisters, who take care of them and watch that they do not interrupt conversation. Besides, it is dessert time. Nuts and chestnuts are being shelled; they are feasting on an apple pie; everyone knows how such agreeable occupations calm down even the wildest.[4]

The communal banquet draws on a very different tradition than the official banquets of the Third Republic: the tradition of religious meals stretching all the way back to Antiquity and revived by the French utopian socialists of the nineteenth-century, and reenacted by the *compagnons*, the skilled craftsmen who toured France in a rite of apprenticeship. What is significant about the *compagnonages* is that they constituted families by elective affinities rather than by blood; the communal meals taken by the compagnons constitute the paradigm of both a counter and a pseudo-familial grouping; it is a fraternal association where the vertical association of father and son is replaced by the horizontal association of brothers. As George Sand explains in *Le Compagnon du Tour de France*: "The *tour de France* is the poetic phase, the adventurous pilgrimage, the wandering ride of the artisan. Someone who has neither house nor heritage [*patrimoine*] takes to the road to find a country [*patrie*], under the aegis of an adoptive family that abandons him neither during life nor after death"[5] Communal meals recur frequently in Sand, notably the reconciliation banquet that brings closure to an old family feud at the end of *Le Péché de Monsieur Antoine*: "Dinner, served in the shade of the park was made splendid with flowers and exquisite in its dishes. Old Marin, whose master had warned early in the morning, outdid himself in the arrangement of the service. Sylvain Charasson was admitted with the honor of working that day under his orders and he would speak of it throughout his life."[6] In fact the reconciliation dinner is also a dedication dinner, inaugurating the foundation of a utopian commune on the castle grounds: "I was willing in the future that this vast property be destined to found a *commune*" (372) says Monsieur Antoine.

Sand's "politics of food," as I have called it elsewhere, bear witness to the influence of Pierre Leroux on her writings. For according to Jacques Rancière, the communal meal is Leroux's "master image" and one might add, Rancière's, as he entitles a chapter of *La Nuit des prolétaires*, in homage to Leroux, "Le banquet interrompu." In the second part of his 1838 treatise *De l'égalité*, Leroux devotes several chapters to what he terms variously the "repas des égaux," the "repas communs," and the "repas égalitaire," an ancient institution that constitutes, according to him, the basis of Christianity. In instituting the sacrament of the Eucharist, Jesus, the apostles, Paul, the universalist, took a decisive step: they extended the Spartan common meal, which was reserved to a minority of Spartan citizens—for not all men were equals in Sparta—to all men. By establishing a link between the banquets of classical antiquity and those of early Christianity, Leroux took another, though obviously less decisive step: he made of the modern communist and communautarian banquet a sacrament on the order of the Eucharist. But Leroux neglects to mention that there were in fact two meals patterned on the Last Supper, the Eucharist and the Agape. In modern French, agape has come to mean something like a feast among friends. However, in its original meaning, which Christian theologians have great difficulty in distinguishing from the Eucharist, agape, from the Greek word for love, designates a "love feast," patterned on the gatherings attended by Jesus and his disciples. In agape, community and commensality are linked and, around 1847, the agape of early Christianity fuses in France with the fraternal banquets of early Republicanism; the occurrence of several Republican banquets are attested to in 1848. Just as bourgeois excretory digestion contrasts with Des Esseintes's anal ingestion, the bourgeois feast is to the Republican as the Eucharist is to Agape. The religious metaphor prevails in both instances, but the Christian meal referred to differs. Speaking of *L'Education sentimentale*, Bancquart comments:

> A religious comparison is in order. It is explicit in the presentation of the "buffet-altar" during the big reception at the Dambreuses'. Gleaming with precious metals and piously "served" like a mass, the food here and only here, is not the object of minute detail: a holy wafer is not being described. But this silence is that of supreme respect. (14)

What characterizes the agapes of antiquity was the fact that they were meals of fellowship to which the poor were invited; what characterizes those of the nineteenth century was that they were meals of fellowship that brought together rich and poor, master and servant, man and woman, parent and child. The Republican banquets of the mayors of the Third Republic were no love feasts, they were, on the contrary, eminently secular occasions.

If Sand, as a loyal disciple of Pierre Leroux, adheres to the tradition of pseudofamilial banquets, Zola, notably in *Fécondité*, appropriates the banquet and places it in service of the celebration of an extended nuclear family, thereby lending the family the legitimacy of early Christian commensality and by the same gesture the imperialist politics of the Third Republic that of an earlier agrarian society. On the occasion of their diamond wedding anniversary, Mathieu and Marianne Froment, the patriarchs of the Froment family, preside over a huge, indeed biblical meal, bringing together all their numerous progeny and held under the spreading branches of the oak tree they had long ago planted at Chantebled. The crowning event on this occasion is the arrival of an unknown descendant, Dominique, the son of Nicholas, the son who had gone off to participate in the colonization of Africa. Describing his family's life in "the other France," he tells his assembled aunts and uncles, nephews and nieces: "—Oh! We live in a republic; we are the community each of whose members must work in brotherly labor" (675). Similarly, as we have seen, in the closing banquet of *Le Tour de la France par deux enfants* a place is made at the table for M. Géral's son, who has just returned from Annam, where he was engaged under the auspices of the Institut Pasteur in the fight against the plague.

For all its roots in primitive communism, agape participates in legitimating the ideologies that we now consider conservative: familialism, agrarianism, colonization, and religion. Ways of eating are embedded in the social formations of an era. The abstinence of medieval women cannot be conflated with modern anorexia, as Carolyn Bynum has powerfully argued, or at least not without taking exquisite precautions to take changing cultural contexts into account. And, to a lesser extent, the same can be said of decadent inappetence. The ways of eating popular at the turn of the century are far more complex and varied than the expression "the banquet years" would allow. Decadence is not, as some would have it, synonymous with excess. Hence I would question the breezy assertion of Wayne Koestenbaum in the *New York Times Magazine* millenial issue: "Systematic gorging is a quintessential decadent activity. . . . Aren't vulgar desserts served at mediocre, expensive restaurants inevitably called 'Chocolate Decadence?'"[7]

The turn of the century plays out through its rituals of food consumption some of the larger issues of the day: the cleavage of church and state, the redefinition of the family, the politics of imperialism, the

bureaucraticization of the body social. But above all the turn of the nineteenth-century marks an important chapter in the ongoing saga of the
regulation and the deregulation of the body and its appetites. At the turn
of the twentieth century, regulation seems to be ascendant in societies
where food is abundant, but perhaps more significant is the closeting of
excess and the concomitant loss of commensality. Feasting on the eve of
the second millennium is not as it was in the first millennium an expression of collective love, nor as it was one hundred years ago in Paris the
occasion for public display: aside from some pockets of surviving agrarian
communal feasts, we feast but we feast in isolation. This is the era of the
loveless feast triumphant.

NOTES

1. Pascal Ory, *1889, L'Expo Universelle* (Paris: Complexe, 1989), 68–69. There
is some disagreement among the experts on the exact number of participants:
thus in *Le Mangeur du XIXe siècle*, Jean-Paul Aron writes of the Potel et Chabot,
founded during the Restoration: "In 1889, he served this meal to the 18,000
mayors gathered at the Palais de l'Industrie" (108). The menu follows: *potage à la
parisienne; truites saumonées sauce françoise; filets de boeuf à la gelée; galantines de poulardes
truffées; dindonneaux nouveaux rôtis—pâtés potel; salade printanière—soufflés glacés;
gâteaux des Iles—babas au rhum.* This meal is accompanied by: *madère vieux, graves,
médoc, pommard, champagne frappé, café* and *liqueurs.*
2. Charles Rearick, *Pleasures of the Belle Epoque* (New Haven: Yale University
Press, 1985): "Almost all the events were free. The banquets were kept at low
cost, but even the few francs charged were beyond the means of the poor" (11).
3. J.-K. Huysmans, *A Rebours* (Paris: G-F, 1978), 77.
4. G. Bruno, *Le Tour de la France par Deux Enfants* (Paris: Eugène Belin, 1994),
302.
5. George Sand, *Le Compagnon du Tour de France* (Paris: JCM, 1979), 100.
6. George Sand, *Le Péche de Monsieur Antoine* (Meylan: Aurore, 1982), 372
7. Wayne Koestenbaum, "Angelina Jolie, The Indiscreet Object of Desire,"
The New York Times Magazine, The "Me" Millennium (October 17, 1999), 96.

6. Colette's "Écriture gourmande"

BRIGITTE MAHUZIER

> If you are not able to practice a little witchcraft, there is
> no point in getting into the art of cooking.
>
> *Prisons et Paradis*

Colette's infamous gourmandise, a trait that connotes both Frenchness and femaleness, has been instrumental in the creation of her myth, a creation in which she participated and which came to be publicly hailed by the Third Republic. For this petit bourgeois republic, with its optimistic belief in progress and the future enrichment of all its citizens, Colette played the rebel, the necessary salt of a pretty bland earth. But where her predecessors, like Hugo and Zola, had grand causes, Colette had none, nor did she ever claim one. Where they spoke from a position of exile and imprisonment, their voices heard most clearly from afar or between prison bars, she remained the provincial woman whose discovery of Paris coincided with its kitschification, its becoming a center for touristic attractions and large popular cultural events. Where Hugo's and Zola's lives seem to have obeyed a centrifugal force, the better for them to strike and be remembered for their deeds and words against social and political injustices, hers, as her latest biographers are quick to point out, seems on the contrary to have obeyed a centripetal movement, never venturing very far from her native land, conserving with a few choice provinces some very close ties and ending her days in the closed square of the seventeenth-century Palais-Royal. For Michel del Castillo, in *Colette: une certaine France*, her life coincided with the rise and fall of the Third Republic, with its narrow, conservative, myopically egotistical quest for happiness.

By 1940, the bewitching, precocious girl, Gabrielle Sidonie Colette, had turned into a crafty woman of letters.[1] As she became old and feeble, partly because of her great weight due to a ferocious appetite, magazines and newspapers took a sadistic pleasure in representing her either in photos where she would pose, until the end, with her oblique and charcoal lined glance, as the "gamine" she no longer was and yet always remained, or else in the cruel drawings where she would be pictured as half old hag, half animal. She was, for the Third Republic, a rebel without a cause, a witch in the sense often given to that recurrent female figure: a rebel whose function is less to overturn the order of things than to conserve age-old traditions and history. For del Castillo (21), she is now "the Madonna of the Palais-Royal, fixed for eternity between her crystal paper-weights and her butterflies, between her cats and her blue paper, she is what the Eiffel Tower is to Paris, haunted as it is by nostalgia for its provinces."

In the wake of sexual liberation and the rise of feminist criticism in the 1970s she has offered a liberating image for women looking for role models in an attempt to free themselves from the prison of puritanical or petit bourgeois ethics.[2] She did, after all, defy an impressive number of social rules and sexual taboos—incest, bestiality, age, and gender, while exhibiting a remarkable lack of concern for public opinion. More recently, and also due to the rise of lesbianism on the market of literary criticism, she has also found a place as a lesbian icon in Claude Francis and Fernande Gontier's *Colette*.[3]

As the institutional beloved rebel, Colette then became, in the French national unconscious, a sort of Joan of Arc of French letters. It has never been forgotten, any more than it has been for Joan, that she was a woman and that she represented a mythical France, a certain flattering idea that France had and still has of itself when it turns toward its past. And as a woman of letters of a very bourgeois republic, what better place to situate this image than in the world of food, what more flattering and appropriate terms for such a "femme de lettres" than to speak of her prose in culinary terms, as a kind of "écriture gourmande"? Like Proust's Françoise, the Michelangelo of French cooking, the creator of crystal clear aspic around her "boeuf aux carottes," her writing could be construed as the outcome of a mysterious cooking process, transforming carefully chosen ingredients into something ineffable. But the difference between Colette and Françoise in the kitchen is that while Françoise's "genius" as a chef is presented as male, Colette's "écriture gourmande" has been considered as a "natural" outcome of her sexual female relation to the world. What has tended to be effaced in the making of Colette as a national monument, yet resurfaces when the "witch" appears under a negative light, is the biting edge of her original creation, starting with *Claudine à l'école*.

We do not know whether Willy, before he took the manuscript of *Claudine à l'école* to Ollendorf, asked her to spice it up or water it down. Two stories coexist that appear at first glance to be mutually exclusive, each casting a very different light on Colette. In *Mes apprentissages*, as well as in other more fictional texts such as *La Vagabonde*, she portrays herself as goaded by a decadent, lubricious, and money-hungry husband who would ask her to answer to the public's taste for pornography in which sapphism played an essential part (a version she later modified in her "interviews with André Parinaud" after her rage against Willy had long subsided). In the other, a letter written by Willy to a newspaper, the latter appears genuinely surprised by an already spiced-up novel that, according to him, needed to be rendered somewhat more palatable to the public.

Although Colette appears as pure and innocent in the first one and precociously perverse in the second, both stories can happily coexist because what shocked Willy was not the standard pornographic elements or scenes that his contemporaries expected to read in the libertine literature he was promoting. What was probably a bit too spicy for Willy and prompted him to write this letter is Claudine's simple and primordial sadomasochistic relation to the world and the other, a relation which has a gastronomic equivalent in the condition known as *pica*.

Pica is a perversion that consists in eating "non-foods" like dirt, glue, paper, erasers, pencils, and crayons; they are materials related more to touch than to taste. The term *pica*, which comes from the Latin *picus* and the French *piquer*, meaning both to prick and to steal, is related to the word *pie* in French and *magpie* in English: the bird that steals shiny objects. The OED describes this perversion as typically feminine since it is mostly found in hysterics and pregnant women, but if asked, many people of both sexes will admit to this unnatural fondness. It is most often relegated to a "youthful error," a primordial need to devour everything in sight, a happy, polymorphous relationship to the world linked to a taste for discovery and adventure. Pica does not refer to an unlimited, voracious "appetite of pleasure," but to a more intellectual and refined relationship to the world, combining the pleasure of ingestion with that of discrimination. If gourmandise consists in considering the world as one's oyster, this perversion of gourmandise, in tune with Colette's "unnatural" way of writing, in which the shell is preferred to the oyster, offers an ironic twist to the portrait of the most medal-decorated writer of the "République des Lettres."

In *Claudine à l'école*, snails, or more specifically slugs, are the heroine's father's life. Totally absorbed in his scientific research, this Fabre of malacology, has with his creatures of choice, whose main interest for him resides in his study of their eating habits, a love that Claudine, noticing a trace of slime in his beard, would prefer not to investigate, too busy herself in the discovery of her own eating habits.[4] Clearly, the ingestion metaphor is describing a vital, primordial being in the world, which Claudine and the slugs share as they are both avid little creatures, living under the bemused eye of this benevolent observer who never ceases to wonder at their common appetite for life.

Here we are right at the origin of Colette's mythological creation where gourmandise bordering on gluttony [*goinfrerie*], is seen by many of her biographers as the original sign of the writer's devouring appetite for life in all its facets: sex, money and all forms of material possessions, praises, medals, titles, etc. Mona Ozouf attributes Colette's "gluttony" to her mother from whom she learned some very enduring lessons about women's tireless resistance, their amazing aptitude at surviving catastrophes, at picking up the pieces of a shattered life: "Sido is a woman who makes the best of everything and arranges her daily life the way a Dutch painter fills his canvas, gluttonously, never tiring of adding an oyster shell or a lemon" (Ozouf, 176). Colette, the writer, is the true daughter of the woman she has reconstructed in her writing, Sido, the oyster-shell displayer. And what she "inherited" is a noncomestible "gluttony."[5]

Analyzing *Claudine à l'école*, we find a kind of gourmandise that is not typically feminine, indiscriminately gluttonous and devouring, as del Castillo would have us believe in his demythologizing yet essentializing portrait of Colette-the-woman, but more akin to a Baudelairian, dandy-like, unnatural or denaturalizing attitude toward life and art, a piquant version of Colette-the-author, what may have perturbed Willy and prompted him to provide his edulcorated pornographic (for his time, kitschy for ours) additions.

In *Claudine à l'école*, almost every school girl eats school supplies provided by the *commune*. But the girl's school is particularly costly to the community for the students consume vast amounts of writing and drawing material, especially in the sole person of *La grande Anaïs*, who ruins the *commune* by her excessive pica perversion:

However much they forbid her these strange comestibles, all day long
her pockets and her mouth are filled with pencil stubs, filthy black
India rubber, charcoal, and pink blotting paper. Chalk, pencil-lead,
and such-like satisfy her stomach in the most peculiar way: it must be
those things she eats that give her a complexion the color of wood and
grey plaster.[6] (*Claudine in School* 23)

Claudine, who may not have read Brillat-Savarin, but who instinctively
knows that "you are what you eat," is quick to mark her distance from
Anaïs, the repulsively ugly girl, as tall, angular and grey as the pencils she
eats. Although she admits to sharing the same perversion, hers is very discriminating: "At least, I eat only cigarette paper and only one special kind
of that" (23).

Yet the two girls have much more in common than Claudine is ready to
admit: namely the same avid appetite and rebellious attitude toward life as
well as the same sadistic desire to conquer and make their mark. Indeed, it
becomes clear that this adolescent perversion is linked to a sadistic relation
to the "other," whether it be the inanimate world defiantly devoured or the
object of abuse lovingly terrorized.

As they move into the new school where girls are seated two by two,
Anaïs and Claudine, known as the "dégourdies" (the smart and worldly)
are paired with Marie and Luce, known as the "engourdies" (numb, slow,
naive, and easily dominated). The pairing is perfect. The mean, ugly, and
wickedly smart "grande Anaïs" can terrorize the sweet, plump, and pretty
Marie Belhomme, while the no less mean and devious Claudine can take
revenge upon Luce for her failure to conquer Luce's beautiful sister Aimée.[7]
So, as the two "dégourdies" mark their new territory and take over their
new space, they exchange gastronomic appraisals of their new surround-
ings like two gourmets discussing the merits of a new restaurant not yet
classified in the Michelin guide:

— Whatever are you eating—old crab-apples?
— Lime buds, old thing. Nothing so good. Now's just the moment,
   when it's getting on for March.
— Give us a bit? . . . Really, it's awfully good. It's sticky like the gum on
   fruit-trees. I'll get some off the lime on the playground. And what
   other hitherto unknown delicacies are you stuffing yourself with
   nowadays? (80)

Anaïs, who has a conservative Frenchness in her taste, is, however, the true
adventurer of the two. In a monologue, while she deplores, like a picky

French gourmet, the loss of good quality supplies that forces her to move from swallowing the world to simply masticating it, she shows her ability to adjust to a changing world and try something unknown: "'I can't even eat colored pencils any more. This year's lot are gritty. Beastly—absolute rubbish. However, to make up for that, the blotting-paper's excellent. There's also something good to chew, but not to swallow . . . the samples of handkerchief linen that the Bon Marché and the Louvre send out" (80). Claudine replies: "'Ugh! That doesn't appeal to me in the least," and then turns to Luce and digs her nails into her hand to test her own power and mark her own territory. This sadomasochist relationship between Claudine and Luce is perfectly illustrated in terms of food. To provide Luce with the pleasure of pain and keep her coming back for more, Claudine feeds her the most peppery mints she can find: "For ten sous' worth of too-hot English peppermints, she would have sold her big sister and one of her brothers into the bargain. She opened her mouth, breathed in the air so as to feel the cold of the peppermint and exclaimed: 'My tongue's freezing, my tongue's freezing,' her eyes rapturous" (84).

Such is the world according to Claudine: a place to explore and redefine, starting with what one ought to eat and not eat, accept or reject, in a sadistic need to control and dominate. She grows up, marries, leaves Montigny, discovers Paris, and remains from 1900 to 1907 the hungry and sensual little creature she was in school, her bisexuality eventually recognized and avidly explored.[8] What happens to Proust's Marcel, whom we see as a wizened old man on the brink of death, does not happen to Claudine, who becomes caught in her Belle Époque time frame, forever "gamine," and gourmande.

Colette herself admits that she participated in her own typecasting as Claudine; she created a type, that of the "ingénue libertine," which then pursued her with a vengeance; and she even reaffirmed this type as something essentially French in her 1944 creation of *Gigi*, the schoolgirl ingénue of the Belle Époque, seduced by Gaston's chocolates and champagne. "Colette," life and work together, has been essentialized as feminine and as French to the point of caricature. It is not surprising, then, that terms pertaining to the pleasures of food are often seen to characterize her writing. André Parinaud, who interviewed her in 1949, summarizes her style in gastronomic terms: "her 'prose gourmande' is perfectly illustrated by her delectable and confident choice of words as she speaks" (*Colette: Mes vérités*, 1996). What is more essentially French and feminine than "gourmandise," a term for which there is no equivalent in the English language?

Combine food and sex in a large bowl, add language, and you have some-thing essentially French, as French as Brillat-Savarin with his *Physiologie du goût*, Proust with his "petite madeleine," or Colette with her "écriture gourmande" and her "tasty and juicy words." Colette fits into a tradition, even more so because, as a woman, she is supposed to have a direct and nat-ural access to orality, to the pleasures of the tongue and the mouth.

From the other side of the Atlantic, Colette's "gourmandise" is another favorite product of exportation, and like all made "for export only," it answers to a particular preconceived idea in the mind of the importer of what the product should connote: in this case, its "Frenchness" (Ladenson). Robert Phelps, the main editor of Colette's works in English translation, is quite aware of the mythologizing that has taken place despite or rather because of the author's tendency to display her life in view of all. His *Colette's Earthly Paradise*, described as "the autobiography of her myth," "drawn from the writings of her lifetime," is a judicious way of circum-venting the difficult task of getting at the truth about Colette when all her "secrets" are so flagrantly open ones.[9] There are no "truths," Phelps seems to say; there are only myths, and they can be reached directly through the texts, which together draw a better portrait of her than any fact-based biography. However, this genre has its flaws because editorial choices have to be made and myth-making (especially about paradises) is an unending process, necessarily depending upon the way the myth is recounted, or in this case edited. Among the many texts on food Phelps could have chosen to include in his pseudoautobiography, we find, under the title "gastron-omy," four short works that reveal as much about Colette's discriminating taste as about the American appreciation of what compose the best of French earthly gastronomical paradises: wine, cheese, and, inevitable, the sexy truffle. Colette, in the United States, is never very far from *Gigi*.

Just as there is a Colette for export, there is a Colette for home con-sumption, especially according to the French's soft spot for its peasantry, the incorruptible, unimpressionable, solid part of France's stock. Colette, as a true "paysanne," may be temporarily bedazzled by the savoir-faire of a Willy and the flashy demimonde in which they will live, but deep down, she is true to her "race, milieu, moment," and translated in culinary terms, this means that she will resist the perversions and the fads which cooking has rapidly undergone in her time. Colette would no more be attracted to the concept of "nouvelle cuisine" than she was to that of the "nouveau roman," suspicious as always of anything with the ring of pre-tentious novelty.

Although Colette was never the traditional *femme au foyer*, there is something very traditional in her culinary tastes, that critics, encouraged by Colette herself, link with the way she writes and talks. When hearing recordings of Colette, one is struck by her low guttural voice and her very thick Burgundy accent. In more ways than one Colette reminds her public of her attachment to Burgundy, the province where she grew up, and her later attachment to Provence, her father's birthplace. On the surface, it seems that Colette's gastronomical map remains pretty much limited to Burgundy and Provence. Although she did travel in Europe during her career on stage and was on the maiden voyage of the *Normandie* in 1935, she was unimpressed by continental foods and remained cold under the "basilica ceiling" of the *Normandie*'s first-class dining room. She seems, by contrast, to have taken a particular liking to North African fares. Her Moroccan notebooks are replete with comments about traditional food, lavishly described as they are served in the palaces of sultans and Pashas. In "A Moroccan luncheon," she describes "pale girdle-cakes soaked in sugared butter and sprinkled with almonds; pigeons bathed in succulent juice with green olives, chick peas melting in flour, sweet onions; chickens buried under fresh beans with wrinkled skins and lemon cooked and recooked and reduced to a savory puree" (92).

And the list goes on. Sometimes, Colette stops to offer a recipe or adds a comment reflecting her philosophy as a gastronome. About the preparation of a "Shoulder of mutton *en musette*, she insists on the importance of adding "sugar as desired" because recipes are to be treated with freedom and anticipatory delectation, and because, above all, one must never think about such petty hazards as one's weight or one's fragile stomach" ("Moroccan" 93). Although the picture of Colette that emerges from these writings from North Africa corresponds to the image we have of her—the hedonistic, free-thinking woman whose appetites for life are displayed in her prose—this image has been more often linked to her roots in her native land. In her introduction to *Places*, a collection of essays Colette wrote later in her career, Margarete Crosland (5–6) is quick to point out that although Colette writes with color, movement, humor or nostalgia about places where she has been, "she writes perhaps with most depth about her own country and more particularly about the places where she lives for a long time." In Colette one finds a true respect for regional traditions, the age-old traditions of "la France profonde," for the simple foods of her youth, such as the chestnut, which she describes with lyrical empathy, in *Paris de ma fenêtre*, a text written in 1941 when food was very scarce: "Admirable white flesh of the white chestnut, providential complement of our diminished meals! You are the delicate bread brought by this cold season, sparse in lentils and dried haricot beans; you abound when all else becomes scarce, when the earth closes" (*Looking Backwards* 117). The *flognarde* is also a source of lyricism for Colette, who after giving its recipe ("two eggs only, a glass of flour, one of cold water or of skimmed milk, a good pinch of salt, three spoonfuls of sugar"), describes it as it cooks: "With twenty minutes' cooking, the *flognarde* becomes an enormous puffiness which fills the oven, becomes golden, then brown, bursts here, swells there. . . . At the finest of its eruptions remove it, sugar it lightly with caster sugar, and divide it still boiling" (*Looking* 145).

Later on, in the same text, she adds the pleasure of etymology to the pleasure of description, and calls herself a "gourmet etymologist." The name *flognarde*, she explains, comes from Mme Flogny, the postmistress of the Flogny relay (in the department of Yonne), who used to cook it as the travelers were waiting for their coach. Thus, she claims, it comes from Burgundy, and not from Limousin, as some would have it, where *flognarde* means lazy and spineless, for how could a lazy, spineless bum be compared to "a crisp brown tidbit, still emitting little splutters of laughter as its leaps out of the oven" (154).

Marie-Christine and Didier Clément's *Colette gourmande* corresponds to this traditional image of Colette, the provincial gourmande whose epicurean philosophy is so attuned to the simple and joyous pleasures of food, that even in the dark of winter, in the deprivation of war, or in the confined quarters of a Parisian apartment, these pleasures can be evoked and celebrated with words. Food and language, all French will agree, have a natural affinity that makes writing or reading cookbooks a poetic experience. The Cléments' *Colette gourmande*, lavishly illustrated with many black and white pictures of Colette and assorted friends and lovers, and many color pictures of natural landscapes and prepared dishes, is part biography, part cookbook, a genre that aims at giving gastronomical writing its titles and pedigree. In the same vein as *Proust: la cuisine retrouvée*, a contemporaneous cookbook with a biographical bent, it is the sum of collaborative efforts between a (male) French chef and a literary critic (female), a cookbook finding its justification and founding its appeal on the life and work of a major literary figure. In both cases, the book is divided into two parts: a first part more properly biographical and textual and a second part offering a collection of recipes. In the case of Colette, the recipes are announced as hers ("Les cahiers de recettes de Colette" is its title) and comprise the major part of the book, whereas in the case of Proust, they are simply "recipes."

The second part also offers similarities with unsurprising differences. Both begin with "the tastes of childhood" (the "petite madeleine" for Marcel and melted chocolate for Gabrielle), associated with the mother and the small town idyllic image of the province (respectively Illiers-Combray and St-Sauveur). Differences are also predictable. In the case of *Dining with Proust*, the main chapters, arranged according to a number of high society dining experiences—whether it is with the lady in pink, Madame Verdurin, or the Duchess of Guermantes—never lead us very far from the Parisian center. In the case of *Colette gourmande*, the chapters, divided into a large "Gourmandes provinces" and a smaller "Un goût authentique," remind the reader of the author's attraction to the provinces and her feline attachment to places rather than people as indicated by the titles of the "Gourmandes provinces" part: "Saint-Sauveur-en-Puisaye," "Les Monts-Boucon," "Rozven," CastelNovel," "La Treille-Muscate," "Le Palais-Royal." From this gastronomical portrait of the writer as a gourmande, it is clear that, for most of her compatriots, Colette embodies a feminine attachment to things past, especially in their mythically simple and authentic state.[10]   The enfant terrible of literature, who never fitted into a bourgeois mold, she represents, especially for the postwar generation, a kind of good witch version of the keeper of the hearth, close to mother nature in her tastes for its bountiful fare. Like Sido, who could not bring herself to kill and eat the little red hen, she presents herself as more vegetarian than carnivorous, although she admits to the pleasure of eating meat, and maliciously compares it to eating babies. She would happily, she claims, trade the "revered and ineluctable meat, monotonous center of every Parisian gathering" for "a plateful of *fromage blanc*, well-peppered" or "the hallowed tomato, the stout onion" (*Looking* 34).[11] She sneers at the typical Parisian tourists in Provence who "reject the magnificent Provençal vegetables: peppers, tomatoes, the glossy aubergine, sweet onions" (*Looking* 34). In a film made of her at the end of her life, she ostentatiously takes great pleasure in shocking middle-class attitudes with her peasant table manners as she bites into a large onion brought in fresh from the open market, appreciatively pronouncing it "sweetness itself."

There is something undeniably conservative in Colette's attachment to the good food of yore, which makes her sneer at the inauthenticity of what is now served as "traditional cuisine" (in "Récriminations," *Prisons et paradis*), and makes her shiver at the thought of any form of pretentious stylistic effect such as found in the "nouvelle cuisine." She would probably have laughed at the recent "food fight" in French cuisine between traditionalists and eclectic creativists, for being typically bourgeois "academic" turf wars.

In her reverence for the past and traditions, for simplicity and refinement, Colette is purely ancien régime, she is the aristocrat inhabiting every peasant (or vice versa). She has, with Françoise and the Duchesse de Guermantes, the same aristocratic attachment to a place, the same "noble taste for the country." In a short piece entitled "Moi, je suis gourmande," (written late in her life), Colette clearly defines her gourmandise as a taste for simple things of the past: "when I speak of gourmandise, you always expect me to lecture you on stuffed partridges, foie gras or dressed soles."[12] No, she claims,

> my gourmandise is of rustic origin . . . a twelve-pound loaf of dark country bread, with a thick crust, its dense and even, linen-grey inside still fragrant with the smell of new rye, and a slab of freshly made butter, still oozing with milky tear drops under the knife, perishable butter, not machine-made, but hand-pressed, rancid after two days, as perfumed, as ephemeral as a flower, luxury butter.

Thus, it is easy to take Colette's avowed love for traditions and authenticity, her reverence for nature and natural food, as the sign of conservatism, going hand in hand with her feminine nature, her bursting sexuality. In *Amoureuse Colette*, Geneviève Dormann's amply illustrated story of "the thousand and one nights of the one who was one of the greatest writers of our century" (jacket cover, my translation), gourmandise, a sign of her vitality, is intricately linked to her amorous life. While recounting Colette's passionate and tormented story with Henry de Jouvenel and her love for food, her inability to resist temptation and her propensity to gain weight, Dormann maliciously interpolates four pages of recipes illustrated with pictures of Colette mostly cutting, buttering, and tasting a very large slice of bread. The result is remarkable, especially since this mini-cookbook interrupts a sentence written by Colette in 1923 from Rozven where, noticing an abundance of large toads, she compares them in size to her behind: "there are toads," she writes, "as large as [mini-cook-book inserted here] my ass [*ma fesse*]" (177–82).

Colette as Claudine, the devourer of school supplies, later the devourer of young lovers and husbands, and the old Colette, still coyly devouring an onion in front of the camera: it all seems to fit in. Colette is a gourmande and she writes with gourmandise, the *péché mignon* of children and old people, but also of women who are, by nature, voracious.

But "gourmande" for Colette is nothing to sneer at. Well understood, it is in fact an aesthetic and an ethics. It is the same kind of reverence for the past and sense of timeless perfection that also dictates her writing. The hand of the writer is like the hand of the baker, "a rustic hand, inspired, or simply respectful of ancient traditions." Thus, Colette is full of admiration for her Provençal housekeeper who, although illiterate, respects the usage of the imperfect subjunctive: "Should we have left him dying on the road [*Fallait-il que nous 1'eussions laissé mourant sur le chemin*]?" she asks Colette rhetorically of the victim of a bicycle accident. Which prompts the writer's appreciative comments for such "a fine phrase, redolent of the seventeenth century, that nevertheless flourishes on illiterate lips," adding that she admires this kind of resistance to vulgarity: "I admire the fact that a syntax of such style should be able to repulse the alluvium of slang, sporting patois and pretentious humor that floods in from all sides." In "Moi, je suis gourmande," she makes sure that she is not mistaken for what she calls a "gourmette romantique," the kind who loves to expound endlessly and with great flourish on the merits of haute cuisine of the past. There is nothing worse for a true "gourmande" than "littérature gastronomique," the bastard daughter of gastronomy, especially when it is only dictated by the art of writing ("l'art d'écrire"). Just as there is nothing worse, for a true writer, a writer with a sense of self-respect, than what she calls with intense disgust "la littérature." There is nothing worse than complacency, whether in art or in life, the two being indissociable.

For Colette, writing had never been easy, and she quickly dispels André Parinaud's misconception of her writing as the natural result of some sort of (feminine) instinctive attunement with her senses. "You have a musical ear, a richly nuanced sense of touch and your sense of taste is that of a *gourmande*. All these qualities together make up for what I see as the virtues of your style," says Parinaud to the woman he often calls "la grande Colette." "It's easy to see," replies Colette, without missing a beat, "that you are not here when I am hard at work, painfully revising my manuscripts" (*Mes Vérités* 184). Although she admits that her olfactory sense is crucial ("I am delighted I still have the flair of dogs or cats"), hard work and a refusal of complacency are the keys to her writing. These, she claims, she owes to her parents, but as a kind of negative heritage. She did not inherit Sido's natural epistolary talent, for Sido could, in the most uncomfortable places, write the most charming letters. Nonetheless, she gets from her mother her lack of self-indulgence, for Sido pointed out to her daughter that her real talent was not for "facilité," but for "lucidité" and that she must use this gift accordingly. She did inherit from her father a difficulty of writing linked to a fetishistic attachment to "stationery supplies" which was a source of amusement for her naturally gifted mother: " 'She is a chip off the old block,' Sido would say teasingly to my father" (Phelps 49–50).

In *La Cire verte*, Colette describes how, like her father, she had a religious fascination for all forms of writing tools, which she names "the objects of my worship": "I was about fifteen years old, going through a *fournitures de bureau* (office supplies) crisis. I was only imitating my father for whom this mania lasted his whole life" (*Cire* 237—my translation). As is the case for Claudine and her schoolmates, her desire for possession and control took on the form of a lusting after writing material. She begins by stealing a few things from her father's table, "a little mahogany set square that smelled like a cigar box, then a white metal ruler." Meeting the blazing gray eye of her "rival," she just prowls,

> hungrily, with my mind full of evil thoughts, around all these treasures of stationery. A pad of virgin blotting paper; an ebony ruler; one, two, four, six pencils, sharpened with a penknife and all of different colors; pens with medium nibs and fine nibs, pens with enormously broad nibs, drawing pens no thicker than a blackbird's quill; sealing wax, red, green and violet; a hand blotter, a bottle of liquid glue, not to mention slabs of transparent amber-colored stuff known as "mouth glue." ("My father" 48)

But, as she reaches a climactic moment in her debauched *tour de table*, when everywhere on the table she sees "reams of paper, cream-laid, ruled, watermarked," there she spots it, the paper-devourer itself, "that little stamping machine that bit into the white sheet and with one snap of its jaws adorned it with an embossed name: J.-J. Colette," the name of her father, Joseph-Jules Colette (48–49).

Colette, the devourer of office supplies, grew out of her frenetic adolescent phase. Unlike her father, who "dissipating his desire in material arrangements," never wrote more than a few lines, she became at once one of the most prolific and the discriminating writers of French literature. She may have eaten, for good measure, as she prowled over her father's treasures, the white (and only the white) "sealing wafer" on his desk, but the beautiful and fragrant green sealing wax, inherited from her father, "very old [. . .] and speckled with gold dust," the equivalent of Proust's "boutons d'or," she never ate.

NOTES

1. Del Castillo, who marks her death as a writer in 1940 so that it coincides with the end of "une certaine France," discards the last ten years of the writer's production and more than ten major works.

2. See Marks, whose work opened the way for women scholars with an interest in Colette's life story. See also, Crosland, Mitchell, Joanna Richardson, Thurman. In French, see Sarde, Dormann, Ferrier-Caverivière, and Francis and Gautier.

3. Male biographers, if not seduced like Jean Chalon (*Portrait d'une séductrice*, 1976; *Colette, l'éternelle apprentie*, 1998), tend to be more detached, like Claude Pichois and Alain Brunet's scrupulously documented *Colette*, 1999, more skeptical, and in some cases, like del Castillo's Colette, 1999, downright caustic. In typical Proustian fashion, del Castillo separates "l'homme" (as it were) whom he hates from "l'oeuvre," which, for the most part, he loves, and presents a portrait of the author in a less than flattering light.

4. Contrary to what could be expected from Colette's declared love for the food and wine of her native Burgundy, she could never get the famous "escargots de Bourgogne" down her throat. To Adrienne Monnier ([1976] 197), the American literary journalist and chronicler of the in-crowd of the Parisian literary and artistic circles, Colette declared over lunch in 1942: "It's the only thing I have never been able to eat. I've tried to enjoy them, but nothing goes down except the juice." Taken out of their hard little shells, covered up in garlic butter, or smothered in Burgundy wine, snails are not for everyone.

5. Michel del Castillo's abrasive portrait of the writer depicts her as a glutton, so turned toward her appetites, which are totally woven into her writing, so in tune with them, that she remained all her life myopic to history, often reducing her characters to animality or to the timeless figures found in fairy tales. In Mona Ozouf's *Woman's Words*, Colette appears under one of the ironic title headings mimicking the ten capital sins here attributed to women, as "Gabrielle or Gluttony." Yet, contrary to what the title seems to indicate, there is very little allusion to Colette's famous gourmandise. The portrait she paints, while sharing with del Castillo a lack of interest in Colette's real gourmandise, is a lot more generous and

less reductive, less essentializing despite the title of the whole collection, which clearly announces that the author will attempt to extract some essential, singular trait among French women in order to establish a sense of a certain "French singularity."

6. References from the Claudine novels will be to Antonia White's translation of the works. Minor modifications in the translations of Colette's work will be made silently.

7. Aimée is herself in a sadomasochistic relationship with the headmistress, Mlle. Sergeant, who, while posing as the tyrant, is being capriciously tormented by her, to the great delight of Claudine.

8. In *The Sentimental Retreat*, Claudine's liberated alter ego, Annie, takes over.

9. Another way is through irony and distance vis-à-vis a genre that can no longer cling to the idea that biographies simply unveil the truth of the subject under study. Judith Thurman, well aware of the difficulties of such an enterprise, especially concerning Colette who displays her private life in view of all, mentions in her introduction the "aspect louche" of her title, emphasizing that it "is intentional—my own ironic bow to Colette's reputation" (*Secrets of the Flesh*, 1999).

10. In *Colette gourmande*, Proust keeps hovering over the portrait of Colette as the master storyteller of bygone days, Proust with his sophisticated madeleine and Colette with the simple chestnut: "The *cornuelle* is for Colette what the *madeleine* is for Proust. It symbolizes the place of origin and childhood C . . . It abolishes time and encompasses all at once her youth and the tastes of her native province" (35).

11. I have restored the French *fromage blanc* for the translated phrase "white cheese."

12. In *L'Étoile Vesper*, she says that gourmandise is "the most essentially French quality," but indicates that it has been dishonored by the French propensity for ostentatiousness.

7. Monsieur Marcel's Gay Oysters

FRANC SCHUEREWEGEN

We are in Balbec, in the dining room of the Grand-Hotel:

> "But I don't believe I've ever seen you eating oysters," she said to us one day (increasing the sense of disgust which I felt at that moment, for the living flesh of oysters revolted me even more than the viscosity of the stranded jelly-fish defiled [*ternissait*] the Balbec beach for me). "They are exquisite on this coast!" (*JF* 2:56; 2:218)[1]

The oysters are exquisite, and yet the hero refuses them. For now, that is. For this is a bildungsroman; many things will change and this is merely the starting point. Here is the same character one hundred and fifty pages later, in the same dining room, having just finished his lunch:

> I would now happily remain at the table while it was being cleared [. . .] I sought to find again in reality, I cherished as though for their poetic beauty, the broken gestures of the knives still lying across one another, the swollen convexity [*la rondeur bombée*] of a discarded napkin [. . .] the promenade of the antiquated chairs that came twice daily to take their place round the white cloth spread on the table as on an altar at which were celebrated the feasts of gourmandise, and where in the hollows of the oyster-shells a few drops of lustral water had remained as in tiny stone baptismal fonts. (*JF* 2: 224; 2:519)

Granted, the shells, and not the flesh are recalled. Common sense, however, would indicate that if the shells are left empty on the table, the flesh has been eaten. And who would have eaten it but the very person who is addressing us?

Evidently, the visit to Elstir's atelier that precedes this scene is not without significance. The great painter teaches the hero how better to observe

"common things," and not to scorn the banality of daily life.[2] Elstir, however, is a master of the gaze, an aesthete, and our subject here is culinary. It
is true that the two are linked in Proust: to better observe is also, in part,
to better savor; and this is the lesson we are being taught. Nevertheless, we
would be hard placed to imagine Elstir offering a course in gastronomy to
the Proustian narrator. The hypothesis that "it is the great painter who
changed my life" does not explain everything. Another element is of
import, and it is up to us to say what it is.

Let us leave Balbec for now and go to Doncières. In another restaurant,
some men in uniform are seated around a succulent meal. Our hero has
joined them at the invitation of his friend Saint-Loup. Marcel is very
happy, beatific. Never in his life has he eaten so well. Interestingly, the
menu features oysters:

> I felt cut off [. . .] from all external preoccupations [. . .] by the
> warmth of that little dining-room, by the savor of the refined dishes
> that we were being served. These gave as much pleasure to my
> imagination as to my gourmandise; sometimes the little piece of
> nature from which they had been extracted, the rugged baptismal font
> of the oyster in which lingered a few drops of brackish water, or the
> gnarled stem [sarment], the yellowed branches of a bunch of grapes,
> still enveloped them, inedible, poetic, and distant as a landscape,
> evoking as we dined successive images of a nap in the shade of a vine
> and of an excursion on the sea. (CG 2:416; 3:128-29)

Once more, the shell is recalled along with its physical qualities. Yet let us
again appeal to common sense: all empty oysters were once full. Our hero
has a responsibility in this story; he participated in this feast. It is not
important that he is not shown consuming the milky flesh, savoring it
fully. "Imagination" and "gourmandise" are both present: Marcel accepted
and enjoyed the oysters.

The context is surely a factor, for we are in a small private room. Everyone is comfortable in this small private room permeated with a warm glow
of friendship; the hero is really quite euphoric. The military men who have
welcomed him show him great esteem and appreciation. In fact, this provokes a slight fit of jealousy in the friend who invited him.

> "I'm jealous, I'm furious," Saint-Loup said to me, half laughing, half in
> earnest, alluding to the interminable private conversations which I had
> been having with his friend. "Do you find him more intelligent than me?

> Do you like him better than me? Ah, well, I suppose he's everything now
> [*Alors, comme ça, il n'y en a plus que pour lui*]." (*CG* 2:417; 3:129)

Proust adds, to ensure that there is no misunderstanding: "(Men who are
enormously in love with a woman, who live in a society of woman-lovers
[*hommes à femmes*], allow themselves pleasantries which others, who would
see less innocence in them, would never dare to contemplate)" (*CG* 2:417;
3:129).

Honni soit qui mal y pense: shame on him who thinks ill of it. Nevertheless, we think of it, due to the narrator's allusion, due to this warning we
get and whose motive we do not know. If this is all innocent fun, why
speak of guilt? Would the narrator himself belong to the category of
"men" that he brings up, those seeing "less innocence," because they know
a bit more and because their conscience is uneasy? As kids say in France,
"C'est celui qui le dit qui le fait": Whoever said it did it. Children know
that not everyone can say just anything.[3]

Note how the narrator qualifies his friend's intervention as jest [*plaisan-
terie*] even though he precedes it with a remark that Saint-Loup is only
half-joking. If we read further we realize that the term "ladies' man" is not
fully appropriate to this military group. For we remember some revela-
tions of Aimé, the maître d'hôtel at the Hôtel de Balbec, those that refer to
the time that where a friendship is struck between the narrator and the
marquis: "'Why, of course, Monsieur,' he said to me, 'it's common knowledge, I've known it for ever so long'" (*AD* 4:259; 5:785).

Let us not too hastily determine, however, the nature of this delicate
matter. What counts is the path to be retraced and the step that has been
taken. Oysters engender nothing but disgust in the young hero when he is
at the seashore with Mme de Villeparisis and his grandmother. Yet, when
he dines at Doncières amongst men, disgust no longer exists. The ostrophobe becomes an ostrophile. He has grown, matured. Brave young man.

In the famous section on homosexuality at the beginning of *Sodom et
Gomorrhe*, Proust remarks that: "there are cases where, as we shall see,
inversion is curable"(*SG* 3:26; 4:29). He really is quite silent about cures,
and the statement has no follow-through. This is because the section he
alludes to was not included in the published version of the text, and one
must read it in the section of "Esquisses"—a genetic accident among many
in Proust. What is relevant for us is that our oysters appear in this section:

> In some rare cases, the problem is not congenital, [. . .] and in this
> superficial case, it can be cured. Sometimes it arises from a difficulty

of making love with a woman, because of an anatomical weakness. Indeed, certain kinds of asthma can be cured by destroying adhesions in the patient's nose. Other times, the cause of the problem is a disgust towards women, a repulsion caused by their smell, by the quality of their skin, a repulsion that can be overcome, just as with certain children who do not feel well upon seeing oysters or cheese and then wind up really liking them. ("Esquisse IV," *SG* 3:951)

Thus, some are cured of homosexuality just as others can overcome their repulsion to certain foods. The two are linked. Learn to eat oysters; and become hetero. That is accomplished in much the same manner; the path is the same. If we now read the same passage in the official version of the novel, we notice that the oyster has vanished. In its stead is the jellyfish [*méduse*], the other object of disgust in Balbec.[4] A slippage has thus occurred, a slight metaphoric and metonymic shift of interest to us. In the next passage, Proust describes a quite specific category of invert which he names the "solitary":

> Then the loner languishes alone. He has no other pleasure than going to the neighboring watering-place to ask for some information from a certain railwayman there. But the latter has obtained promotion [. . .] the loner will no longer be able to go and ask him the times of the trains [. . .] and, before retiring to dream, Griselda-like, in his tower, loiters upon the beach, a strange Andromeda whom no Argonaut will come to free, a sterile jellyfish [*méduse*] that will perish on the sand [. . .] (*SG* 3:27–28; 4:30–31)

Proust has confused myths: Andromeda was rescued by Perseus and not by one of the Argonauts. But "argonaut" is also the name of a mollusk—the nautilus—and we can surmise that the author has deliberately used this terms in order to remain in the register of marine biology. Thus, we get the idea that the oyster is part of this mythological seaside play being staged for us.[5] In his letters we should note that Proust compares himself to Andromeda. What he retains in particular in this allusion to mythology is the image of the captive "attached to the rock."[6] In short, it is the oyster that appears again. The author is himself a type of oyster, and this is the reason he speaks of it so knowingly.

Proust does not identify the seaside resort where he places his daydreaming loner. It is more than likely another Balbec, for Balbec appears shortly thereafter in the same passage: "When I followed only my instinct, the jellyfish [*méduse*] would revolt me at Balbec; but if I knew how to look at them, like Michelet, from the viewpoint of natural history and aesthetics, I would see an exquisite azure girandole" (*SG* 3:28; 4:31).

Here, again, the oyster has been forgotten; Proust mentions only the *méduse*. Yet we now know the interchangeability of both terms: the oyster is but another name for the *méduse*. From this perspective, the oyster is there, even though it is not named. Many other images, other figures, could be added. When Proust undertakes the chapter on inversion, it is to deploy a vast metaphoric web in his text, a veritable interlacing of tropes and figures whose ornamentation can be sighted throughout the *Recherche*. In *Du côté de chez Swann*, the narrator describes the culinary talents of Françoise:

> [. . .] but what most enraptured me were the asparagus, tinged with ultramarine and pink which shaded off from their heads, finely stripped in mauve and azure, through a series of imperceptible gradations to their feet—still stained a little by the soil of their garden-bed—with an iridescence [*irisations*] that was not part of this world. (*Swann* 1:119; 1:143–44)

We are inland at Combray, on terra firma, yet the atmosphere is ultramarine. For even the commentators on this passage had no difficulty in demonstrating that Proust was amusing himself in a pastiche of a section of Michelet's *La Mer*, a section where the great historian refers to the medusa: "The delicious creature with its visible innocence and the iris of its soft colors" (152).

Behind the asparagus lurks the medusa; the asparagus is another medusa. Proust disguises it, as a painter would pose a model in a period costume. Of note in this passage we again find the motif of disgust that is itself linked to Balbec. But Proust has displaced this motif toward other characters: the narrator is "delighted" by the beautiful asparagus. Their odor, however, triggers asthma attacks in the servant-girl who has to peel them.[7] And we must also remember, in another register, the statements of the Duke of Guermantes vilifying a painting by Elstir: "There was nothing else in the picture, just a bunch of asparagus exactly like the ones you're eating now. But I refused to swallow M. Elstir's asparagus" (*CG* 2:791; 3:578).

Are we not reminded again here of the scene in Balbec with Mme de Villeparisis and the grandmother? The Duke is physically repelled by the painter's asparagus. Similarly, the hero of *A l'ombre des jeunes filles en fleurs* cannot stomach the flesh of oysters, nor the medusas. But the young man will be cured of his ostrophobia and ends up acquiring a taste for the "mauve orchids of the sea" (*SG* 3:28; 4:31). As for the Duke, he will surely find a way to get used to the unacceptable painting. For we must recall the remark made by his wife in reference to Manet's *Olympia*, a painting that was deemed to be shocking at first, but which now everyone has fully assimilated: "'It looks just like an Ingres'" (*CG* 2:812; 3:604). Without a doubt the same will occur with Elstir's work. For all can be learned, and everything is eventually assimilated. Disgust is often the precursor to digestion. A kind of law can be formulated, let's call it the ostreical law, or the medusan law: the more an object disgusts you, the better are the chances that you will end up loving it.

It is opportune moment to recapitulate: Three series seem to be interwoven: a taste series, an aesthetic series, and a sexual series. In the three cases, the series is recalled to stage a *Bildung*, an apprenticeship. For these series that we are distilling function as part of an ascending force in the novel which, as we know, recounts the story of a vocation: a young man with little will ends up a great writer. Each of the series prepares and accompanies this path in its own way. Through them, we can see how a character who is initially limited, trapped in his habits and fears, overcomes his initial frame, and goes beyond it to something more: something more in terms of gastronomic pleasure in the category of taste, something more in aesthetic emotions, something more—better health—in the category of the sexual. What is a bit problematic is how the third series might relate to our hero. For the young ostrophobe of Balbec is not an invert but an active hetero seducer. While he failed with the double task of cultivating his palate and his gaze, sexually speaking, his education is complete, and he has nothing more to learn. His romantic life is far from happy, and his liaison with Albertine ends disastrously. Nevertheless, his "orientation" is "normal": this young man is already on the "good" side. And we breathe a sigh of relief (phew!). Here is one, at least, who has escaped from the peril running wild everywhere else in this book!

Yet, almost immediately, we are uneasy. Are we certain which side is the "good" one here? What is inversion in Proust: a "plus" or a "minus"? For the hero of the novel, heterosexuality exists from the outset, as does his ostrophobia and his aesthetic insensitivity. If all the elements evolve, his sexuality presumably evolves in the same direction. Furthermore, in a bildungsroman, we necessarily proceed from a "minus" to a "plus"! Tell me what you eat and I'll tell you how you love, Proust instructs.[8] Thus, we must recognize that despite his initial repulsion, our hero becomes a lover of oysters and a connoisseur of medusas. A similar transformation is therefore possible with his aversion to homosexuals. For our three series are intertwined, and proceed at the same pace and in the same direction.

Whether or not the scenario we are imagining remains hypothetical, that Proust does not "tell" us so in his book would not appear to us a valid objection. It is true that we do not see Marcel pass over to the side of Sodom. But we also do not see him become a great writer! Yet it is precisely becoming a writer which is the goal of this bildungsroman! From a literary standpoint, if the essence is situated in the subtext, why would it not be the same in the realm of Eros?

Let us not be too hasty. Proust tries to interest us in a certain ambiguity that he locates at the very heart of the notion of "taste": the ostreical or medusan law, i.e., no gusto without disgust. That which disgusts, attracts. Swann, for example, is physically repulsed by Odette, yet he will madly fall in love with her (*Swann* 1:193; 1:234). The same principle applies to the homosexual universe. There is a passage in *Sodom et Gomorrhe* where the Verdurin "loyals" travel with the Baron de Charlus in the narrow-gauge train to Raspelière. They are indisputably fascinated by him and see him as a fetish or totem:

> But when all was said, if M. de Charlus did not appear, they were almost disappointed to be traveling only with people who were just like everybody else, and not to have with them this painted, paunchy, tightly-buttoned personage [*ce personnage peinturluré, pansu et clos*], reminiscent of a box of exotic and dubious origin exhaling a curious odor of fruits the mere thought of tasting which would turn the stomach. (SG 3:429; 4:509–10)

"Just the thought of tasting it would turn your stomach," writes Proust. Yet the idea is very much present. There is a desire to taste at the heart of the disgust. Here, Charlus is compared to an "exotic fruit" and even might be said to resemble an oyster that is closed and rounded. This reminds us of our seafood [*fruits de mer*]: oysters and medusas. Of course, Charlus is a repulsive old invert, his beauty long gone. But we can imagine the same scenario with a younger man garnering the same sort of attention. The outcome would be the same, we would encounter the same dialectic, the same mixture of attraction and repulsion. Proust states this very clearly in the following excerpt, which remains at the level of the subtext and where we also see an other "solitary" walking on the beach:

> I was pleased to see one day that numerous jellyfish had been washed up on the sand by the inclement weather. I enjoyed seeing the sun shine through the opalescent luster, I even touched their delicate lilac belt with the same joy I would have touched the scarf of Iris. I had no disgust, because the aesthetic sensation enables us to transgress limits which are imposed on our tastes by the preferences of our bodies. It is thus that a great artist will be delighted to make comparisons to beautiful Muses, charmed to look at some young men which would nauseate a club man, won over by the restrictive repulsions of the sexual instinct. (*JF* 2:var. 1488)

The same text appears a second time with some minute changes (Proust works in this manner, accumulating successive versions):

> I was pleased to see one day that numerous jellyfish had been washed up on the sand by the inclement weather. I enjoyed seeing the sun shine through the opalescent luster, I even touched their delicate lilac belt with the same joy I would have touched the scarf of Iris. I felt no disgust because the aesthetic sensation enables us to transgress limits imposed on our tastes by the preferences of our bodies. It is thus that a great artist will be delighted to make comparisons to beautiful Muses, charmed to look at some young men which would nauseate a club man overcome by a restrictive repulsion of the sexual instinct. (*JF* 2:1489)

Every word is important: the "muse" is linked to the *méduse*, both phonetically and also from the point of view of the referent (the club man is, with respect to the "young men," akin to the Argonaut in connection to the medusa in the *Sodom et Gomorrhe*, a passage discussed above); the "belt" that is "touched" is a metaphor for the sexual encounter (Bloch with regard to Odette: "I picked her up a few days before that on the Beltline railway, where, speaking of belts, she was willing to undo hers for the benefit of your humble servant."[*JF* 2:136; 2:414]; the motif of iridescence refers us, among other things, to the description of the asparagus of Combray, the opalescent luster is reminiscent of the "lustral water drops" in the passage about lunch at the Grand Hotel, and so forth.

In the context of our study, the thought to keep in mind is above all that art, if it is to be true, if it is to be "grandiose," is not "sexually correct." In other words, that the aesthetic experience shatters the frames of normality. The premise being that those who seek to conquer a "sexual repulsion" should not address themselves to a specialist, for the "great artist" is the only one who can be of help. Thus, a kind of quid pro quo is deliberately created: substitute "sexual experience" for "aesthetic experience" and see what happens. What transpires is rather curious: Proust is nearly suggesting that in a good bildungsroman the hero has to learn how to go against his sexual instinct, just as he will have to go toward art.

We conclude with an ultimate warning addressed to those who would prefer to misunderstand us, despite the effort we have made not to create any false—or forlorn—hope: the admission "yes, I am a homosexual" does not appear in the novel, despite all that has been said on the subject. However, he leaves us begging, here lies the difficulty. As Antoine Compagnon has shown, we are condemned to an "interminable perplexity" (Compagnon 142). There are various reasons informing this "perplexity": narratological (writer and narrator resemble each other but do not coincide), genetic (censure appears in places, as we have noted, when we pass from the subtext to the text), stylistic (Proust is a novelist, and not a sexologist; homosexuality is a spectacle that he seeks to describe rather than explain.) In this sense, the work of the metaphor, the succession of figures and images that we have sought to evoke here, are without a doubt more important than any "literal" content to have been illustrated. Proust's job is to write, to ensure that his writing itself progresses.[9] This is what we sought to recount.

NOTES

1. For the original French, the four-volume Pléiade edition has been used; for the English translation, the Scott-Moncrieff has been cited and modified when necessary. In all instances, the French page numbers precede those of the translation.

2. Here Proust takes up an ancient study that remained unpublished in his lifetime, "Chardin," in *Contre Sainte-Beuve*: "Oyster-shells, light as cups of mother-of-pearl, cool as the seawater they offer us, lie about on the cloth like charming fragile symbols on the altar of gluttony" (Pléiade 375; translation 245).

3. On the fundamental principle of the hermeneutics of childhood, see A. Compagnon, "La dernière victime du narrateur."

4. The French for "jellyfish" is "méduse," which is also the word for "Medusa" (translator's note).

5. Perseus is also the hero who kills Medusa. To name him here is to introduce a type of lexical inconsistency: the conqueror of "Medusa" cannot at the same time be the rescuer of a "medusa [jellyfish]." This does not impede the metaphoric and metonymic link the author makes between the marine animal and the mythological monster.

6. Here is one example among others: "[. . .] a masculine Andromeda is always attached to his rock and suffers at the sight of Antoine Bibesco fading away" (letter to Antoine Bibesco, June 1902). For other examples, see the note by the editors of the Pléiade, *SG* 3:1285.

7. A Proustian sickness we hesitate to mention, so as to refrain from referring to the biographical. Jean-Pierre Richard puts himself between a textual reading and a biographical one, when in *Proust et le monde sensible*, he speaks of the "tender phallism" associated with those stalks (133).

8. A better example: Albertine, who adores oysters, desires the whole succession of products she hears offered by the fishmonger (*AD* 3:633; 5:136).

9. Lawrence R. Schehr has found an efficacious and concise formulation: "homosexuality is an excuse for discourse" (*Shock of Men* 71).

8. Savory Writing: Marcel Rouff's *Vie et Passion de Dodin-Bouffant*

LAWRENCE R. SCHEHR

B y 1924, the joyful feasts of Marcel Proust's first two volumes were already yesterday's news. As the remaining volumes of his monumental *Recherche* were published at the end of his lifetime and in the years following his death, the gastronomic symphonies, the gustatory memories, and the culinary remembrances of the early volumes had been replaced by concerns of middle-aged men and women rapidly turning into the senescent characters of the *matinée chez la Princesse de Guermantes*. By the end of Proust's novel, many things have changed, not the least of which are the characters themselves. Gone are the foods of the early years and early pages: gone are the days of madeleines and linden-tea, of *boeuf à la mode* and pineapple and truffle salad, of Françoise's torture by asparagus of the scullery maid nicknamed Giotto's *la Charité*. Gone too are the teas *à l'anglaise* given by Odette Swann and the bread bought by the Princesse de Luxembourg, noblesse oblige, for Marcel to offer his grandmother, as are Françoise's "New York ham," her "sale bête" that, though beheaded, refuses to die, and the sensuous fish and seafood of Balbec.

Proust's reflections on food are part and parcel of the memories of the past, the most atavistic ones for him (taste and smell), spurs to writing, joggers of memory, culinary flying buttresses that helped to support the massive cathedral that becomes the novel in four dimensions in which all of Combray emerges out of a cup of tea. Despite the author's trips to the Ritz for a midnight beer, despite the intense supportive role played by food as a means of resuscitating a randomly remembered past, the world of the culinary in this novel remains firmly anchored to the feminine, the familial, and to home. It is a safe cuisine, resplendent and rich if not inventive, consonant with bourgeois cooking and thinking. As is always the case in Proust's writing, the various accreted layers expand this initial moment. As the narrator's social sphere grows, so does his exposure to a wider world of culinary relations that includes hotel food (in Balbec) and restaurant food (with Robert de Saint-Loup and his mistress, Rachel). And yet food never quite gets beyond the relational; food is never there for the sake of food; it recalls, repeats, reinscribes, and remembers for the narrator what he has forgotten and what he will, through the pricking of involuntary memory, now remember and write.

Proust's use of food contrasts with a "food novel" from his own era, Marcel Rouff's *La Vie et la passion de Dodin Bouffant, gourmet*. Today its author is remembered for the series of books on gastronomic France he coauthored with the pseudonymous Curnonsky ("Why-notsky") and this unique volume, while never wholly forgotten and while having remained a cultural touchstone, has not really secured a place in literary history. Written before the war, but published only in 1924, this light novel has never been considered high literature, though its many editions attest to a popular following and the work has given its name to a famous Parisian restaurant. One would do well to turn to the work as a literary document because of the way it challenges our received knowledge of description and the way in which it offers us a hybrid work that sits somewhere between fiction and cookbooks, menus, and Food TV.

Aside from its value as a curiosity and as a slight, if generally respectable piece of literature, *Dodin-Bouffant* demonstrates how novelistic discourse seizes, includes, and ultimately assimilates another discourse into its realm. Rouff's work is a happy, unexpected marriage between two sets of discourses: a straightforward narrative with an episodic and fairly predictable plotline and a developing discourse of gastronomy that reaches its own height in codification in this very time period. First the story: set in an unnamed provincial town in the Franche-Comté, not too far from Dijon, Geneva, and Grenoble, the novel concerns a singular figure, the title character whose entire life is devoted to gastronomy.[1] When the novel opens, we are treated to a sad sight, the funeral of his beloved cook: "Eugénie Chatagne, Dodin-Bouffant's cook was dead. In the full development of her genius, she had just passed away, an incomparable artist, the blessed dispenser of all culinary treasures of which, for ten years, at the table of the master celebrated throughout France, they were the cherished beneficiaries"(27).

Dodin-Bouffant is despondent, for she has been the center of his life and the focus of his being. Her talent was her art of cooking, and her capacity as an individual woman is regularly subsumed, indeed sublimated, under her position as female servant to a male master. Thanks to her talents, Dodin-Bouffant and a few friends have eaten resplendently for a decade.[2] And now he looks forward to a bleak future: "sautéed chickens smothered tactlessly under mountains of tomatoes, shamefully rushed hashes, dry, tough partridges, veal fricassees with neither enrichment nor succulence, saddles of hare without broth, crunchless French fries, unbrowned beans" (50). Eventually another culinary wizard comes along, and despite her country ways and often eccentric manner, she rises to the occasion.

The occasion in question, which forms the central episode of the novel, is a culinary joust. Having heard of Dodin-Bouffant's singular passion and dedication to gastronomy, His Highness, the Prince of Eurasia (an entire continent, no less), invites Dodin-Bouffant to a dinner in which the prince shows off his wealth and his cooks' talents. The menu for the meal runs to over four pages in the novel and includes everything from pigeon bisque to stuffed pike to young boar [*marcassin*] to pheasant terrine stuffed with green truffles. And this, all in the first service. Other dishes include a leg of lamb with four sauces, carp roe with béchamel sauce, hazelnut pâté, and, in a nod of the head to Orientalism, a dish of cocks' combs in the shape of a pagoda (with Champagne sauce, naturally) (83–86). Alas, Dodin-Bouffant is not impressed, finding the meal on the whole, despite the talent used and the expenditures made, rather a series of false notes: no logic, no light, no clarity, no order (91). The Prince has violated the laws of gastronomy, those of science—what Brillat-Savarin years before called the "physiology of taste" in the book of the same name—and those of nature: "Is it also allowed to suffocate the divine perfumes of nature under the uniformity of such sophisticated sauces?" (93). For Dodin-Bouffant, the Prince is nothing short of a "false artist" (93), for whom money has replaced knowledge and balance.[3]

Both by his constitution and by his knowledge, Dodin-Bouffant is up to the task: "This gourmet feared no menu, even if it were to keep him at the table the entire day and night, but he knew how to eat it with a grace that made one forget his great capability" (87). Solid physically and ready for any challenge, Dodin-Bouffant is also armed with the knowledge of gastronomy and its rules; he has already noted several "solecisms" in the menu proposed by the Prince d'Eurasie (88). The gastronomic faux pas show how the culture of gastronomy had become refined by Rouff's time. The gravity of the errors starts with these solecisms and is followed by "faults" in the order and selection of wines: gastronomic grammar is at the basis of all decisions and recommendations and the fault of the prince's dinner was that it violated these laws. Aside from the basic grammatical errors that are in themselves inexcusable, Dodin-Bouffant believes that neither logic nor reason was used in assembling the right ingredients (91). It is only then that taste of a higher order comes in: beyond the simple grammatical errors, beyond the lack of reason and line, there are egregious acts tantamount to murder. One might say that the road to capital gastronomic crime starts with simple mistakes in conjugations and goes downhill from there.

Dodin-Bouffant feels obligated to teach the prince a lesson and invites the latter to dinner. But instead of the copious, gargantuan menu orchestrated and offered by the prince, that of Dodin-Bouffant is a comparatively simple one. By today's standards, of course, the pared-down menu offered as the palinodic counter-meal would still seem highly complicated, but in this world of gastronomic dueling, it seems, at first impression, of a severity, a simplicity, and indeed, of a lack of distinction second to none. After some hors d'oeuvres, Dodin-Bouffant will serve a soup named for his cook, some fried morsels named for a writer on gastronomy (*fritures de Brillat-Savarin*), a pot-au-feu, that most fundamental of French boiled beef dishes, an onion purée, and dessert. The wines will simply be two white and three red wines. Of course the meal will turn out to be something splendid, unimagined, unpredicted, a series of masterpieces one after the other. Dodin-Bouffant will win this duel of taste.

Within the framework of the novel and its paradigms, it would have been impossible to describe the meal offered by the prince, for to do justice to it would have required scores of pages to give the specifics of each dish in appropriate novelistic detail. In the meal offered by Dodin-Bouffant to the prince, the relative simplicity allows for expansive prose. The hors d'oeuvres, simple nothings, afterthoughts before the real meal, include crayfish in aspic, chopped pigeon in cream, tiny cold thrushes wrapped with anchovies, and eel stuffed with shrimp purée, among others. While Rouff risks excess here with the number of different "nothings" offered as hors d'oeuvres, he can, because of the rules of gastronomy, if not those of the novel, pass on lengthy descriptions, for these are literally "outside the service"; they are nothing, mere appogiaturas and grace notes. Because he goes into great novelistic detail in the description of the other dishes on Dodin-Bouffant's menu, Rouff can permit himself the conceit of importing the rules and paradigms of gastronomy along with its discourses. That is to say, because Rouff gives full novelistic (and gastronomic) honors to the rest of the meal, the hors d'oeuvres can be mentioned with only a cursory nod at concerns about narrative description.

In Dodin-Bouffant's meal, the soup alone takes over two pages to describe. But the pièce de résistance as one might say in gallicized English is the pot-au-feu. This is normally a humble dish, not even on the level of the justly famous *boeuf à la mode* with its mountain of cubes of aspic and its perfect carrots that marks a memorable scene in Proust's *Recherche*. The pot-au-feu is not a poor dish, because it is enriched with meat juices, stocks, vegetables, various kinds of meat, and must be cooked to perfection; it thus takes a certain culinary talent and savoir-faire to make it right. But it remains nonetheless a humble dish, true to its origins as boiled beef, the eternal pot sitting on the stove or over a fire in the hearth, symbolizing domesticity and mother's cooking (Weiss 1997).

Needless to say, the pot-au-feu transcends its origins, becomes something so totally other from what it is that it is a great success. In an *Aufhebung* of boiled meat, the pot-au-feu becomes the Hegelian "absolute knowledge" of food, the Platonic ideal of perfect cooking. Dodin-Bouffant already has complete knowledge of the metaphysics of cooking, all of which is distilled into and recuperated from this apotheosis of the pot-au-feu. Like Brillat-Savarin's *ozmazôme*, knowledge and gastronomic essence flow from solid to liquid and back again. This pot-au-feu features slices of beef impregnated with tarragon and transparent bits of fat. The beef slices lie on a "pillow of sausage" made of pork and veal, and seasoned with thyme, chervil, and other herbs. Yet that is not all, for this pillow itself sits on a layer of hen, stewed in its own liquid that had been enriched with veal, mint, and wild thyme. That would be all, were it not for the "comfortable layer of fresh goose liver simply cooked in chambertin" (104–05). And of course there are vegetables to accompany this "quadruple enchantment."

The prince has learned his lesson and this has been accomplished with no loss of face or dignity. It is still a hard lesson to swallow, especially for someone who thinks that nobility has its privileges and, while not seeking revenge or satisfaction (in the dueling sense), he still wants some tribute, if not retribution. The envious prince wants to exact a high price: not the hand of Adèle, but her hands, for he wants to hire Dodin-Bouffant's cook as his own. Incapable of going through a second period of mourning, Dodin-Bouffant has no choice but to marry Adèle, and they live more or less happily ever after. After an episode in which he is pursued by a woman in love with him for his epicureanism and whom he visits once, the novel concludes at a more farcical level. Dodin-Bouffant is instructed to go on a diet of moderation to compensate for his many excesses that have literally crystallized in an attack of gout. The doctor recommends, among other moderations, no meat at night. Not to worry, for Dodin-Bouffant will have modest meals, as is evidenced by his first dietetic, meatless supper: a crayfish bisque, gratinéed cardoons, truffles wrapped in pork fat, some cheese, and an apple and cream tart (174). The following meals are just as monastic and include escargots à la provençale, plovers' eggs with cauliflower (à la Du Barry), crayfish, omelettes with asparagus, macaroni with bacon, creamed potatoes, and so forth (175). And if a trace of meat in a stuffing piques his tastebuds, he questions not, for he does not want to incur the wrath of his wife who believes she is following doctor's orders. He follows her therapy without a question.

Finally, there is no choice. They must both take the waters and they go "chez les Barbares," as Rouff puts it, and wind up at the spa of Baden-Baden. The indignities the hapless couple suffers there are endless, for aside from the water cure, they are subjected to the most unspeakable cooking imaginable. No wonder then that the Germans are the way they are; no wonder that literary characters are driven to suicide: "'My God, what could that poor Werther have eaten?'" wonders the amazed and outraged Dodin-Bouffant (208).[4] But the couple gradually recovers its strength, despite the horrors of the food, which included "the infamous mortified meatballs of Teutonic soups," and they return to France to live happily ever after in a world where life is "the joy of knowledgeably and copiously eating the glory of nature accommodated by the genius of mankind" (231).

For Rouff, the question of gastronomy is as much a question of the words with which one eats as the foods themselves. The extensive menu for the centerpiece of the novel, which is the cryptic version of the indescribable banquet offered by the Prince d'Eurasie to Dodin-Bouffant, is testimony to the importance of the discourse. The menu is a singular list, with no narrative or novelistic form, in which the gastronomic descriptions are telescoped into a baroque menu by means of a special language, that is to say, the language of gastronomy. One could call it the inversion of ekphrasis. As is well known, ekphrasis is a familiar literary technique that is defined as an extended description within a longer piece; classic examples are the shield of Achilles described in the *Iliad* and Charles Bovary's singular cap. An ekphrasis stops the narrative time-line as the reader's attention is brought to bear on a single phenomenon deemed worthy of description by the author.

While for Rouff, gastronomy is related to the other arts, and is therefore subject to ekphrasis, the author also proposes a special kind of inverse ekphrasis, one that stops the timeline as well but without a formal description. In fact, the description is absolutely voided as he lists names of dishes; at the same time this is much more than a shopping list or litany, the anathema of narrative. For the four pages that constitute the menu of the dinner offered by the prince seemingly provide only a list that runs the gamut of available foods. But each is prepared, cooked, and garnished according to a well-known (or ostensibly well-known) formula. Instead of a description of the dish or even a mention of the ingredients, there is a title indicating what the dish is. Knowledge of this specialized discourse will be a veritable open sesame for the pages, as the right key to the text will turn these cold formulas into the equivalent of Proustian madeleines and Combray.

Rouff's work operates a magical transformation through discourse and memory, one not at all unrelated to Proustian metamorphosis. Rouff asks us to dip into his text, turning each named dish into a symphony of tastes, a sonata of gustatory pleasures for the palate; we should taste the food much as we should hear a Beethoven quartet by reading the score. Each title becomes a description, and together they should form one giant contrapuntal, orgiastic banquet piece. Part of the means of transformation is our own gustatory, olfactory, and visual memory, the assumption (right or wrong) that we know what carp, pheasant, boar, and a myriad number of other foodstuffs taste like, smell like, and look like. And yet the gargantuan menu as such would tax all but a few readers as given to the pleasures of the palate as Dodin-Bouffant himself. The latter does not read the menu; he hears it, as it is read aloud with great formality by the prince's head steward, his *officier de bouche*, literally his "mouth officer."

Interestingly, there is no written menu within the story itself, for the prince is opposed to such things, as he says that he is not one of those "who think that the order/prescription [*ordonnance*] for a feast must be discovered on a written menu [*carte*]." What is denied Dodin-Bouffant, a written menu, and given him to hear in a flourished announcement, is given to us to read. His hearing is followed by the presentation of the foods and their consumption by the party. The reader however exchanges the protagonist's—or should we say protophagist's?—coenaesthetic experience and displeasure for some gastrographic shorthand. But where is the key to this gastrographic discourse? Let us assume for the moment that all the dishes are, as the French say, repertoried; that is to say, they are meaningfully and logically catalogued according to a system that distributes meaning to names of dishes, and by which we know, for example, that *boeuf à la bourguignonne*, for example, is a beef stew or ragout cooked in red (Burgundy) wine, and garnished with potatoes, pearl onions, and mushrooms, usually thickened with a *beurre manié*. Many dishes are codified by geographic origin as they are taken into the *grande cuisine* or at least the officially repertoried group of dishes served in restaurants and many others are baptized with the names of an illustrious person. In either case, the names of dishes are often ritually coded, with some of the geographic names indicating a type of preparation and/or garnish and some of the personal names indicating either a main ingredient, such as Crécy indicating the use of carrots, Du Barry, that of cauliflower, and Rossini, foie gras. This assumption of a culinary repertory is fair in theory, even if not necessarily true in fact; some of the dishes may have been invented (just as they are elsewhere in the novel), some, even if known at the time, have certainly faded from memory into the dark recesses of some forgotten text in a culinary library or bookstore. These lacunae and fictions do not challenge the basic assumption here.

To read the menu then, one needs a key, the rational alphabet by which this shorthand file can be unzipped. Armed with the knowledge that all French sauces, for example, come from four master sauces, one need only have recourse to a volume that explains the details of the repertory. This repertory itself is the codification of the grand tradition of French cuisine and reached its apogee under Auguste Escoffier. Indeed, in a volume dedicated to Escoffier and published in 1914 (thus at the same time that Rouff and Proust were writing their novels), such an explanation of the codification exists. By Th. Gringoire and L. Saulnier, it is called, aptly enough, *Le Répertoire de la cuisine*. In this slim volume of about 240 pages there are no fewer than about seven thousand recipes, "*of which more than 2600 are collected nowhere else*" (ix). Collecting recipes, organizing them logically, relating all to the bases, to the master sauces, to the ABC's of gastronomy: that is the raw material and knowledge on which the repertory is founded. Thus, to take an example, one may read of *sole à la parisienne*, described in a short-hand (and barely grammatical) way. The repertory tells us that *sole à la parisienne* has five different manifestations. In one of them, "blanketed three sauces: in the middle white wine; one each side genevoise and anchovy." One knows how to cook it (ostensibly by poaching, though one could grill it as in version five, which says "grill. On top Parisian butter" ([105]). The various recipes for white wine, genevoise, and anchovy sauces are elsewhere in the volume and by a careful process of reading and building of a food database, one arrives at knowledge of the dish and its variants.

Thus with each dish offered by the prince, one could unzip the hypothetical food file and come up with the dish. Some are simple, even by modern standards, as we all know what a hollandaise sauce is; some are not. At each point though, the reader has to stop, for the choice is a difficult one: either one skips over the dishes or one tries to understand what the author is saying. Repertory in hand, be it this short one or Escoffier's compendium of French gastronomy, one reads Rouff well-armed (and preferably well-fed) to write his recipes and titles for him, as well as to remember our own gastronomic knowledge and sensations or even to combine ingredients that as yet we have never eaten together. Can we imagine what the novel means, intends, or names at this point? It is hard to say. The result of reading the menu against a repertory, and thus of reading the menu outside the confines of the fictional narrative, is not a series of singular dishes nor is it exactly the errors in judgment that Dodin-Bouffant perceives. Here reader and character separate, despite the best of intentions. For the reader, the menu represents a disorder akin to that detailed in the antique shop of Balzac's *La Peau de chagrin* or the museum of Flaubert's *Bouvard et Pécuchet*. Here however it is literally and etymologically a hodge-podge or an olla podrida of the foodstuffs of the world and not just antiques, fetishes, and the occasional magical skin thrown in for good measure.

The prince's menu then is not only problematic because of the culinary sins, it is also difficult, unreadable, and indigestible, because of its gastronomic excess. If food is to be translated into discourse it must be manageable, easily absorbed by the eye or the mouth, so that the coenaesthetic and synaesthetic effects, that is to say, the general bodily effects and

the effects of senses paired together, are developed in tandem. For gastronomy to work as a discourse within a literary work, there must be the
possibility of an ekphrastic moment, be it either a description or a recipe.
There is a contrast then between a meal that is impossible to digest and
dishes that are capturable as discourse, even if in that discourse, there is a
narrative feint by which one indicates a knowledge in the implied reader
that is surely absent:

> the first *pâté à la Choisi*, which is made, as everyone knows, with boned
> partridges stuffed with their carcasses (mashed with their livers),
> truffles, diced pork fat, ordinary spices, partridges that have been
> wrapped in purged and blanched *foie gras* studded with fresh anchovies,
> and which has been cooked in a light crust, nourished with good butter
> and baptized at the end of cooking with a half-glass of old brandy. (73)

The recipe may seem odd to some because of the disparity of the ingredients. But the author has carefully set the stage for this singular dish with a
remark pages earlier that "Dodin-Bouffant had dared, before anyone else,
to marry fish and fowl, for example, and enchant the perfume of a copiously marinated capon with a stuffing in which shrimp and turbot
dominated" (33).[5] Even if this description does not bear all the hallmarks
of the perfect recipe described by M.F.K. Fisher, it is approachable, readable, and tasteable.[6] The moment in which a dish is named or described in
this book thus allows the reader to digest both with his or her eyes and his
or her gustatory palate. At the same time, the possibility of ekphrasis
means that the gastronomic vocabulary can be married to a novelistic one.
While not reaching the dithyrambic heights of Proust, Rouff can dare to
marry textual fish and fowl and serve up a recipe as a narrative mechanism.
Long before Laura Esquivel's *Like Water for Chocolate*, Rouff has provided a
hybrid hypertext that sits between the purely literary (whatever that is)
and the gastronomic.

   With such an example, Rouff is showing the reader how a specific discourse can be integrated into the novel as the latter generically expands its
horizons to go beyond the representation While the menu is itself a tour de
force and a culmination of the codification of nineteenth-century gastronomic repertory, and while the menu could be used to generate its
signifieds, the dishes themselves, on the level of narration and discourse,
the menu is void and voided of content. It is arguable that Rouff is describing a kind of gastronomic expansion that is, essentially, anti-Carême,

anti-Escoffier, and antirepertory in nature. As we have indicated above, this moment in cooking, with the development of the restaurant industry as an industry, with the various *guides routiers* for food (of which Rouff was one of the most noted authors), and with the advent of Escoffier's systematic exploration of French cuisine, is the moment of pure codification of the gastronomic discourse. It is clearly the moment at which that gastronomic discourse begins to have generalized exchange value as opposed to some local, individual value of "restauration." And yet, the novel rejects the translation of gastronomic discourse into value as much as it rejects the assimilation of that discourse to novelistic. We will see below how Rouff develops a counterdiscourse, that of Dodin-Bouffant.

Arguably, one of the reasons for the shift is the move from capitalist model to speculative model. As David Bell has shown in his discussion of the speculative model in the works of Zola, who obviously remains one of the turning points in this discussion of assimilable discourses, the difference between the two systems is that in the speculative model, the (surplus) value ascribed to an object does not relate to the congealed labor that produced it. Bell's example relates to the inflation of value associated with stock market speculations. In a crude fashion, one could say that the gastronomic model is similarly speculative. Certainly there is the search for refined (*raffiné*) and often costly foodstuffs like truffles, but the creation of culinary value depends neither wholly on the cost of the raw ingredients nor on the amount of labor involved but depends most heavily on the speculative investment in the idea of gastronomic perfection, the search for new dishes, the reputation of a cook, restaurant, or cuisine.

Escoffier, or the figure of the prince who profits from the repertory-like nature of the current state of gastronomy, is the epitome of this speculative adventure. And I would argue that there is a moment in the representation of culinary and gastronomic wealth in which the encyclopedic thoroughness illustrated in Escoffier's work or in the contemporaneous encyclopedia of gastronomy by Ali-Bab, and indeed, in serial form in the work of Rouff and Curnonsky themselves is given over to the speculative. This moment is necessary, but for the protagonist of the novel, it must be outstripped. Just as with journalism in Joyce's *Ulysses*, where the journalistic cant, rhetoric, and discourse maintain their own nonintegrated, heterogenous status in part because of the speculative investment of others in that discourse, so too is the case with the encyclopedic discourse of gastronomy in *Dodin-Bouffant*. As the menu, metonymy of the encyclopedic moment in

gastronomy, can stand on its own with neither a relation to food nor a relation to fictional narrative, the heterogeneity of the discourse remains for
the moment completely other. Only the moment of genius, divine, but
unsuspected marriages, and indeed vatic impulse becomes the one by
which the gastronomic text remains readable.

Rouff sets up his protagonist and his dedication to food in opposition to
the encyclopedia, as the individual heroic gastronome crosses over the
moment of knowledge, goes beyond that knowledge to sublimate it, uses
taste to choose (or reject), and participates in the true creative moment,
which is, for Rouff, the moment of genius. Against the compendium of
knowledge there is a total synthesis; against the repertoried encyclopedia
of shorthand recipes given by name or abbreviation, there is a veritable
library, an infinite set of possibilities that knowledge can combine, but
which should not be read from A to Z, as Jean-Paul Sartre's autodidact
might do. Instead, the infinite library will require the genius to realize the
perfect understated gastronomic moment: "Next to the oven, at the hand
of the officiant, was a veritable library peopled with an infinite number of
ingredients, spices, pepper, aromatics, bottles of essences, vinegars, wines,
syrups, everything carefully labeled" (46). So culinary genius is marked by
the sacred, as the priest or priestess of cooking chooses the right books in
the library, but not all the books, to produce the culinary masterpiece. To
choose all the books, no matter in how many separate readings, is the
gravest error of all.

The great gastronome is the titan, a thunderer shaking the heavens like
the great geniuses of all time: "the Napoleon of gourmets, the Beethoven
of the *cuisine* [which means both kitchen and cooking], the Shakespeare of
the table" (28). Applying knowledge and taste to the world before him,
he selects; he excludes. Indeed like Michelangelo, who said that he
removed everything from a block of marble that was not the statue,
Dodin-Bouffant develops an art that seeks not to show everything in a
baroque extravaganza but to excise all but the essential. It is not only the
comparative wallets that determine the two very different menus of the
book, but also the very philosophical approach to food. Dodin-Bouffant
sees singular, titanic strength in each piece, looks for perfection in each
bite. And Dodin-Bouffant seeks the Hegelian synthesis that resumes all
in one gathering without hurting the various parts of the whole. Where
the Eurasian prince has created a patchwork quilt on the table, Dodin-
Bouffant creates a multilayered singularity, complex in nature, elegant in

every way and exquisite to boot. Indeed, Dodin-Bouffant himself is the perfect Hegelian gastronome:

> Dodin-Bouffant, dizzied by the complex perfection of his happiness, brought the first mouthful to his lips: he had masterfully seized at the same time a piece of marinated flesh, some stuffing, and some crust. In sum, he was going to absorb a synthesis.
>   It was like an attack of vertigo. He was biting into the absolute. (163)

Let us take the soup of the "counter-meal" as an example of Dodin-Bouffant's approach to food. The carefully measured description, even more than that of the *pâté à la Choisi*, is a thumbnail evocation that does not fold down the way the big menu does; these recognizable references form a polyptych of concatenated descriptions and evocations of stimuli. The soup becomes a museum exhibition that we can recognize:

> This soup was simply a masterpiece. Very complex and very medi-tated, with a somewhat old-fashioned charm like Greuze, it had some brutal aspects like Ribera and some unpredicted tendernesses like Da Vinci. Its general allure recalled the development of a sonata in which each theme keeps its own life and taste in the collective strength and harmony of the whole. It had a singular taste, but each part of this taste kept its own natural and personal taste. (100–1)

Whereas the Escoffier-inspired gastronomic litany eschews ekphrases through its shorthand repertory, this soup gives us the possibility of three linked descriptive moments, three painters whose naming permits the work to be savored and the food to be inscribed in a language not its own.

Rouff offers us gastronomic knowledge capturable in culinary ekphrases, in the perfection of dishes, in the absolute knowledge of a library, be it made of foodstuffs or books. Memory itself, in its perfect inscription of the edible, becomes gastronomic, as opposed to visual or auditory: "his memory was eminently gastronomic" (149). Dodin-Bouffant associates the face of a person (Pauline d'Aizery) with the food he ate in her presence (a stew of young boar [*marcassin*]). But how is this perfection attained? Where does knowledge come from? Obviously there is a vatic impulse that brings the king of gourmets and his food to the level of the titans of world culture, for Dodin-Bouffant is inspired as few others are by food, which for him is always a manifestation of the revealed and the divine. At the same time, this divine revelation is always manifested through the agency of the feminine, be it in the incarnation of Eugénie Chatagne, Adèle, or Pauline d'Aizery. For Dodin-Bouffant, and, one may speculate, for Rouff, neither food nor gastronomy is complete without the play of the feminine. Indeed, in the volume on Savoy that Rouff wrote with Curnonsky, they deify the feminine in the form of the female cook, as they elevate her with a capital letter: "There She was" (14). And the authors assure us that "there are some [female cooks] who can rival their great confreres of the stronger sex"(14).

Cultural history as well as practical everyday experience has taught everyone in the Western world that cooking and nourishment form an essential part of the traditional roles given to and assumed by women in the construction of society. Perhaps viewed as a "natural" extension of the woman's maternal role as the giver of milk, food preparation has by and large been considered both the natural and proper realm of women. And yet within the class structure that develops the profession of chef, the role of food preparer becomes masculinized, because it is considered "work" and not natural, biological functioning. Home cooking may be feminine but haute cuisine is masculine in a parade of peacock-like preenings of *pièces montées*, the elaborate desserts, for example, for which Carême was known. The accompanying gastronomy is, needless to say, equally masculine if not to say misogynistic and homosocial.

As gastronomy develops as a body of knowledge and a discourse in the nineteenth century, the topos of food in narrative remains bifurcated. Home food remains the realm of the feminine, whether it is the butter and sugar needed to treat Charles Grandet in *Eugénie Grandet*, "the previous day's coffee-grounds [*le marc de la veille*]" that signifies the state of impoverishment and famine to which the striking miners are reduced in Zola's *Germinal*, or the famous food memories already mentioned in Proust's *Recherche*. At the same time, food scenes do begin to take on a public face as characters go to restaurants and there is a recognition of the role that this new discourse plays. Indeed, in Flaubert's *Education sentimentale*, the characters play on the language itself. Yet there is no real attempt to have the two discourses meet. In an act of decadence Huysmans's Des Esseintes brings a perversion of gastronomy back home, defamiliarizing the home, the safe, and the nurturing in the process. With Rouff, however, a new possibility is brought up: that of the woman as a culinary genius loci. The deceased Eugénie Chatagne mourned by Dodin-Bouffant is replaced by the perhaps even more ingenious Adèle, whose cooking talents are so vast that Dodin-Bouffant makes the ultimate sacrifice and marries her.

While not a masterpiece, Rouff's book needs to be reread and remembered because of the way in which it engages the discourses of gastronomy, normalizes them within the world of heterosexual exchange, and assimilates them to the novelistic. Rouff's book returns to a concept of individual genius who has mastered the discourses, but in which art and love supercede knowledge: "As he walked back and forth, his eyes wandered over the shelves where old books, great classics of the mind and of cooking, were arranged with love" (31). Nostalgia for a simpler time? Not really. Prescience for *nouvelle cuisine?* Perhaps not. Yet somewhere between the two as a *plat de résistance*, a pot-au-feu that is as masculine as it is feminine, as gastronomic as it is home-cooking; Rabelais's "sustantifique os à moelle" made at once literal and gastronomic in the life and passion of a gourmet.

NOTES

1.Priscilla Ferguson has suggested to me that "as a homage to Brillat-Savarin," the novel was set in Belley. I should like to thank her, Allen Weiss, and Michael Garval for their insightful comments and suggestions on this piece.

2. Rouff intertwines gastronomy and friendship as well in his novella "Un soir à Brantôme," included in *Les Devoirs de l'amitié*. Writing of one of the main characters who has a passion for food and who arranges an excellent meal for himself and his fellow travelers, Rouff says, "However great his passion for food was, he never satisfied it completely unless he was in the company of his old friend. It seemed that the sum of their two joys was much more than doubled" (17). Rouff goes on to characterize these events as "the fraternal feasts/celebrations of gastronomy [*les fêtes fraternelles de la gastronomie*]" (17).

3. In his political novel on the development of the League of Nations, Rouff visits the same nexus in which he distinguishes good taste from wealth: "Around the food, essentially classic féra in white wine, Baron of lamb jardinière, truffled chicken around the stemware, the silver, the centerpieces [*surtouts*], the china, around the pieces of his wealth, more imprinted with tradition than with real taste . . . " (*Sur le quai Wilson* 194–95).

4. In a Gallimard collection from the twenties devoted to the "lives of illustrious men," Rouff also published a competent, if overly romanticized, life of Chateaubriand. Rouff's Chateaubriand is as given to women as his Dodin-Bouffant is to food. And yet the two share some points, not the least of which is Chateaubriand's gout (318), inconceivably painful toward the end of his life. Rouff does not fail to quote a younger Chateaubriand, who has been named in 1828 to the French Embassy in London. The quote Rouff chooses is worthy of his own Dodin-Bouffant: "'Also look at purely English or German tables. You eat there, you really drink there, but you don't dine there. . . . In France, you feast! The eye, palate, and mind are excited all at once'" (letter to Marcellus, qtd. in Rouff, *Chateaubriand* 253).

5. This is a literary conceit, for numerous cuisines marry fish and fowl on a regular basis, including Spanish, Portuguese, Cajun, and various Southeast Asian cuisines. And though this is not now a commonplace in French cooking, one could of course point to the historic Napoleonic dish called chicken Marengo, with its apocryphal garnish of crayfish (and its avatar in Michel Guérard's *nouvelle cuisine* dish of poached chicken with crayfish) as well as to many Renaissance dishes in which the two were paired and to numerous Provençal dishes that use anchovies as part of the seasoning. Still the idea is a rare one within the repertory of French haute cuisine and the author takes the time to create the moment of frozen description in order to have the readers savor, measure, imagine a singular dish.

6. For M.F.K. Fisher, writing in "The Anatomy of a Recipe"(13–24), a recipe "is supposed to be a formula, a means prescribed for producing a desired result . . . There can be no frills about it, no ambiguities . . . and above all no 'little secrets'" (20). Fisher "demand[s] to be told . . . the ingredients and the method" (17) and insists that a good recipe also give her the ingredients in the order of their use. She sums up as follows: "A good recipe, for modern convenience, should consist of three parts: name, ingredients, method. The first will perforce give some sort of description: for instance, one does not simply say 'Cake' or 'Bread,' but 'Golden Sponge Cake,' 'Greek Honey Bread.' The ingredients should be listed in one column or two, rather than in a running sentence, according to the order of their use, and with the exact amount of each ingredient given before its names. The method should in most cases tell the temperature of the oven first, if one is needed, and in a real kitchen guide should indicate in the simplest possible prose what equipment will be used [. . .]. In the same way, a true manual . . . should indicate in some way the number of portions a recipe will make"(23). Of course no recipe can ever be full and complete, can ever tell every single bit about the dish.

9. Diet and Ideology in *Corps et âmes*

GERALD PRINCE

Maxence Van der Meersch (1907–51) is not especially well known today, even if both the *Robert des noms propres* and the *Petit Larousse* still devote a few lines to him. Yet this sometime lawyer and former winner of the Concours général (with a paper about Molière on the eve of the first performance of *Le Malade imaginaire*) was once a much admired and very popular writer.[1] His first novel, *La Maison dans la dune* (1932), proved remarkably successful with the reading public. In 1933, *Quand les sirènes se taisent* almost got the Prix Théophraste-Renaudot. In 1936, *L'Empreinte du dieu* won the Prix Goncourt. *Maria, fille de Flandre* (1937), *Pêcheurs d'hommes* (1940), *Femmes à l'encan* (1945), and *La Fille pauvre* (1948) were also widely liked. Above all, Maxence Van der Meersch is the author of *Corps et âmes*, that is, of the biggest fiction seller in France under the Occupation (Lucien Rebatet's *Les Décombres* took the overall title). Awarded a prize by the Académie Française, translated in several languages (including Spanish, German, and English), adapted for the stage by the novelist (1951), and brought to the screen by Curtis Bernhardt as a pure Hollywood soap opera (*The Doctor and the Girl*, 1949, with Glenn Ford and Janet Leigh), this 1943 work in two substantial volumes (I. *Enchaîné à toi-même*; II. *Qu'un amour t'emporte*), whose title and subtitles are suggestively programmatic, sold tens of thousands of copies in a few months and quickly became a precious commodity on the black market. At one point, it could be found only under the counter in most bookstores and purchased only for the most outrageous price (Todd 78). It was also a novel that provoked virulent attacks from the medical establishment. On November 8, 1943, in Paris, over four hundred physicians and students attended the "trial" of *Corps et âmes*, which was chaired by the president of the French bar; and the formal debates and denunciations resumed on December 13.

Corps et âmes, the action of which takes place in many parts of France during the 1930s, is, after all, a novel about medicine and, more particularly, a bomb thrown at the medical corps, its teachings, its treatments, its conformist passion for money and fame. Van der Meersch praises the modest neighborhood doctors who show kindness along with intelligence and who value the heart as much as the mind. He also honors the scientists who work on their research in solitude and poverty. But he has nothing but contempt for the kind of classical medicine dominant in France, for socialized medicine with its clinics, its sanatoriums, its technology, and the tyranny of its specialists and bosses. From the very first pages on, putrid fluids and foul-smelling dejections overflow, ulcers, tumors, cankers, and sores abound, terrifying dissections and horrific operations multiply, urethras are probed, ovaries removed, limbs amputated, hemorrhoids excised. A humanity full of pus is left at the mercy of a world of rakes and fakes. Classical medicine, official medicine has become dangerously specialized, compartmentalized, cut up. It has lost all sense of the general (2:15). It has also forgotten its duty and has paradoxically grown to be the most dangerous enemy of those most in need of it.

More specifically, *Corps et âmes* is a veritable epic of proper nutrition, based on the theories of Dr. Paul Carton (1875–1947), who authored such books as *Traité de médecine, d'alimentation et d'hygiène naturistes* (1920), *Les Lois de la vie saine* (1922), and *Diagnostic et conduite des tempéraments* (1926), who developed a unique kind of therapy (beyond mainstream medical practice but also beyond homeopathy, chiropractic, acupuncture, or pseudonaturopathy), and who stood alone against every single expert of his time. According to Dr. Carton, who served as the model for the novel's Dr. Domberlé, the motor of both health and disease is the humoral state of the individual, a state determined by two fundamental factors: nutrition and corporal energy. Health is simply the condition of the individual who eats what is physiologically appropriate for her. A patient is merely a (weakened) transformer of energy for whom light, diluted nutrients not exceeding his (reduced) powers of assimilation and digestion prove essential. In particular, tuberculosis (which Carton suffered from and which Van der Meersch probably died of, a victim—said his detractors—of the very kind of treatment he had adopted and promoted) usually results from alimentary intemperance (1:265; 2:15). For humoral as opposed to classical medicine, the only way to health is a return to nature and to a diet in which mild ingredients like vegetables, cereals, or fruits predominate. Moreover, for Dr. Carton (or Dr. Domberlé), illness is all one and always caused by a perturbation of body fluids. There are no local diseases but only general pathological factors which manifest themselves locally; and tenacious constipations as well as violent diarrheas, acidic sweats or fetid breaths, congestions and palpitations, gravel and kidney stones, acnes, boils, and rashes have the same origin (1:282–83). Besides, contrary to official dogma, it is important to regard sickness not simply as an opponent but also as an admonitory sign and purifying agent (1:287). It is also important to remember that suffering—whether physical or mental—can be the best of all teachers (1:287). Finally, it is important to understand that the body and the soul, rather than being autonomous, are inextricably linked and mutually affecting. As Dr. Domberlé emphasizes: "if one understood well, medicine and [the Christian] religion would produce the most harmonious of syntheses and depend upon each other instead of being antagonists. The preestablished plan which leads the world toward the Better is one" (1:287–88).[2]

The fundamental contrast between mainstream and humoral medicine is underlined by a series of oppositions. At the level of action, for example, a well-established doctor, Jean Doutreval, causes the death of one of his two daughters when, in order to advance his career, he allows a powerful but aging surgeon of dwindling skills to operate on her. He also lets his other daughter experience the worst kind of pain in an illicit relationship with his political protector. On the other hand, his son, Michel Doutreval, who is also a physician but a disciple of Domberlé, saves young and impecunious Evelyne Goyens from tuberculosis, marries her, and, through honesty, dedication, and charity, attains happiness and truth. At the symbolic level, love of self, a maniacal pursuit of pleasure, and Evil are repeatedly contrasted with love of others, generous striving, and Good (2: 25). At the more purely referential level, the differences are at least as striking. Synthetic drugs, artificial diuretics and laxatives, a frenzy for sugar, tobacco, and alcohol, a veritable cult for gorging oneself and one's (consumptive) patients with quarts of wine, pitchers of meat juice, canned foods and cold cuts, partridge on toast, fish meunière, or peach Melba contend with natural remedies, mild purgatives (for instance, prunes mixed with senna beans), and a gentle, nontoxic diet: spoonfuls of fruit juice, grains of wheat, atoms of meat, a bit of rye bread, a dash of milk, a touch of honey. Food in *Corps et âmes* is almost as prominent as in the average cookbook and I will not resist enumerating a few more items: fried steak or cold pigeon; pheasant, oysters, and lobster; ham, smoked salmon, and foie gras; fruitcake, kirsch souffle, chocolate, and jam; but also plain pasta or mashed potatoes; mushrooms, shallots, and bananas; not to mention Hospice de Beaune and Pommery; Corton 1898 and Chablis 1911; "schnick," absinthe, champagne, and port; or goat's milk and fresh water.

The nutritional concerns of *Corps et âmes* partly explain, no doubt, the extraordinary popularity of the novel during the Occupation just as they partly explain the medical outcry it provoked. Granted, the times were not exactly propitious for denouncing the evils of overeating (cf. Van der Meersch, *Pourquoi* 220–21); but they were certainly favorable to dreams of gastronomic debauchery.

No doubt, too, and in spite of a thesis that often threatens to submerge the story and that I have a hard time exaggerating, several other factors contributed to the novel's success. In the first place, Van der Meersch shows real affection for the weak and the poor. He knows that it is not easy for a wife and mother to make sure that vegetables are cooked very slowly when she is toiling in some factory and running constantly between work and home. He also knows that it is practically impossible for workers earning next to nothing to go back to the land and cultivate its fruit. Besides, for all the redundancies and repetitions of his *roman à thèse*, its exemplary vignettes, its manicheism, its stereotypes, Van der Meersch is a savvy narrator and the combination of his descriptive boldness with his mastery of melodrama frequently proves powerful. Critics praised his "mystical realism" and Alfred Fabre-Luce even said that Van der Meersch "seemed to have been given, in some divine plan, the task of redeeming Zola" (cited in Bordes 108).

Above all, the conformity of the values of *Corps et âmes* with those of Vichy France and the *Révolution nationale* is clear. If that conformity has rarely been pointed out, perhaps it is because the author, whose conduct during the war was quite honorable, had ties with certain groups in the Resistance; or because the Christian dimension of a text placed under the sign of contrition and redemption more than compensated for its ideology; or simply because the medical polemic obscured the text's other properties. Along with the stress on proper hygiene (France must become healthy again!), there is, for example, the recurring opposition between the interests of the group and the selfish passions of the individual, the hatred for parliamentary governance and universal suffrage ("The café owner is the grand elector. France is a bistrocracy"[1:118]), and the call for a return to "natural" hierarchies and government by the elites: "If we do not accept . . . an electoral system that gives the elites of every class a preponderant voice, if we do not come back to religion, morality, a government by the best among the workers, the bourgeois, and the farmers, we are screwed [*nous sommes foutus*]" (2:300). There is also the call for a return to reasonable segregations and a reasonable immigration policy: too many immigrants—Poles, Czechs, Italians, Algerians—are corrupted by urban life and become a burden instead of contributing to the well-being of the community (2:184–85, 300–1). There is the praise of the family as the most important element in a sound society: "in medicine as in every domain nothing will ever be worth the humble familial hearth" (1:136). There is the hostility to women's education ("overly intellectualized women sometimes lose part of their femininity, of their heart" [1:231]) and the criticism of blue-collar women workers ("the factory, for a woman, is the biggest school for abortion [2:293]). Finally, there is the obsession with the decline of France and the West, with a racial deterioration aggravated by nutritional madness and a low birth rate, with a degeneration of civilized peoples, for whom increased material wealth is the surest road to extinction (2:317). The hero of the novel, Michel Doutreval, is almost driven to hope for a defeat in the war that is coming: "for us, morally, a victory will already be disastrous. What arrogance, what frenzied quest for pleasure, what liberation of our worst instincts. . . . It would almost be good if victory left us severely weakened so that it would not lead us to a terrible decadence" (2:317).

If the dietetic rantings of Van der Meersch coexist easily with an arch-conservative vision, perhaps they also, more specifically, betray a kind of (religious) anti-Semitism. The novelist's criticism of urban life, of conspicuous consumption, of cosmopolitanism and skepticism can, of course, be read as attacks against Jews. The same is true of his many reflections about foreigners, however tinged with understanding and pity they may be (2:12, 184–85, 300–1 passim). But even more telling, perhaps (and paradoxically), is the almost total absence of Jews in *Corps et âmes*. There is not a single Jewish doctor in this novel about medicine. Nor is there a single allusion to the anxieties provoked in medical centers (and beyond) by the large number of Jewish physicians or a single echo of the measures taken in the 1930s and 1940s for their progressive elimination. As early as 1930, for instance, a report cowritten by the dean of the Medical School in Paris underlined the growing proportion of foreign doctors—most of whom were Jewish—and deplored its negative effects on French medicine. In April 1933, the "loi Armbruster" required physicians practicing in France to have a French degree. In July 1935, another law required them to be French citizens or subjects (or under the jurisdiction of a French protectorate). In August 1940, still another law stipulated that they had to be born of a French father and, in November, the law was made retroactive. Furthermore, a *numerus clausus* operative in the liberal professions limited the number of Jews to 2 percent of the entire corps of practitioners (Muel-Dreyfus 305–7). Now, the seven hundred pages of *Corps et âmes* contain only two explicit mentions of twentieth-century Jews. The first mention occurs in the description of Jean Doutreval's visit to Aix-en-Provence, "the luxurious and joyful city, with its crowd of cosmopolitan idlers, its cafés, its pastry shops, its jewelry stores, its Jewish dealers of Oriental rugs, and its antique dealers" (2:43). The second mention comes when one of the characters, Julienne Guerran, "spends her day, as usual, visiting the pastry shops of Aix, the jewelry stores, the Jewish boutiques where rugs and furs are sold, the *salons de thé* where there is dancing" (2:56). Each time, the metonymic linkage of Jews with cosmopolitanism, with trade and money, with a surfeit of sweetness, idleness, and the Orient is notable.

Moreover, Dr. Domberlé, whose difference, fervor, and stubborn quest for truth earn him nothing but ridicule, scorn, vilification, and worse, calls to mind the prophets of the Bible and is, in fact, explicitly likened to them (2:28, 200). He even predicts the punishment awaiting a nation of monstrous selfishness and unbridled materialism (2:316), quotes Job ("Even that it would please God to kill me, then should I yet have faith in him" [2:201]), and compares himself to Moses, who could not reach the promised land but whose followers did (2:15). Indeed, the dietary laws that Domberlé promotes can evoke, in the context of *Corps et âmes*, the laws of kashrut. Except that the Jewish God demands absolute conformance to his rules and can crush his chosen people for the smallest breach of principle (cf. Van der Meersch, *Pourquoi* 30). Domberlé and his disciple Michel Doutreval, like the Christian God they extol, are more indulgent. If the prophylactic and curative virtues of a vegetarian diet are often evident, it is also evident that the individual's temperament, habits, and situation must be taken into account. Domberlé's prescriptions are not uniform. They vary with his patients' condition (1:261). The rye breads and jams that can be easily digested by a robust suject, for instance, can devastate a weakened organism (1:284). The healer's art consists in "adjusting the nutriment's degree of concentration to the patient's digestive power" (1:266). For the two good doctors, it is the spirit that counts and not the letter.

In *Corps et âmes*, like in so many other texts, you are what you eat. The truth comes with the pudding and "the writer's mission is, above all, to serve it, and to hasten its arrival" (1:149). During the 1930s and early 1940s, that truth could perhaps not avoid being connected to the notorious Jewish question.

NOTES

1. On Van der Meersch, see Bordes, Jans, and Léliaert.
2. Page references are to the 1943 edition and all translations are my own.

10. Existential Cocktails

GEORGE BAUER

In *L'Être et le néant*, Jean-Paul Sartre insists that we must learn to decipher the choices we make in what we eat, but he cautions us that we must not just look for images, "but also to make very explicit the meanings really belonging to things" (691). His fascination with the "material imagination" discovered by Bachelard is tempting but unsatisfactory because perception and imagination, for him, have nothing in common. His preference is for a psychoanalysis of things. "It is thus a question of applying, not to the *subject* but to *things*, a method of objective deciphering that does not suppose any previous return to the subject" (691). We must focus on "the existential meaning of these foods." He insists that "generally, there is no taste or irreducible inclination. They all represent a certain choice belonging to the individual. It is up to existential psychoanalysis to compare and classify them" (707).

In 1972, in the turn to things sexual and culinary our only guide books were *L'Être et le néant*, *La Nausée*, *Les Chemins de la liberté*, a fragment of *La Reine Albemarle ou le dernier touriste* published as *Nourritures* in *Verve*, and the cocktail origins of Sartre's phenomenology focusing on *things*, recounted by Simone de Beauvoir in *La Force de l'âge*. Recently returned from Germany and intoxicated by Husserl, Aron joins Castor and Jean-Paul for a drink. "We spent an evening together at the Bec de Gaz, on rue Montparnasse; we ordered the specialty of the house: apricot cocktails. Aron pointed to his glass: 'You see, little pal, if you are a phenomenologist, you can speak of this cocktail, and that is philosophy!'" (141). Castor records Jean-Paul's astonished reaction:

> Sartre turned pale, or almost. This is exactly what he'd been hoping
> for for years: to speak of things, as he touched them, and that would

be philosophy. Aron convinced him that phenomenology corresponded exactly to his preoccupations: to go beyond the opposition of idealism and realism, to affirm both the sovereignty of consciousness and the presence of the world as it gives itself to us. (141)

This choice of realism ("the idea of making a philosophy in which one would be realist. And realist was neither materialist nor idealist") was only a confirmation, Husserl's "things themselves," through which Sartre could come into touch with and uncover his "café philosophie." *Sartre par lui-même*, a film shot by Alexandre Astruc and Michel Contat in 1972, was finally shown in 1976. There the Husserlian thing comes up in its alcoholic beginnings. "That's it, that was Husserl. That's why, when Aron told me, 'But we can reason about this glass of beer—'" Castor interrupts: "No, it was not a glass of beer. It was an apricot cocktail." The group, for one reason or another, melts in fits of laughter. Sartre goes on: "Well, that thrilled me. I said to myself: 'Finally there is philosophy.'"

For too long now I have looked at the culinary aspects of fiction and these conflicting tales of phenomenological origins in drinks seen and drunk without paying attention to Simone de Beauvoir in her kitchen, in her own nausea, in her beef as useless mouth. *Les Bouches inutiles* began as part of a novel that ended up as an unsatisfying drama. The incident that struck her dumb centers on the mouth. Her readings of the *Italian Chronicles* of Sismondi in twelve volumes gave her numerous accounts of the same dramatic situation in which the male defenders of the city sustain themselves at the expense of those they defend: "During a siege, to protect themselves against famine, sometimes the fighters chased women, the elderly, children, all the useless mouths, into ditches" (*La Force de l'âge* 602). The question she asked was this: "If they kept one mouth, how would the survivors deal with their despair and their anger?" (602).

What interested her was the suspense that preceded the actual execution of these useless mouths condemned: "What did these victims feel and what did the fathers, brothers, lovers, spouses, sons feel who had condemned them?" Her play failed, she notes, "partly because at that time, it was my bent to slip into moralizing" (603). She should have stuck to her cocktails, but instead she slipped into moralizing.

I have come to the bars of Beaver through the blues of Marguerite Duras's own drunkenness and cure. The bitter Camparis of Sara in *Les Petits Chevaux de Tarquinia* ("with Campari and bitters, it always seems less urgent to me" [82]) and the wine of *Moderato Cantabile* drunk by Anne Desbaresdes in a self-prescribed drunkenness as a cure for their maladies and malaise are Eurasian solutions to exclusion from male society in which they have an unsatisfactory part. Emma Bovary's own unquenchable thirst for life is reflected in the bottles on the bar of both Sartre and Simone de Beauvoir. But well before Castor fell in with Sartre and his pals, she dreamed of a marriage made in heaven with her cousin Jacques. Her Jacques seemed to come to her out of *Le Grand Meaulnes*, but was, finally only a guy who went out to bars with his buddies and used his night howls for a justification for his existence—an existence from which she was barred. She loved him for his poetic accounts of nights on the town, loved him as a disembodied night fowl who endlessly flew from her to be with his peacock dandy friends who only descended from their perches to speak of their cocktail nights.

Her devotion to Jacques and the holy spirits shared by his fellow imbibers finally resulted in her own step up to that communion rail. She had come prepared by her own readings in the catechism of the heady poetry of Baudelaire, Rimbaud, and Mallarmé incorporated by Dada and surrealist men in their poetry of Parisian bars. The critical idealism of Brunschvicg left her "with her hunger" and her "taste for literature" returned. *Sed non satiata*. Baudelaire's useless mouth, his unslaked thirst became her own: "One must always be drunk. Everything is there; it's the only question. In order not to feel the horrible burden of Time that breaks your shoulders and makes you bend toward the earth, you must get intoxicated without interruption. But with what? Wine, poetry, virtue, as you wish. But get intoxicated" (*Oeuvres complètes* 286). Her complaint: "Philosophy had neither opened heaven to me nor anchored me to the earth" (*Mémoires* 239). In her ennui at her nadir, she first thought that Gide would be her guide as she drowned in her philosophical studies and success. Then she was really down, a drunken genie appeared out of the "avant-garde publications that had the life-span of a fly in those years." She tells how she fell in love with the texts of Breton, with Aragon. "Surrealism conquered me. Concern, after a while, was pale; I preferred the outrageousness of pure negation. Destruction of art, morality, language, systematic disruption, despair pushed to the point of suicide: these excesses thrilled me" (*Mémoires* 232). Her conversion to cocktails was surreal, a descent into the hell of pure negation through words and alcohol, into drunken words and words drunk. She began to live the scripture of the city, returning again and again to the park of *Le Paysan de Paris*:

> I loved the evenings, after dinner, when I went alone in the metro and got out at the other end of Paris, near the Buttes-Chaumont. Often, I returned on foot. Boulevard de la Chapelle, under the steel of the el, women walking the streets, men teetering out of lit-up bistros; on the movie marquis, the signs yelled out. The world was always an enormous confused presence around me. (*Mémoires* 239)

In those days she almost seemed to want to become Breton's Nadja: "The streets, the cars, the people on the street were only a parade of appearances among which my nameless presence floated. I sometimes told myself with pride and fear that I was crazy: the distance is not very long between severe solitude and madness" (*Mémoires* 258). Finally she returned to her Grand Meaulnes who spoke to her of "unknown spots where one met people different from everyone else and where things happened, things that were a bit tragic, sometimes very beautiful" (*Mémoires* 261). Jacques had never traveled, but he had his bars. Simone was struck by the fact that "a lot of young novelists—Soupault among them—affirmed that one could have astonishing travels without leaving Paris. They recalled the upsetting poetry of those bars where Jacques spent his nights. I took to loving again" (*Mémoires* 261).

In the spring of 1927, she passed her exams in moral philosophy and psychology. Brunschvicg advised her to do her thesis on *The Concept in Leibniz*; "Jacques found a haven in the bars of Montparnasse" (*Mémoires* 264). She cried herself to sleep at night: "How I would have loved to dive into the night, listen to jazz, elbow people. But no, I was walled in; I was stifling; I was eating myself alive; I wanted to bang my head against those walls" (*Mémoires* 265). Jacques was soon to be off to Algeria for his military service leaving behind Olga with whom he was having an affair, Simone, and an extraordinary woman called Magda.

As if he were Breton, Jacques enigmatically added: "It was a story that cost us deeply." Magda was, she writes, one of those "disquieting prodigies one meets at night in bars. I didn't wonder what role she had played in Jacques's life" (*Mémoires* 266). Eight days before he left, Jacques took her to a bar—so long desired from reading Soupault and Aragon and from Jacques's own episodic tales of Parisian bar nights. This was the Stygian threshold she was carried across. Jacques used the movies as a way to get her out of the house. Marriage had never been mentioned. Simone lost herself, not in Aragon's Certa Café/Bar, not at the movies, but in the Stryx on the rue Huyghens. The tale of the cock and the cocktail took her over.

"Les affiches criardes" were not those of the movies seen and drunk, but the poetic bar texts of Aragon, now. In Aragon's book the Certa was a Dada spot. "To be dada is not a dishonor; it merely designates a group of regulars, some young people who are sometimes noisy, but nice" (*Paysan de Paris* 95). He adds: "And dada has even become so much a part of daily life that here dada is the name of a cocktail. I'd like to write a long paragraph of gratitude for the drinks in this café" (95). In his lyric praise of these "boissons déconcertantes," the porto is unique, and before words fail him he recommends the Mousse Noka, the Théatra Flip, and the Théatra Cocktail "for various uses." The ultimate poem is the "Tarif des consommations" itself and he reproduces its art in typographic font and fountains of poetic names and situates it on the wall of the bar in which he muses.

> A painting in the small room, above which, for a drink whose name I
> forget, a sign painted by one of the former waiters in the style of the
> mechanical paintings of Francis Picabia, and which disappeared a while
> ago. One of the charms of cafés is in the little signs hung all around,
> lots of which are in Certa, proclaiming Martini, Bovril, Carola Water,
> or W.N. Youngers Scotch Ale. Sometimes there is a whole series of
> them. All of that is excellent and above reproach. (*Paysan* 98–99)

The movie they were supposed to see was *L'Équipage*, but Simone joined another crew and writes up her adventure story in the Stryx Bar inspired by Aragon's Dada cocksure recommendation of the starred Certa. Simone's account is a starry-eyed inscription of her initiation to membership in the suborder of nocturnal birds: the *striges*. The owl is one of its members. Here are the lyrical words of her first hoot:

> We didn't go to the movies. Jacques took me to the Stryx, on rue
> Huyghens, where he was a regular, and I perched on a barstool
> between him and Riquet. He called the bartender by name, Michel,
> and ordered a dry martini for me. I had never set foot in a café and
> there I was one night, in a bar, with two young men: for me this was
> truly extraordinary. The bottles with calm or violent colors, the bowls
> of olives and salted almonds, the little tables, everything astonished
> me. The most surprising was that this decor was familiar to Jacques. I

rapidly slurped up my cocktail, and as I had never drunk one drop of
alcohol, even wine, which I did not like, I soon left planet earth.
(*Mémoires* 266)

She was in heaven. She dumped her second martini behind the counter,
broke a few glasses, and the crew went on to the Vikings. Flanked by her
new drinking buddies, she felt only Jacques. "I marveled knowing
Jacques with a physical intimacy that symbolized the confusion of our
souls." There he bought her a gin-fizz with very little gin and she slipped
through drink into an amorous blur. Time was of no consequence. A two-
o'clock *crème de menthe verte* at the Rotonde was seen through new eyes.
"Around me flitted faces come from another world; there was a miracle at
every corner. And I felt myself linked to Jacques by an indissoluble com-
plicity, as if we had committed a murder together or crossed the Sahara
together on foot" (267).

Jacques left for North Africa, but he left her in the good hands of
Riquet. Clearly her readings of *Le Grand Meaulnes* and *Le Paysan de Paris*,
of Gide, her immersion in the ballet, her philosophical readings, and the
movies failed to come together. In a Proustian search for her first physical
intimacy, desire unstoppered, but bottled up, she spent her time and
money on booze, on cocktails, at the Rotonde, at the Vikings, drinking gin
fizz after gin fizz, searching for the right neon light, only to end the night
with a yawn. Her only unfathomable cocktail was offered by the barman at
the Rotonde. His act was a miracle: "But when I wanted to pay my sherry-
gobler, the big redheaded bartender refused my money. This incident, that
I never cleared up, discretely touched prodigy and encouraged me" (268).
She vomited food but went on. The bar replaced her church; the absence of
God and the absence of Jacques fizzed into one. The Aragon Bar and its
men were inexplicable in their artistry of the cocktail miracle. In his
Paysan de Paris those *garçons* who drew their typographical, mechanical
Picabiaesque invitations to drink were artists in their own right. His hymn
to them unconsciously marked Simone in her coming nights. Of these tender men he says, "almost all were the incarnation of politeness and
discretion; they made cocktails well, were more or less artists, and showed
talent in doing errands" (*Paysan* 99). They were acolytes, if not priests, as
the smell of cigarette smoke and the ash drifted into and onto her communion robes. She is explicit. She went in search of sin in the cocktail bar in
order to find the miracle of Saint Jacques or, at least, to stumble into an
adventure that might slake her thirst.

> I remained convinced that sin was the gaping spot of God and I
> perched atop my barstool with the fervor that had made me prostrate
> as a child at the feet of the Holy Sacrament. I touched the same
> presence; jazz replaced the booming sound of the organ and I waited
> for adventure just as I had once waited for ecstasy. "In bars," Jacques
> had told me, "one can do anything and something will happen." I did
> anything. (*Mémoires* 269)

But there were other artistic encounters as she played at being the flirt,
the tart, the teaser. Those men, unlike the gentle Dadas and the Corta bar-
tenders, brought her down to earth. That didn't stop her. A "boiteux" gave
her lessons in her cocktail game; drawing on an available napkin he
sketched out what the little bourgeoise must taste in her bohemian role.
"'It's very badly drawn,' I said. 'It's a likeness'; he opened his fly and this
time, I looked away" (269). Despite this obscene drawing lesson she went
on ("helped by the alcohol"): "All I needed was a gin fizz and my solitude
melted. All men were brothers; we understood each other; everyone loved
everyone else" (270). The attraction to "bars and dance-halls arose mostly
from their illicit nature" (270–71). She grew bolder and literature was the
guide that brought her the temptation of devils in the flesh. The certified
cocktails of the Carta, the Pick me Hup and the Kiss Me Quick, led her to
strangers who did just that. The spinster decided to go for a spin. "I had
principles: Live dangerously. Refuse nothing, said Gide, Rivière, the Sur-
realists, and Jacques. Fine, I said. Place de la Bastille, outside a café, we
drank cocktails sadly" (271). Back in the car, he went to her knees and then
on. She fled on foot content in yet another cocktail adventure of surreal *Lits
et Ratures* with Sugar Daddies. "I realized that I'd gotten away. However, I
congratulated myself for having committed *a true free act*" (271—my
emphasis). Her Pick Me Hup and Kiss Me Quick cocktail nights wore a
different kind of instruction. "I was a soul, a pure spirit, I was interested
only in souls; the intrusion of sexuality blew this angelism apart" (291).
Her escapades ended. The academic year too. Sartre failed his examinations. Next year she would work harder. Her fling scared her, but restored
her, but after a summer of *nourritures*: "oeufs en gelée, comets, aspics et bar-
quettes, ballotines, galantines, pâtés, chauds-froid, daubes, terrines,
confits, tourtes, tartes, frangipanes," "where all these women had fulfilled
their social obligations with zeal" (277), she again bellied up to the bar:
"As a believer, following a dry spell, wallows in the odor of incense and
candles, I sunk again anew into the smells of alcohol and tobacco" (291).

She went against the grain of a thesis on Spinoza and marriage. Her choice was daily reasoned. "At Picard's, I looked through the *Eleven Chapters on Plato* of Alain. That cost eight cocktails: too expensive" (292). At certain moments "the poetry of bars" (306) like some cocktails drunk seamed to lose its flavor, but only temporarily. In her diary she questions her addiction.

> Jazz, women, dances, impure words, alcohols, touching: how could I not be shocked, but to accept here what I would accept nowhere else, and joke with these men? How could I love these things with that passion that comes from afar, that holds me so tight? What do I seek in these spots of troubled charm? (307)

Clearly it was sex; she explained her escape from one church to another with her embodied spirit in confrontation with the violence of the flesh and its crudity: "In fact, I remained dirty, sexual taboos survived, to the extent that I imagined being capable of becoming a drug addict or an alcoholic, but I never even thought of sexual freedom" (308). This was her own experience of the "tragic sovereignty" (309) of the flesh. If Jacques's poetic bar knights initiated her into sipping, only to leave her thirsty in a new Sahara, her desires for philosophical drink and bonding went unsatisfied. "Only the clan formed by Sartre, Nizan, and Herbaud remained closed to me" (310). Her curious reservation in the need for this threesome showed her second thoughts about men and bars. "Sartre didn't have a bad head, but they said he was the worst of the three and he was even accused of drinking" (310). She want back to the men's bar and the barmen. He was not only a cocktail artist but he and his *bande à part:* "on every occasion—in their words, attitudes, jokes—showed that men were not spirits but bodies driven by need and thrown into a brutal adventure" (336). Herbaud was her date, but Sartre picked up the tab. "Sartre, whose generosity was legendary, put us in a taxi and in the Falstaff on rue Montparnasse, poured cocktails into us until two in the morning. They were rivals in kindness and he told me a lot of stories. I was in seventh heaven" (337). She sipped her way into his life. He became her new bartender. He was a real displacement for her Grand Meaulnes and her Dada/surreal men. She abandoned the man and proposed gratuities and gratuitous acts. "Sartre answered exactly the wish I made when I was fifteen; he was the double in whom I rediscovered, brought to incandescence, all my manias" (344). She escaped the Church. She escaped the family. She preferred workers eating out of lunch pails. "I was thrilled to escape from those ceremonial family dinners; in reducing food to its truth, I seemed to take a step toward freedom" (283). These were moves toward her partnership in bar and café philosophy. They did drink together replacing Dada and surrealist concoctions with their own "Passions inutiles" for "Bouches inutiles." Their *tarif des consommations* was different.

In *Cérémonie des Adieux*, Simone returned to the philosophy of things drunk. She went back to cocktail beginnings, but her reservation is still there. Sartre's hero Pardaillan ate little and the discussion turns to drink.

> S. de B —And drinking. You liked to drink quite a bit
> J.-P. S—I really liked to drink, but it's too complicated; it has no relation to the body.
> S. de B.—To the body?
> J.-P. S.—Well, if it has relations, they aren't many. I don't see it that way. Obviously, I don't drink for ideas, for the beauty of the ideas that will emerge, but for a certain kind of imagination nevertheless.
> S. de B.—What do you mean?
> J.-P. S.—Subjectivity becomes, in a certain way, inventive. It invents bullshit [*conneries*], but in the moment they are invented, the bullshit is amusing.
> S. de B.—To be precise, you never drank alone.
> J.-P. S.—Never.
> S. de B.—You liked to drink with friends, with people.
> J.-P. S.—With you. (404)

Here is her guarantee of their tenderness in drinks drunk, echoing her first dry martini with Jacques. Through cocktails, the "we," the "nous" fizzes where the ingredients are shaken into one.

To return to alimentary beginnings and Aron, that other "petit camarade," is to return to the tale of bar, beer, and cocktail origins. Simone, in her insistence on the apricot cocktail is a very real presence in the male bar scene from which she had so long been excluded. Her cocktail history, I think, is critical for any understanding of phenomenological origin. Herbaud, who named her Beaver, did not understand the communion of cocktails drunk by Simone and Sartre alone, when he seemed to pour a drink over her head with this comment: "'You'll never be a little pal; you're the Beaver" (*Mémoires* 336). She became Sartre's only drunken pal and to the end it still scared her, but she used her fright, pushing away the body of cocktail proximity in order to bring him closer in their ceremonial adieux.

Just now, to end, I will not retrace etymological mysteries of the cocktail, but will dish up, ladle, a saucy receipt of *Adieux*, ceremonially. The dropped "T" is a tale that begins in the death of a lusty rooster from M. F. K. Fisher's *The Art of Eating*. This is a clue and recipe in the psychoanalysis of things, of cocktails and cocks become ale ingredients:

> To make Cock Ale, instructs one ancient recipe reprinted in 1736 in Smith's *Compleat Housewife*, "take ten gallons of ale and a large cock, the older the better. Parboil the cock, flea him, and stamp him in a stone mortar until his bones are broken. You must craw and gut him when you flea him. Put him into two quarts of sack, and put to it 3 pounds of raisins of the sun stoned, some blades of mace, and a few cloves. Put all these into a canvas bag, and a little while before you find the ale has done working, put the ale and bag together into a vessel. In a week or 9 days' time bottle it up, fill the bottles but just above the necks, and leave the same to ripen as other ale." (54)

As Simone de Beauvoir sat between two "petits camarades" at the Bec de Gaz, she listened silently, than recorded the origins of their French existentialism, but her own cocktails in this bar light dazzle us with the fizz and pizzazz of German philosophy sipped in a different light. And with a new zest, a different twist, added by Simone tending bar.

11. The Betrayal of *Moules-frites*: This Is (Not) Belgium

STÉPHANE SPOIDEN

The destiny of nations depends on how they nourish themselves. Tell me what you eat, and I shall tell you what you are.

Brillat-Savarin

Inasmuch as the scope of French gastronomy extends far beyond its national boundaries, it is certainly not out of place to conceive of Belgian cuisine as one of its numerous regional varieties. Indeed, French gourmets often view Belgium as a high spot of French gastronomy; and the Belgians, notorious for their dedication to food, take pride in such a compliment. From this point of view, Belgian specialties—whether they come from the sea, such the *waterzooi* of fish (a fish soup with vegetables), or from the forests of the Ardennes in the south, such as old recipes for game—are to be considered along with the foie gras of the Dordogne or the bouillabaisse of Marseilles as regional products of a French gastronomy that is infinitely more varied and diverse than one might think in these times of eclectic fusion cuisines.

Like Belgium's cultural and artistic expression in general, Belgian cuisine is undeniably dependent on and inseparable from the international field. The characterization of Belgian culture and its image abroad is mainly subject to structures and processes of definition imposed by an international context. For instance, Belgian artists' apprehension of reality—which often verges on magical realism with its unique exaggeration of the real—has consistently been perceived as a variation of French surrealism. But it is only a variation, since some minimal distinction from the French movement, in the sense that Bourdieu used the term in *Distinction,* is proving indispensable for the sake of its own existence. Without doubt, René Magritte is the best known example. Considered surrealism the world over, his work is viewed in Belgium as a familiar approach to reality, often characterized as a sur-representation of the real, or even as a recognizable reality.

A similar process of "assimilation," not to mention the ambiguous and ingratiating co-option that comes with it, is found in the realm of gastronomic definition. Belgian gastronomy is contiguous with French cuisine in the order of classification, as it is geographically, and has to occupy a specific niche that has not already been cornered by the dominating cultures that surround and confine it. Belgium produces the largest variety of top-quality beers, exceptional chocolates, and delicious Belgian fries, just to cite some of the most popular products of an incomparable gastronomic culture. Unfortunately, it is established that Germany has the best beers, Switzerland the best chocolates, and, well, France the renowned French fries. The origins of these famous fried potatoes—are they Belgian or French?—is the object of an ongoing controversy that seems to play itself out beyond the borders of the countries involved, since it is well implied in France that fries, known around the world as French, were invented in Belgium. The case of French fries is evidently the most striking example of a French gastronomic hegemony over what is considered its cultural margins being imposed mainly by the forces of an international market, rather than by the French themselves who have always acknowledged the high quality of Belgian gastronomy. The notable exception is Charles Baudelaire who affirms in *Pauvre Belgique* that food in Belgium is deplorable and that there are no respectable restaurants in the country. Jean-François Revel in his noted book on food *Un Festin en paroles*, comments that the poet was either "égaré" or that food in Belgium must have improved tremendously since the nineteenth century (24).

These introductory remarks, anecdotal as they may be, are nevertheless revealing, and bring us to the "meat and potatoes" of the discussion. That is, what is the Belgian classic dish? Were you to ask any Belgian this question, he or she would respond without hesitation, *steak-frites*. The bad fortune of this rare assurance is that it will not travel very far, even within the confines of this cramped country. Again, French gastronomic sphere *oblige*! It is the very same *bifteck-frites* that the French, too, proclaim as their national dish. And the addition of a salad as in *steak-frites-salade* often encountered in Belgium changes the complexion of the question very little. Especially after the Barthesian consecration of this French icon, Belgium has had to content with the leftovers granted by a sort of obscure and unconstituted, but nonetheless powerful, Culinary International. Thus, the *moules et frites*, Belgian steamed mussels with fries, were conferred, as it were, with the title of Belgian national dish by a cosmopolitan vox populi. Of course, this approbation does not offend the good-natured Belgians in the least, given that *moules et frites* are indeed very popular in Belgium. Besides, the somewhat outrageous commercial exploitation of this dish by the tourist industry has certainly played a role in its international recognition. If you ever visit Belgium, you will see restaurants all over the country advertising *moules et frites*. The *moules*, also named *moules marinière* in France, are simply mussels steamed with aromatics, often presented in a casserole with broth, accompanied by a plate of crispy Belgian fries. Mussels can be served with bread to dip in the broth, but the real Belgian experience commands an order of fries and a portion of mayonnaise to dip them in, as one would ask for ketchup in North America. At first, it may not seem appetizing to an American palate; but rumor has it that once you have tried the fries-mayonnaise combination you are addicted for life. For a try, you don't have to rush off to Belgium: a place in New York's East Village offers an authentic experience of Belgian fries with mayonnaise served in a paper cone just as if you were wandering around Brussels's Grand Place. For culinary advice on Belgian food, I have been guided by one of the few, and most recent, Belgian cookbooks available in the United States, written by Ruth Van Waerebeek.

CULTURAL IDENTITY

Curiously enough, *moules et frites* constitute an epiphenomenon of the dynamics that delineate Belgian culture at large. From its historical creation to its contemporary cultural production, Belgium has constantly been defined by outside forces that it attempts, for the most part, to channel for its own best interests. In other words, *moules et frites* typify and perfectly represent Belgium, not in spite of the fact that this signature dish has been attributed to the country from outside, but precisely because of it. In response to Brillat-Savarin's aphorism that alleges, "Tell me what you eat, and I shall tell you what you are [*Dis-moi ce que tu manges et je te dirai* ce que *tu es*]" my point would be summed up by asserting that *moules et frites* make you Belgian as an object (defined by exterior forces) as well as a subject. Indeed, "ce que" in French here can refer to nationality as an object, as in: "What are you, French or German?" From an historical point of view, being Belgian as a subject, is first and foremost being the object of outside forces.

A brief historical and cultural detour is required here. Although its cultural identity dates back to the sixteenth century with the Catholic reconquest of the southern provinces of the Low Countries (present-day Belgium), Belgium can be said to be a by-product of nineteenth-century European diplomacy. Belgium was declared independent from the Netherlands in 1830 with the support of France and England after a brief period of revolution against the House of Orange in Holland. The country was, and still is today, comprised of two distinct communities: the Walloons, who are French-speaking, and the Flemings, who are Dutch-speaking. There is also a small German-speaking community of about 65,000 people along the German border in the east of the country. The artificiality of its conception has led many observers to believe that Belgium is a country without national identity because its creation did not significantly reflect cultural or national character. The idea of Belgium as a non-nation has recently gained considerable currency among Belgians themselves who, witnessing the fragmentation of their country and the concomitant rise of an antagonistic biculturalism between the two major communities, have more and more difficulty discerning cohesive cultural or national forces within the country. This undiscoverable country on the map of Europe is therefore merely an idea or afterthought. Many consider this notion only "logical" since Belgium was born culturally in the Middle Ages (a thesis popularized by the famous Belgian historian Henri Pirenne in his classic *Histoire de la Belgique*), and nationally in the nineteenth century as the result of foreign powers that have always maintained strong political and cultural influences on this small country.

How can Belgium still cultivate a semblance of cultural identity despite the powerful influence of surrounding cultures? The answer to this question has often been found in what has become a cliché concerning the cultural particularity of this nation. Belgium is a country that lies at the crossroads of the two major cultural types in Western Europe—Latin and Germanic—a crossroads that served for centuries mostly as a battleground, but that also gave rise to a bastardized or hybrid culture. However, as a Belgian sociologist suggested in a recent article, the precondition of being able to absorb so many heterogeneous cultural elements and influences is generally the constitution of a solid identity (Lacrosse 13). In this case,

Belgian identity has to be either well hidden, or manifest itself in odd ways, perhaps as an identity-through-nonidentity.

Belgium's receptivity and ability for assimilation make it difficult to discern what constitutes deliberate borrowings from impositions. But however that may be, the definition of Belgium by negation engenders an absence of chauvinism toward the outside, whereas the tensions, divisions, and self-doubt that prevail within the country translate into scathing self-derision. In what could be called the positivization of a deficiency, this untenable situation linked to hybridity explains the tendency among Belgian artists to attempt to transcend reality through the imaginary and dreamwork in a society that is otherwise known for its pragmatism and matter-of-fact mentality.

Yet amid everything that divides Belgians, elements of cohesion remain, sometimes prosaic, and impossible to ignore. These exceptions center on essential ingredients or pillars of national cultural expression: king, hearth, food, and, perhaps, sports. Since Baudouin I (1930–95), the King of the Belgians has become the embodiment and ultimate symbol of national unity, the last defense against the forces of secession. This symbolic locus was both affirmed and authoritatively revealed by the spontaneous gathering of millions of Belgians, who do not ordinarily display the least patriotism, in homage to the king upon his death. Observing the occasion, some cynical commentators noted that Belgians are given to such displays of national identity only spasmodically and at rare emotional events such as the death of the king (although he always has a successor), a sporting victory such as Belgium's third place (!) in the 1986 World Cup soccer tournament, or more recently the "white march" in memory of the victims of a pedophile ring. It is not surprising to see that a country in relative decomposition attempts to recreate a semblance of unity around a crime that reminds us of Sigmund Freud's fable in *Totem and Taboo*, or René Girard's commentary on this notion in *Violence and the Sacred*.

More relevant to my thesis is that, regardless of ethnic or linguistic distinctions, it is often said of the Belgians that they "have a brick in their bellies." That is, they are obsessed with the construction or acquisition of a home. Home and stomach, the obsessive quest for Belgian identity culminates ultimately in the question of food, a question which perpetually preoccupies the Belgian as a brief stay in the country would confirm. Daily conversation is always centered between these two immovable poles in a country where personal comfort and security, characterized by a good table and a good roof, have been set up as the supreme goals. A Belgian author wrote recently: "I love Belgium for its magnificent dishes, the glory of its beers and because in Belgium a good meal and a good wine are daily staples. I loathe Belgium because all anyone ever talks about is eating and drinking" (Istendael 431). No one will really be surprised to learn that Belgium is eminently proud to hold the per capita European records for the number of bistros, cafés, and restaurants of all types.

In sum, Belgium exists and remains somewhat unified only at its most domestic. Therefore, it is fundamental to become familiar with the home: hearth and table. Belgians are bound together by the artifacts of their culture and not for example by language or an illustrious past: objects of their culture are the only symbolic heritage through which they feel interconnected, and where food plays a central role. If a war of secession— an entirely peaceful one I hasten to add—is presently underway in Belgium, then the dish of *moules et frites* symbolizes the cultural or even anthropological unity that persists in a country in the process of disappearing, where the two major groups are generally at loggerheads.

MOULES-FRITES

It is thus important to consider the conjunction or hyphen in the name of the dish *moules et frites* or *moules-frites*, and how they unify the two disparate elements, *moules* and *frites*. Even if the two main components of the dish taken separately do not represent one or the other of the two linguistic communities, the meal as a whole (wasn't it *the* example of Belgian cuisine?) is nonetheless an incontestable sign of unity. Neither of the two major linguistic communities has ever shown enough bad taste, which would certainly be incongruous in the matter of food, to claim cultural ownership over a dish like *moules et frites*. Food, the quintessential element of conviviality, is in effect the best-shared thing in Belgium. Every dish known precisely for its regional origins is cooked in the same way and just as well in the north as it is in the south of the country. Nothing here, as in all Belgian artistic expression, identifies itself antagonistically as a product of either Flanders or Wallonia. For example, Flemish beef stew cooked in beer, which originally seems to have come from Antwerp, is prepared and consumed as much in Wallonia as it is in Flanders. A history book reports that Flemish beef stew even played a role, albeit bizarre, in the creation of a united Belgium. Beef stew was poured from a balcony over Dutch troops invading Brussels streets during the riots that led to Belgian independence in 1830 (Vandersypen, qtd. in Martens 40). These remarks might seem odd, or even absurd; however, we must place them in the worsening context of excessive regionalization [*communautarisation*] in a country where even social security is threatened with division along linguistic lines. If one cultural constant exists in Belgium, it touches on the fact that cultural expression transcends linguistic regions, although I realize that many artists deplore the so-called *communautarisation* of cultural funding in Belgium. Cultural expression remains nonetheless devoid of any regional sense of belonging. In Belgium, culture—as the symbolic heritage that alone constitutes the nation—remains national, or even international as suggested in the introduction.

Belgian cultural unity goes beyond a simple conjunction and has more to do with the fusion, if not confusion demonstrated in the popular name given to the national dish. *Les moules et les frites* are often reduced to *moules-frites* with a more unifying hyphen. This never means that *moules* are sometimes cooked like *frites* as visitors who have not been forewarned occasionally believe. The hyphen in *moules-frites* is testimony to the symbiosis expressed by the dish in question.

FROM A PARADOXICAL COUNTRY, A PARADOXICAL SIGNATURE DISH

And yet the unity of the dish is not obvious. What strikes you immediately when the server brings a meal of *moules-frites* is the baroque mixture not only of *moules* and *frites*, curious in itself, but also the composition of the mussel casserole. For here you have these magnificent, shiny, blue-black shells—at once elegant, hard, and breakable—contrasting sharply with their soft orange-yellow insides, accompanied by the green vegetables of the broth, when cooked together at the same time the hard and the soft remain.

Moules-frites are no less of a baroque aberration from a gastronomic and dietetic point of view. The *moules* part of the dish looks like some New Age concoction designed to promote weight loss and healthy eating habits. Here you will find nothing but healthy ingredients. In fact, *moules* are well-known for being perfectly nutritious: they are high in proteins, relatively low in calories, extremely low in cholesterol and fat; they contain various vitamins, minerals, and omega-3 fatty acids that are thought to help fight heart disease and cancer. Besides, they are prepared with an arrangement of fresh vegetables. But as if the dish proved too healthy, the

Belgians, not known for their dietetic food or reasonable portions, add one of the most formidable enemies of the current cholesterol-correct cuisine. The addition of mayonnaise, one of the most decried artery cloggers, to the light mussels seems to bear testimony to the heavy side of Belgian culture, so often mocked by the French since Baudelaire. From a paradoxical country, a paradoxical signature dish. And don't even think of dispensing with the mayonnaise because, as any Belgian will tell you, *moules-frites* without mayonnaise is like Belgium without Brussels! Without it, the dish would not make sense!

A hybrid and bastardized specialty that cultivates paradox like its country of origin, *moules-frites* is a dish without unity. Take a moment to observe a casserole of mussels when it comes to the table: All the open-mouthed mussels in frightening disarray, piled one upon another as if they had been thrown carelessly into the casserole (which is often the case), decorated here and there with limp vegetables. To paraphrase Ponge, who had his own, uncanny way of looking at an oyster, *moules-frites* forms a complete world, but not any world, a Belgian world where chaos emerges from a simple dish (43). As renowned filmmaker Jaco Van Dormael (*Toto the Hero*, *The Eighth Day*) said when asked in an interview what he, as an artist, thought of Belgium, he said: "We [Belgians] are utterly disorganized [*Nous, on est* brol]" (491), using an expression that conveys the "odds and ends" aspect of Belgian culture. Like its country of origin, *moules-frites* are the product of bricolage, a sort of constructive mess, in short a resourceful, positive disorganization (491–93).

This dish-that-is-not-one, as Belgium is a country-that-is-not-one, could bring to mind the carnavalesque delineated by Bakhtin. This idea is not without merit since specialists have retraced one of the original influences on Belgian culture to the medieval period and to the Renaissance. Barring the anachronism of potatoes in Renaissance Europe, it is very easy to imagine the people depicted by Brueghel the Elder (1525–69) eating meals of *moules-frites*, since it is not rare to find living elements of contemporary Belgian culture with a direct lineage from the Brueghelian era. And of primary importance among these elements is the notion of revelry, the famous *kermesses* or fairs and, of course, the famous beers, and food.

In effect, Belgian gastronomy owes much to its medieval and Renaissance roots, an element that possibly differentiates it from the typical gastronomy of France, despite its numerous influences. By the Middle Ages, Belgian territory had already been invaded by virtually all the peoples of Europe, who brought with them different cooking techniques, ingredients, and spices. The High Middle Ages and Renaissance were also a time when Flemish culture flourished in the commercial cities of Bruges and Ghent. Van Waerebeek acknowledges that "Belgian cuisine is still deeply rooted in medieval cookery" (ix). The medieval use of spices and condiments—she cites in particular mustard, vinegars, and dried fruits—originates in this era and is still clearly recognizable in Belgium today. Beer making and the survival of hundreds of artisanal breweries—the microbrewery is not a recent market phenomenon in Belgium—is also a remnant of Belgium's medieval heritage. This explains why Belgian brewers still use ancient techniques unique in the business.

Finally, Belgian food finally can be said to be a curious compromise between the traditionalism of preserving age-old recipes and techniques (although they themselves result from foreign imports), and the influence of world cuisine that spices up reputedly conventional dishes. A case in point is precisely mussel dishes prepared in dozens of ways, with curry or Indonesian ingredients for instance, now served in many *moules-frites* restaurants. This dish, whether in its traditional form with fries, or in a more exotic guise, inescapably hints at a compromise *à la belge*, elevated to an absurdist art form in Belgian politics. It is a state of mind that goes back to the very creation of Belgium when the two main political factions in the nineteenth century, the Catholics and the Liberals, agreed to secede from the Netherlands by forming the country. This foundational event was consecrated by the adoption of the national motto, "Union makes strength," that today still puzzles millions of Belgians in face of the dizzying discord that reigns in the country.

BELGIAN FRIES

Now I would like to address briefly the culinary aspects of this matter, and the uncertain origins of *moules-frites*. Let's begin with the fries that Europeans are most likely to associate with Belgians, even though it is ingrained throughout the world that they are French fries. Again, note the derisive irony, for a country known for its modesty, attributing its only truly reputed global product to another country.

However, cooking fries is probably the one and only thing really taken seriously by everyone in Belgium. It is for this reason that Belgians, who are so accustomed to and accepting of the Frenchification of their culture, fiercely defend the national origin of *frites*. In my view, this is why the paternity of fries is attributed to them in Europe, although the practice of cooking fries emerged more or less simultaneously in several places, including possibly the north of France, and their invention probably extended over a number of years in the nineteenth century before spreading out.

But what makes fried potatoes authentically Belgian and correctly fried lies in the method of cooking them as it has been done in every Belgian home since the nineteenth century, and at the famous *fritures-frituur* (or *friteries*), the roadside and street-corner stands where heavily salted Belgian fries can be bought wrapped in a paper cone, usually accompanied by mustard, mayonnaise, or any of the popular local condiments. First, you have to start with the right kind of oil and potatoes. Until quite recently, Belgians would cook fries in heavy animal fat, like suet or lard. Though this method was definitely superior for giving a unique flavor, you are better off using a vegetable oil like corn or sunflower oil with a high smoking point. Many Belgians now use solid vegetable shortenings. As for potatoes, Belgians are fond of the Bintje variety because they are very starchy and usually large enough to make long and thick hand-cut fries. In America, the varieties closest to Bintjes are the Yukon Gold and Idaho or Russet baking potatoes. In any case, the ultimate rule is to use older and softer potatoes, not young firm ones that do not contain enough starch to fry correctly.

> Peel the potatoes and cut them to your liking; the one centimeter-wide (⅜ inch) and five to eight centimeter-long (2 to 5 inches) fries are standard. After drying them in a towel, the cut potatoes should be cooked for about five to six minutes in a deep fryer, half-filled with oil heated to 160° C (300–325° F) so as to partially fry them. Every household in Belgium owns an electric fryer or *friteuse* with a thermostat, but these may be less common in the United States. As an alternative, you might want to use a traditional deep fryer with a basket and monitor the temperature.

Here lies the secret of making Belgian-style fries that was revealed to the world only a few dozen years ago: *Potato frying is a two-part process.* The initial part is designed to cook the fries inside and not brown them. The partially fried potatoes are drained and should rest for at least twenty minutes before they are ready for the second frying, also called "shocking." In French, this process is called *saisir* as in "to seize," which indicates that the potatoes will be fried for a brief period, about one to two minutes, at a very high temperature, around 190° C (375° F), which is very close to burning the oil. This final step is evidently designed to brown the fries, making them crisp on the outside and yet softer on the inside. If you use frozen fries, you will be disappointed with the result, and wonder why go through this trouble instead of going to your local McDonald's, which, in fact, uses the two-step process and makes decent fries from frozen potatoes.

One story has it that French fries were served at the White House in Washington around the turn of the nineteenth century at the request of Thomas Jefferson who would have brought the idea back from France. This, I think, is hopelessly off-track in the sense that these "French-style" potatoes would have been nothing more than browned potatoes (*pommes rissolées*) or potatoes fried in a pan with abundant fat. It is notorious in Belgium that until the 1960s, the vast majority of French people had still not acquired the technique of double-frying and the majority of restaurateurs continued to prepare their fries in a pan as still seen in some countries (which is not to say that they would not be good, if greasy). The method imported by Jefferson cannot possibly constitute proof that fries are French in origin since the proper method was still unknown in France a century and a half later.

It is more likely that the First World War was the event that most helped to propagate the Belgian fries beyond the country's borders with the movement of French troops within Belgium and the immigration into France of a Belgian population. More recently, it is the unprecedented globalization of *French* fries promoted by fast-food restaurants, which have learned good fry-making techniques—even if they do use frozen fries—that has made them one of the most-consumed food in the world.

MUSSELS

If, on the one hand, Belgians claim cantankerously that French fries are not French but Belgian, France, on the other, is closely associated with the discovery of mussels as a source of food. Like most innovations, raising mussels or *mytiliculture* emerged out of a combination of necessity and chance. Mussel farming was "discovered" by an Irish sailor, Patrice Walton, who barely escaped a shipwreck on the Vendean coast of France in 1235. The starving Walton, who had set up bird traps on the beach, noticed that the wooden stakes he had driven into the silt were covered with big mussels after each high tide. One day he opened one of them and tasted it. This delicacy must have left a good impression on the courageous man. Walton quickly devised a simple system of stakes and tree branches to retain more mussels. To this day, the Atlantic coast of France remains one of the main centers of mussel production in Europe. The technique is, of course, much more sophisticated nowadays. Most mussels are now grown in parks (enclosed spaces along the coast), hence the name *moules parquées*. Most mussels served nowadays in Belgium come from neighboring countries, mostly from the Zeeland province of the Netherlands. Therefore, by their foreign status and origin, mussels counterbalance the more nationalistically inclined Belgian fries in the *moules-frites* dish.

Mussel preparation is simple, and yet it can be tricky. It should be handled like a fish dish: the less you do, the better! Like fries, mussels should be cooked with great care. Live mussel flesh is flaccid. The heat causes the muscles inside the shell to flex; but overcooking makes them stunted and dry. Overcooked mussels become too rubbery and overcooked fries become too hard. This is hardly a desirable combination. Softness in mussels and steamed vegetables, and crispiness in fries, complemented by smooth mustardy mayonnaise are what you should be looking for if you ever visit Belgium. Keep in mind, however, that the season for mussels usually begins around July 15. Before that time, mussels are said to be milky. Any *moules-frites* served before the season officially opens, an event widely reported in the media in Belgium, should be approached with caution. Here is my personal recipe for Belgian steamed mussels:

> 4 to 6 pounds mussels, thoroughly cleaned and bearded
> Unsalted butter or oil
> 5 large shallots or 1-2 medium onions, finely chopped
> 2 ribs of celery, finely chopped
> 3 cloves of garlic, minced
> 2 carrots, cut (optional)
> 1 teaspoon fresh thyme or ½ teaspoon dried thyme
> 1 bay leaf
> ⅓ cup parsley, finely chopped
> Freshly ground black pepper
> 1–2 cups of dry white wine or Belgian beer such as Duvel or Gueuze (optional)

Ingredients, especially the vegetables can vary. I personally like to add carrots and more vegetables than indicated in the traditional recipe.

Soak the mussels for an hour in salted water. Scrub and beard the mussels, and clean them under cold running water, even if they are sold ready-cleaned. Discard any that are not fully closed.

In a large soup pot, sauté the vegetables in butter or oil, stirring occasionally until soft. Add the mussels and bay leaf, sprinkle with thyme and black pepper. Pour wine or beer over the mussels. Bring to a boil and cover. Lower heat to a simmer and steam the mussels until the shells open (3 to 5 minutes depending on the size of the mussels). Shake the pot or stir the mussels for consistent cooking. Do not overcook the mussels. Discard all mussels that have not opened. Sprinkle with parsley.

Serve in soup dishes or small individual pots with some of the broth.

Although appreciated by specialists, Belgian cuisine suffers from a problem of representation, much like the country itself (Lacrosse 13). As a nation that has always been unable to determine its own fate, Belgium, however, has nevertheless taken advantage of a contingent situation by drawing out of its existential condition a most fascinating cultural production. And *moules-frites* as its designated signature dish have indeed found a remarkable place in the culinary order of national dishes.

If there is one thing to retain from this Belgian gastronomic diversion it is, as Magritte informed us, not to trust obvious depictions. If the *moules-frites* appear to be the classic Belgian dish, it is certainly not for simple and manifest reasons of deliberate national affirmation. Rather, it is by negation, since, as it is constantly repeated in this country-that-is-not-one, nothing in Belgium exists but by negation.

12. Eating Your Way Out:
The Culinary as Resistance in Ferdinand Oyono's
Le Vieux Nègre et la médaille

FRANCIS "PIM" HIGGINSON

Food is increasingly being recognized as a major trope in the Western literary canon. The present collection and this essay are an example of the growing focus on literary discussions of food. In this discussion I have chosen to investigate food and, more specifically, what I call the culinary as a leading trope in African literature. Because the novel I will be discussing here was written in French, I will largely limit myself to French literary history and to the particular implications of French literature's engagement with the culinary and its other.

The novel I have chosen to examine, Ferdinand Oyono's *Le Vieux Nègre et la médaille*, depicts a specific moment in the colonial history of Cameroon and therefore addresses that moment and its colonial occupier, France. As such, the novel's modes of address and its literary tropes, while adaptable to a broad range of Western discourses, are notably attuned to France's cultural landscape of which food is a primary feature. In other words, if food is a salient feature of Oyono's novel, it is precisely because, for France, one of the most meaningful registers in which cultural ascendancy is assessed is the culinary.

In this essay, I will differentiate between food and the culinary, and be using the culinary to connote the process by which the raw ingredients with which we nourish ourselves are transformed and integrated into the social sphere. As we will see, implicit in this nuance is the battleground of the cultural, or, more specifically, whether or not Africans will fall within the parameters of civilization or beyond its pale.

This site of contention is particularly significant because France it would seem, is, throughout its entire modern history, engaged in a quasi-philosophical deliberation on the meaning and importance of the culinary. While Roland Barthes, in *Mythologies*, notes the mythological proportions of the culinary for contemporary France in his two essays "Le vin et le lait" and "Le bifteck et les frites," one could go much farther back in time. Indeed, this mythification of the culinary begins during the Renaissance when the first stirrings of French nation-building are occurring and this same impulse remains operative to this day.

If, for example, we were, albeit somewhat arbitrarily, to cite François Rabelais as ground zero for modern French literature, that is, the birth of the French novel, then the importance of the culinary as a central and guiding trope should be clear. As the father of the French novel, Rabelais depicts many a bacchanalia of a remarkable magnitude. These provide him with an almost archetypal ground in which to produce his caricature of French culture. The first character we encounter in Rabelais's text, Gargantua's father Grandgousier, is introduced to the reader as an eating machine. And this introduction provides Rabelais with the opportunity for one of his famous encyclopedic lists. In this case, it is a list of the things Grandgousier, whose name means big gullet, ingests:

> Was a festive soul in his time, enjoying drink and willingly eating savories. With this in mind, he usually had a good stock of hams from Magence and Bayonne, a load of smoked beef tongue and an abundance of chitterlings sausage when in season and salted beef with mustard, a back-up of salted roe, and a larder full of sausages from Bigorre, Lonquaulnay, Brene and Rouergue. (18)

This list, as every other in which food is the object, shows that Grandgousier's, Gargantua's, and Pantagruel's feasts are not so much unusual in their elements as in their volume: the details, despite their proportions, are recognizably French. Indeed, they are not only French, but as the above passage indicates, specifically regional thereby demonstrating the richness and diversity of France and French culinary/cultural production. "Frenchness," in other words, can be determined through the prism of the culinary.

Rabelais's hyperbolic abundance notwithstanding, what he posits at the outset is the specifically French aspect of his characters. In addition, the extensive list of the "dishes" that these characters ingurgitate provides Rabelais with the opportunity to produce a catalogue in the French vernacular (rather than the Latin that had previously been the norm) of a specifically French national identity, through a medium whose guarantee of Frenchness is for Rabelais self-apparent: for Rabelais food, France, and the French language go together. Ultimately, the novel as Rabelais conceives of it is an essentially national cultural project in which French identity will be explored. Tellingly, he chooses food as one of its first and most important cultural signifiers. Subsequent French literary endeavors follow similar trends—though perhaps not so dramatically.

Another author whom Rabelais greatly influences with his groundbreaking work is Michel de Montaigne. Montaigne also studies the effects of drink and diet and he too conceives of food as a singular sign of one's identity. His *Journal de Voyage en Italie* meditates at length on the culinary habits of the peoples and places he encounters thereby suggesting the importance of these habits in understanding the cultures of others. Similarly, his *Essais* constantly parallel the consumption of food and drink with national and individual characteristics. For Montaigne, "you are what you eat."

Montaigne is particularly important to the present study, because one of the best known of his essays considers food and drink in their connection to culture and identity in the most radical terms possible: "Des Cannibales" (Of cannibals). If, for Rabelais and Montaigne, there is a French culinary identity, likewise, there is the culinary "other"; and in "Des Cannibales," Montaigne chooses the culinary practice most radically alien to his Western reader. Yet, as we know, this is also a ploy. In "Des Cannibales," Montaigne, in a brilliant reversal, alienates the French public from itself and serves up a rhetorical apologia for a ritual that will become increasingly associated with (and used to designate) alterity: the eating of human flesh. Without dwelling on Montaigne's strategy here, it should be noted the extent to which Montaigne cryptically equates the ritual consumption of "flesh and blood" warriors in the New World with the readerly "consumption" of books. Concerning his project, Montaigne, in his "Au Lecteur," states that he is himself the "material" of his book. In essence, Montaigne sees the act of reading and the act of eating as symbolically aligned. Through a process of symbolic transcription, Montaigne familiarizes us with these apparently alien cannibals from the New World. This process of translation also demands a literary transcription in which analogy plays a central role; their "breuvage" resembles "our claret wines" and their food is reminiscent of "pickled coriander" (205). In order for the other to become recognizable, his/her similarity to ourselves must be established in a common currency which for Montaigne becomes the culinary. In this analogical relationship, the other's life magically corresponds to Montaigne's idealized concept of the untainted human subject.

Food and/or eating serve as the starting point for the dialectical play between ourselves as fallen in opposition to the "noble savage" and that binary's negation in which the Western man is enlightened and the other is a brutal and man-eating savage. Thus, at the same moment as Montaigne is penning his essay, the increasing pressure to exploit the non-Western world is suppressing the Montaignian glorification of the other and substituting the genocide and exploitation of the West's "other" that will become the coin of the realm. Historically, a local ritual and literal cannibalism is transformed and reversed by the West into an international cannibalization of the "other" by the West that is to a large degree justified by the literal cannibalism it condemns.

One of the primary justifications for this genocide, particularly in Africa, will depend on the identification of the "natives" as "man eaters."[1] In the place of Montaignian elevation of the other as the Platonic ideal man, Europeans began arguing that: "In dealing with a race composed of cannibals for thousands of years it is necessary to use methods which will best shake their idleness and make them realize the sanctity of work,"as the Belgian King Léopold put it about the Belgian Congo when speaking to a reporter (Hochschild 118). Ritual cannibalism metamorphoses in its reversal into economic cannibalism in which the machinery of capitalism consumes the disposable body of its enslaved labor force.

As proof of this dialectical play, it should be noted that a signal example of the symbolic exploitation of the other are the elliptical culinary references in Hegel's *Phenomenology of Spirit*. For Hegel, one of the marks of the primitive "[pre-]subjectivity," is an oral engagement with the world that fails to recognize the mediating quality of alterity. The primal or "primitive" reaction in the face of alterity, like the behavior of the animal before "the other" is to not "stand idly by," but "despairing of their reality, and completely assured of their nothingness, [. . .] fall without ceremony and eat them up" (65). Later in the *Phenomenology*, in place of this cannibalistic impulse, Hegel instead, albeit cryptically, proposes slavery—that is, the preservation of the other as other (and therefore inferior)—as the rational (i.e., Western) alternative to cannibalism. As I had intimated, "the culinary" becomes a cultural buffer between the raw (and debased) act of consumption and the enlightened European subject—the culinary is to stand in legible contrast to the animal act of ingestion or nourishment.[2]

Freud later recuperates this Hegelian evolutionary paradigm as the "oral stage": "In an infant, the first impulses of sexuality make their appearance attached to other vital functions. His main interest is [. . .] directed to the intake of nourishment" (313), a "[. . .] more primitive stage of organization, in which the erotogenic zone of the mouth plays the chief part" (327). For Freud, as it had been for Hegel, the instinct to consumption (or ingestion) marks the evolutionary lack of a differentiating instinct between the self and the other—a differentiation that is marked for the West by the culinary arts.

If philosophy and psychoanalysis dwell on eating as a primitive and unmediated impulse, likewise anthropology spends considerable energy discussing food. For Lucien Lévy-Bruhl, cannibalism and culinary traditions play a central role in his notoriously racist *La Mentalité primitive*. Likewise, in what can be conceived as a deliberate response to Lévy-Bruhl's questionable analysis, Claude Lévi-Strauss, in *Le Cru et le cuit*, produces a new anthropology in which the essential mythological structures of humanity as a whole will be read through the mythological structures of nourishment. For Levi-Strauss, the archetypal human activity, it would seem, lies in the culinary. In a word, rather than it being the exclusive domain of the West, all humans share the impulse to culturally mark the consumption of food as more than the mere ingestion of nourishment.

This long, but necessary, contextualization has established the cultural and historical weight that both guarantees the importance of the culinary and the extent to which the "other" is the one who stands in absolute contradiction to that culinary tradition. This is one of the primary sites where Oyono, in *Le Vieux Nègre et la médaille*, wages his struggle. If, by the twentieth century, "France is the western country in which the culinary art has occupied the most eminent spot" (Derenne 27), Oyono's argument finds it imperative to (re)situate Cameroon's own culinary tradition within parameters that are symbolically charged for the occupying colonial power. Oyono retraces the epistemology of the culinary backwards and forwards.

In response to the French culinary tradition, Oyono's strategy works on two distinct fronts. The first, which is in part based on an economic analysis, functions in two ways. On the one hand, Oyono defamiliarizes Western food and drink, particularly as they appear in the colonies. This process in itself consists of a depiction of Western food as denatured, particularly in the way that it is marketed to Africans. But Oyono significantly, and somewhat cryptically, also expands this aspect of his critique in the correlation he makes between contemporary Western tastes and the economic exploitation of the "other" who supplies the raw material for the West's increasingly diverse culinary palate.

Simultaneously, and this is the second facet of his approach to food, Oyono describes the Cameroonian culinary tradition as culinary and deeply embedded in a complex and ancient culture. In other words, where someone like the explorer and colonizer Henry Morton Stanley would see nothing but "available space," Oyono fills in the blank lying before the Western gaze with a rich cultural tapestry in which the African is no longer a cannibalistic savage, but a highly sophisticated, culturally complete, and ontologically rooted human being. And this cultural sophistication becomes manifest in an elaborate play of signifiers in which nourishment is intricately allied to the mythical and the social.

The denatured aspect of the Western culinary tradition and its incompatibility with Cameroon are particularly evident in a number of scenes in which Oyono produces a dissonance between the culinary object and his protagonist, Meka, the "vieux nègre" of the title. The most glaring examples of this clash occurs when Meka is invited to see the white commander where he is told that he will receive a medal for his sacrifices to the French colonial cause. Following this encounter, Meka meets the Greek merchant Krominopoulos who has learned of Meka's award. Krominopoulos asks Meka to pick out something, anything he wants, from the store as a sign of his respect: Meka chooses a case of tinned sardines. While the reasons for this choice are never made explicit, what Meka's gesture implies in the symbolic register becomes apparent when, having made the journey to town using his preferred route through the woods, and by his usual means of transportation, on foot, he returns home to the village on the main road in a car.

Meka's entombment or incarceration, one which anticipates his later jailing in the novel, is clear both in the "tin can" in which he is driven home, and in the canned fish he brings with him. If, until then, Meka had been in his own setting and an active member of his village community, his life has just changed dramatically: here life and food/drink mirror each other. As with the little fish packed side by side and preserved in a sterile and alien environment, Meka has lost himself and is drifting in an artificial world in which he has no part—one in which he is merely an object of exploitation. The sardines also serve to remind us of the commodification involved in the industrial production of food in the West. While the novel

never says it outright, it intimates that, whatever the West's dubious relation to its own means of sustenance, Africans following this model will
suffer a slow and steady cultural genocide in which the individual will be
caught up in a machinery whose production, direction, and function are
outside of his/her control.

Symbolically linked to this scene is the blind consumption to which
Meka will fall prey after the medal ceremony. One of the most significant
moments in the novel occurs when Meka and a handful of other
Cameroonian participants are with the white medal delegation. Meka and
his companions get drunk on champagne and whiskey instead of their preferred beverage, the locally made *arki*, an alcohol made of corn and
bananas. This scene provides a kind of split screen of interpretation in
which what appears as confirmation of an African lack of culture to whites
becomes a clash of *two* cultures when Oyono gives Meka's perspective:

> Meka tried analyzing the taste of this wine that he had never drunk
> before in his life and that fizzed all the way into his guts [. . .] He
> thought of the *Eno* that he took in a goblet of water when he had eaten
> too much [. . .] He was surprised that the others had not drained
> their glass of champagne in one gulp without pausing to breathe as he
> had. The Whites and ["evolved"] Blacks barely skimmed the glass
> with their lips. They drank like birds at the edge of a pond. Ah! How
> could these Whites, these chiefs, and the functionaries call themselves
> men? (114)

Where Meka is used to a drinking ritual in which manliness is established
by the rapid downing of the contents of one's glass, he is confronted with a
social performance that he doesn't recognize and that he reads instead as a
failure to follow the proper codes of behavior. Meka sees not his *own* failure
to follow proper etiquette, but the *Whites'*. The white commander's servant, reading the situation through the eyes of his employer, wonders in
turn, "How could this peasant without socks or a tie permit himself to
think he was in his hut?" (114).

Though Oyono provides a double perspective of events in the passage
above, the discrepancies in power between the two groups mean that it is
ultimately the rules of the white ritual that prevail. Thus, when the villagers, lost in what they see as a challenge to the feeble drinking of the
whites, get drunk and unruly, the whites leave and the party is broken up
by the police.[2] The white interpretation of the occasion wins out. For his

part, Meka, passed out in a drunken stupor, is forgotten in the mayhem. He loses his medal and, staggering around in the dark, is finally arrested for being in the white neighborhood after dark.

Meka's imprisonment (in the car, and later in the jail) is compounded by his self-incarceration (reflected in his choice of the sardines and his acceptance of the white commander's medal/liquor) and is in turn thematically linked to his economically subject status. Meka is given the sardines by the Greek merchant, Krominopoulos. Yet, Krominopoulos, in letting Meka choose a case of sardines is, we soon learn, simply returning a fraction of what he has stolen from Meka over the years while "purchasing" his crops.[3]

Meka grows cocoa beans and Krominopoulos regularly underweighs the cocoa beans that Meka brings in. Thus, the subtext here is that, where millet, sorghum, ground nuts, and plantains used to grow, there is now only cocoa, an alien monocrop brought from the new world to satisfy the jaded West's jaded palate. In addition, Meka's "exchange" with the Greek merchant is not even that, but rather a mark of his ever-increasing entrenchment in an economically exploitative system in which he is the victim on every front.

Meka is alienated from his own culinary tradition, as suggested by the monocrop of cocoa as a substitute for the African subsistence crops that preceded them which were the basis of the Cameroonian diet. And Meka increasingly purchases staples that are not part of his traditional diet, staples that are, by their very appearance denatured (canned/packed/preserved). All the while, in each transaction, whether he is selling or buying, Meka is being robbed by an economic system whose principle of profit and surplus value is entirely foreign to him.

Tellingly enough, Meka is also simultaneously enlisted into an economic system that is supplying a French culinary "tradition," one that increasingly relies on the exploitation of foreign lands and people designated as inferior. This exploitation is what brings sugar, coffee, and cocoa to the French table. Thus, the debasement of the Cameroonian culinary tradition and culture is simultaneously contributing to the enrichment of the West's ritualized diet in which abundance and the "exotic" have increased at the same rate as colonial expansion. In the process of distancing itself from the raw materials it ingests, a distance that it claims as a mark of its civilization, France is symbolically cannibalizing its colonial subjects.

This reversal in which the West is depicted as cannibalizing Africa is reinforced by the white characters in the novel. Two of the principal figures, Father Vandermeyer and Gosier d'Oiseau, are described in terms that attest to their cannibalistic impulses. The chief of police Gosier d'Oiseau's name ("Bird Gullet") suggests that he is a cannibal figure who, in his brutal treatment of the villages, symbolically eats those he is ostensibly hired to protect. Likewise, Father Vandermeyer is described as a carnivorous cat who induces Meka to give over his best land to the Catholic church so that cocoa may be grown on it. Vandermeyer's concealed cannibalism only becomes apparent when he "imprudently revealed his claws" (108). This is same priest who has impelled Meka to give away his best cocoa-growing land to the church.

Thus, on the one hand, Oyono suggests that the rich and nourishing culinary tradition of Cameroon is being slowly expunged only to be supplanted by the industrial processed foods of the West.[4] On the other hand, he illustrates the degree to which non-Western labor and resources are being exploited in an economic cannibalism that provides the raw material for the culinary tradition of which France is so proud. In the process, the exploitation of Africans produces the "cultural richness" of the West while magnifying the "cultural disparity" between these two worlds. Perpetuating this cycle, the ever-increasing disparity between the West and Africa ultimately increasingly serves to legitimate Africa's exploitation.

If Oyono gives the lie to the West's claims to civilization and demonstrates the degree to which that seeming richness results from exploitation, he also challenges the interpretation of Africa that would see it as culturally barren. Thus, in the second step of Oyono's challenge to the symbolic emptying of the African space by the colonizer, he provides his reader with an overview of Cameroonian culture in which virtually its every feature is considered in a kind of encyclopedic tabulation of the social and natural worlds reminiscent of Rabelais's text.

Le Vieux Nègre et la médaille can be conceived as a specifically African interpretation of the Rabelaisian project. Oyono begins the process of establishing a specifically Cameroonian literature by filling in the blanks left by European writers.[5] In addition, as with Rabelais, a substantial feature of this project depends on the depiction of a rich natural world that is then vectored into the culinary. That is, the culinary serves as the cultural realm in which the interaction between the human and the natural is substantiated—in which creativity and social sophistication, or civilization, become manifest.

Specifically, Oyono succeeds in providing an astonishing list of the zoological world in which Meka's village is placed, with close to a hundred animals named throughout the novel, one almost every other page. He also provides his reader with a powerful insight into traditional religious and social codes throughout the novel. Where this becomes significant, however, is when animals are related to the social, the mythical, and, particularly, the culinary. The result is that Oyono's novel counters the claim of an African emptiness with a prose that deliberately fills every aspect of the Cameroonian social and geographic landscape, thereby challenging what André Gide in his "Voyage au Congo" describes as "the absence of individuality, of individualization, the impossibility of arriving at a differenciation" (175). And Oyono does this with respect to both the people and the landscape. He begins both to fill in the void that is Africa in the Western imaginary and to delineate its contents with respect to both its people and its landscapes. If, for example, Meka shows his alienation from whiskey and champagne, as we have seen, this does not mean that there is no African drinking culture. We already see this when, on the way to the white commander's office at the beginning of the novel, he stops at Mami Titi's bar where he drinks *arki* and participates in a communal ritual of drinking in which his age and status assure him a seat among his peers. Significantly this scene will be the last time until long after the medal ceremony when Meka will be a fully integrated member of this world.

Oyono notes that "the distillation of their banana and corn alcohol had been forbidden the natives in order to push them towards the European liquor and red wine that were saturating the Supermarket" (15). But he also demonstrates how this economic exploitation is not simply filling in a blank space, but is displacing an existing cultural ritual. What will be lost in the apparently benign outlawing of local *arki* is the space in which it is consumed and the social bonds that this space guarantees.

Though I began this section speaking of Meka's alienation when, at the beginning of the novel, he returns with his case of sardines, there are nevertheless moments that indicate what the sardines are displacing. For example, in a caricature of a French culinary exegesis, Meka's brother in law states, "To appreciate a palm-rat cooked with lemon-grass, wild eggplant and hot peppers such as this one, you must eat it with nothing else" (82). With this explanation, Oyono tells us, albeit jokingly, the extent to which Cameroonians do not simply eat food, but have a *cuisine*. In addition, as Meka's wife Kelara reminds us, the consumption of this cuisine is marked by rituals concerning both the dish and those who eat it:

> —The women will eat with me. The men will go eat with my husband. The woman will eat with their mothers.
> In a fraction of a second, two circles had formed around Meka and Kelara. It was rather a group of two concentric circles among the men. (82)

The food involves a complex preparation and those who eat it are organized in a complex social pattern that reflects gender, age, and standing.

Likewise, the conclusion of the novel shows Meka, now aware of his condition, reintegrated into the village community. This moment is important to my analysis because we find the villagers consuming not European alcohol, but Cameroonian palm wine. Likewise, during this symbolic reunion, one of the most important moments in the novel occurs —the villagers argue about a specific culinary ritual: the eating of sheep's entrails. Here we not only get a greater insight into the complexity of the Cameroonian culinary tradition and the extent to which it implicates everything from religion and gender to social standing, but Meka and the villagers regain their symbolic freedom in the process.

In this discussion, attempting to get the right to speak,

> —oh my elders! Mvondô said timidly who, his eyes lowered, fiddled with the knot of his wrap. I know that I do not have the right to speech among you, but I have eaten the entrails of sheep. (168)

With this declaration, Mvondô claims that he has the status of an elder and therefore the right to speak. Instead he triggers an angry discussion about the loss of tradition for it is taboo for a boy his age to have eaten a dish that is reserved only for the elders of the village:

> —It's an outrage! It's an outrage! protested the audience. A hostile murmur arose from the crowd.
> —Is the young turtle old because it is wrinkled? Who allowed you to eat sheep entrails? Poor Mvondô was being asked.
> —Comments were flying from all sides. Where was this village going if, even the kids, those who only yesterday were running around naked, allowed themselves to eat it! And without the consent of the clan! [. . .] So there were people who were pretending to be White in

the village! What an outrage! Eating a whole sheep in hiding and authorizing the young to eat its entrails without warning the village. (169)

The culinary marks one of the most significant features of the cultural landscape of Meka's village. The disappearance of this culture is finally equated with the presence of the colonial power. This moment marks Meka's return to the fold and his realization that he has been a victim of white manipulation.

The sheep's stomach becomes the cultural signifier for an elaborate and ancient culture that is being eradicated by the colonial occupier. It is specifically the sheep's stomach that reminds Meka of his own world and values, and its invocation also challenges any assumptions the Western reader of *Le Vieux Nègre et la médaille* might have had about Cameroon's lack of history and culture. Significantly, it is the culinary that allows this moment of cultural self-recognition and of ritual bonding to occur.

Thus, Oyono tells us, rather than an empty landscape ready for exploitation and a people who, in the words of Hegel "despairing of [the world's] reality, and completely assured of [its] nothingness, [. . .] fall without ceremony and eat [it] up," there is instead precisely the opposite: an elaborate ceremony in which the animal is partitioned and prepared according to an elaborate culinary code.

In conclusion, Oyono, in *Le Vieux Nègre et la médaille*, answers the debasement of Africa in the most powerful terms he can muster. He uses the West's most prized weapon, writing, to counter the depiction of the African as a culturally backward object. In the process, he answers the West's literary elevation of its own culinary tradition and the debasement of its other point by point. To accomplish this, Oyono's argument runs through two major steps. On the one hand, Oyono demonstrates the extent to which the African's adoption of Western culinary traditions amounts to a denaturing of his/her own culture. In the same gesture, Oyono also shows the extent to which the West is exploiting Africa in order to enrich its own culinary culture. This double gesture allows him to counter the image of the African as a cannibal and instead, in an echo of Montaigne's essay, to reverse the stereotype so that it becomes the West that is cannibalizing Africa.

The second aspect of Oyono's project involves filling the African landscape that Europeans have historically read as empty. Instead of a barren land filled with a barbarian people, Oyono provides an image in which the African people and world live in a symbiotic and ancient relationship in which a culinary culture plays a pivotal role. Where the West sees a void, Oyono counters with an image in which eating is not the mere ingestion of the "other" that was behind the West's conception of the African as a cannibal. Instead, the use and nourishment provided by the natural world undergo a symbolically charged transformation by which they become part of the African *cultural* landscape. Finally, while this interpretation of Oyono's novel has largely limited itself to the culinary and to a primarily binary relationship between Africa and the West, it should be noted the extent to which Oyono himself, as the figure of the interpreter, already knows that the process of literary and literal translation is orienting both Africa and the West toward new and uncharted culinary frontiers. But that is a whole other kettle of fish.

NOTES

1. In addition, Montaigne's discussion takes place in terms that speak directly to the violence that surrounds him. The Saint Bartholomew's massacre had just occurred in which Protestants had been butchered by Catholics. As we know, one of the primary differences between the two religions lies in the interpretation of the host and the wine during mass. For Catholics, they are literally transformed into the blood and flesh of Christ whereas, for Protestants, they are symbolic substitutes. Thus the murder of hundreds of Protestants was itself undertaken, in part, in defense of a form of ritual cannibalism. Yet Montaigne's understanding of cannibalism's profoundly entrenched symbolic importance in Western culture would largely go unnoticed. Subsequent thinkers would go on to exploit the image of the cannibal as the symbol of alterity or prehumanity, largely ignoring the symbolic lines of communication that Montaigne had opened.

2. White drinking is also marked by hypocrisy since the narrator notes that while whites perform a ritual of drinking in public where they do not get drunk, they nevertheless do get drunk at night when they are hidden from the "native gaze."

3. The novel teaches us that the Greek community in Cameroon is largely a merchant class that does the colonial power's dirty work. This intimate alliance becomes particularly clear in two instances. The first occurs when another Greek character, Pipiniakis, receives a "Légion d'honneur"—a real symbol of France's recognition for his services—during the same medal ceremony in which Meka is awarded what we suspect to be a mere trinket. In the second, recapping the party afer the ceremony, its African participants note that "the High Commissioner and all the French Whites from Doum were seated on the bench with the Greeks, the very ones who prevented the Backs from becoming rich" (124).

4. To understand the degree to which the West has been successful in this regard, one need only look at the ever-increasing consumption of Western products in Africa—even such simple ingredients as peanut butter, which demands no expense or technological sophistication at all. Yet Africans are exporting their peanuts to places like Holland and then importing the processed product for several times its initial value.

5. My present analysis begs the question of Rabelais's use of the vernacular. One of the noteworthy elements of Rabelais's writing is that it is in French. There remains a significant debate in Africa and in other non-Western countries about the use of French in a project of national self-determination. While I cannot address this complex question here, one reason for this is clearly is that, where Rabelais is addressing his own countrymen, Oyono is speaking as much to the French as to Cameroonians.

13. The Politics of Food in
Post-WWII French Detective Fiction

PIERRE VERDAGUER

Judging by the frequent mention of food and cooking in current detective fiction, it would seem that investigative activities and interest in cuisine are not only compatible but complementary. Since this is particularly true in the United States today, it is useful to look first into representative American gastronomic mysteries. The specific use of food references in French fiction can then be examined with these models in mind. In this country as well as in France, it is not unusual for an investigator to take a keen interest in well-prepared and tasty dishes, and attention to food in detective fiction on either side of the Atlantic is not new. As early as the mid-1930s, Rex Stout's hero, Nero Wolfe, became the prototype of the American detective with gastronomic taste, with the series that began in 1934 for *Fer De Lance*, and which ended in 1975. Wolfe is distinguished by a hearty appetite proportional to his impressive weight (he is usually described as weighing a "seventh of a ton"). Although he leaves food preparation to his cook, Fritz, he is a true connoisseur and does not hesitate to launch into indignant diatribes when he considers that gastronomic faux pas are committed by fellow citizens with less discerning palates. For example: "Millions of American women, and some men, commit that outrage every summer day. They are turning a superb treat into mere provender. Shucked and boiled in water, sweet corn is edible and nutritious; roasted in the husk in the hottest possible oven for forty minutes, it is ambrosia" (*Murder is Corny* 94). Wolfe's Parisian contemporary is Commissaire Maigret, who appeared in a series of seventy-five novels by Georges Simenon and published from 1929 to 1973. Maigret is by far the most famous of all French investigators, is portly as well, and is similarly endowed with a healthy appetite and a penchant for satisfying cuisine, although his taste is somewhat less upper-class than Wolfe's, as shall be seen.

Over the past years, and noticeably since the 1980s, what used to be an occasional motif or a character's idiosyncracy has become a central theme. Publications have even been devoted to the food and crime combination, particularly in Great Britain and in this country (Manson; Haining). Furthermore, novels usually referred to as "culinary whodunits" by newspaper critics have come to constitute a subgenre. In the American culinary whodunit, characters display more than a liking for tasty dishes. Their interest in food is taken a step further. More often than not, the story is interspersed with complete recipes, which can be as carefully laid out as in a cookbook and may even be printed on separate pages, although they have nothing or little to do with the story line. Their main function is to reinforce the culinary aura of the novel. As would be expected, in such books kitchens become loci of paramount importance and are described in great detail. They are eminently revealing of the cook's personality. For example, in Dr. Scarpetta's kitchen, the appliances are "modern but few" (Cornwell 28). Goldy Schulz, a caterer, has a "commercial-size kitchen," complete with "walk-in refrigerator" (Davidson 4); and wealthy Angie Amalfi's kitchen is "a food columnist's dream," with the latest and most expensive equipment including a "fire engine red stove imported from France" (Pence 5). In its most extreme form, the culinary whodunit signals itself by the very title of the story, which as a rule is a play on words suggestive of its double orientation, both murderous and gastronomic. Some examples: *Something's Cooking, Too Many Cooks, Cooking Up Trouble* (Joanne Pence); *Prime Cut, The Grilling Season, Dying for Chocolate, The Cereal Murders* (Diane Mott Davidson).

This subgenre has therefore acquired specific and recognizable traits, but its most salient feature is that it emphasizes cooking (i.e., the act of defining oneself through food preparation) rather than epicurean pleasure. This shift is very logically reflected in the investigator's professional occupation. For example, Diane Mott Davidson's Goldy and Joanne Pence's Angie are respectively a caterer and a food columnist. It is hardly surprising, therefore, that an actual food critic, the *Washington Post*'s Phyllis Richman, tried her hand at this subgenre: *The Butter Did It: A Gastronomic Tale of Love and Murder*. As for Patricia Cornwell's Kay Scarpetta, she may be a chief medical examiner by profession, but she is also a *cordon bleu* who finds much needed solace in the privacy of her kitchen. In *Postmortem*, Cornwell's first novel, cooking is revealingly declared to be the best antidote to life's many miseries (108). Kitchen work—as a creative, liberating, and satisfying pursuit rather than a family obligation—and investigative work have thus become parallel and sometimes closely interconnected occupations.

One would assume that the culinary whodunit would have developed as a subgenre in countries with both a well-established gastronomic tradition and a strong interest in detective fiction. The example of Spain comes to mind. Manuel V. Montalbán's character, private eye Pepe Carvalho, is known like Nero Wolfe for his hearty appetite and discerning taste, but his interest in cooking and recipes mark him as more of a contemporary of Joanne Pence's Angie Amalfi or Patricia Cornwell's Kay Scarpetta. In France, although detective fiction has developed into a literary phenomenon of impressive proportions, the culinary whodunit does not constitute a subgenre, though *polars gastronomiques* have been published. Chef Jean-Pierre Xiradakis's *Fricassée de meurtres à la bordelaise*, written in collaboration with journalist Pierre Leterrier, is a case in point.[1] This story is very much in the style of the American culinary whodunit (it even includes a recipe), but it serves a very different cause: within the context of the ongoing gastronomic battle between *les anciens et les modernes* (in other words the defenders of traditional taste and the proponents of *nouvelle cuisine*), the authors valiantly take the side of traditionalists.

This novel, however, is not representative of a general trend. The paucity of *polars gastronomiques* may seem paradoxical in a nation which takes so much pride in its culinary achievements. One explanation is that today's French detective literary scene is dominated by politically conscious writers, who are often former Marxists, Trotskyists, or anarchists, and who denounce social evils through novels in the tradition of the *roman noir*.[2] This leaves little room for novelists without a political axe to grind. In fact, Jean-Pierre Xiradakis's *polar gastronomique* is not really an exception in this respect since it also defends a cause, although hardly an ideological one. Furthermore, from a cultural standpoint, refined cuisine, considered a part of high culture, does not logically fit as a central theme in popular literature. To put it differently, since detective fiction is viewed as nonmainstream, and since haute cuisine is a societal preoccupation and a matter of national pride, bringing them together would seem culturally incongruous. According to the same paradigm, however, this pattern of incompatibility would not apply in the case of less refined forms of cooking, and the fact is that plebeian dishes are much more likely to be mentioned in *romans policiers* than are sophisticated ones (the Maigret series is emblematic of this pattern).

In the United States, where gastronomy is not regarded as a national priority (though this does not mean that it is without importance), there is a good chance that the pursuit of culinary excellence will be perceived as a "minority" interest. This in turn may explain why there is more cultural compatibility between cuisine (as a literary topic) and detective fiction (as a nonmainstream, although highly popular, genre) in America than in France. And in the American culinary whodunit, sophisticated food preparation is very likely to be linked to a woman's search for self-assertiveness, fulfillment, and autonomy. Diane Mott Davidson's character, for example, is described as an abused wife whose life blossoms once she leaves her husband and launches herself in her catering career. In this country, culinary activity can therefore symbolize a woman's quest for independence, which would not be the case in France, where the kitchen is hardly perceived as the place for a woman's emancipation.

Clearly, the use of culinary references in French detective fiction is dictated by cultural criteria that differ from American ones. As a rule, mentions of food and cooking tend to complement the social backdrop of the story and reveal the milieu described by the author, very much in the nineteenth-century tradition of realism. Food references also reflect the cultural orientation of novels, which range from ethnocentric to multiethnic, and are therefore indicative of conservative or liberal perspectives, such as Pierre Magnan's or Daniel Pennac's, respectively (Verdaguer, *Séduction* 23–137). By and large, in a country where detective fiction is commonly used as the literary means to denounce injustice, food references are designed to reveal inadequacies caused by society's ill-conceived priorities. Junk food and bad food are constant reminders that present-day capitalism is at work to produce a tasteless and depressing environment. In France, food can frequently acquire an ideological flavor.

Within post-WWII French detective fiction, Belgian-born Georges Simenon (1903–89) remains the best known of all novelists, and his character, *Commissaire* Maigret, although introduced in the late 1920s, is still the dominant and archetypal figure in contemporary *romans policiers*. Maigret continues to be perceived as the epitome of the French investigator, who solves mysteries by letting himself be suffused with the atmosphere of the place where a crime has been committed as a way to understand the motives of his suspects.[3]

Looking into the culinary preferences of this eminently French character is therefore essential. Why is Maigret considered to be so representative of French investigators? One of his noteworthy characteristics is that, like most other French fictional policemen, he comes from humble stock.[4] Even though *commissaires* are solidly middle class, Maigret tends to feel uncomfortable in the presence of the well-to-do and is far more at ease with the have-nots of the world (servants, low-ranking employees, and the like): "It was not his kind of case. He was not familiar with that kind of milieu, and found it difficult to comprehend it" (*Maigret se fâche* 65). Maigret, throughout his Parisian career, remains faithful to his rural origins, and not surprisingly, once he retires, he returns to his ancestors' ways. He is shown in retirement tending to his vegetable garden "barefoot in wooden sabots," wearing blue cloth pants like all French manual workers and a peasant-style shirt "open on his hairy chest" (*Maigret se fâche* 14). As would be expected, a bourgeois woman who has heard of his investigative talents and who calls on him to ask for help mistakes him for the gardener and, incidentally, believes that Madame Maigret is the maid.

These details are revealing: they emphasize class barriers and imply that regardless of how successful one may have been in one's professional life, differences related to a person's upbringing cannot be eradicated. This is clearly an indication of the rigidity of the French class structure, but from a more symbolic point of view, it also reflects the need for policemen who serve the French Republic to be mindful of the underprivileged. In France, it is clear that inspectors must remain true to their humble origins so that justice and equity may prevail.

Maigret's culinary taste, therefore, very logically reflects his social background: he prefers hearty and unsophisticated homemade dishes, as evidenced in this allusion to the couple's daily routine:

> It was Tuesday, hence the day for macaroni au gratin. With the exception of Thursday's pot-au-feu, the menu on other days would vary from week to week, but for years, Tuesday's dinner had been reserved for macaroni au gratin to which was added finely chopped ham and, on occasion, a truffle that had been even more finely minced. (*Maigret et le clochard* 84)

Macaroni au gratin is typical of Maigret's milieu. It is a plain, tasty and nourishing dish, very much like pot-au-feu, whose preparation does not require particular skills. From a class perspective, it can be described as democratic or rather, "Republican," to use the preferred French term that evokes unity against aristocratic exploitation.[5] Even the name "macaroni au gratin" lacks sophistication in French and makes it difficult to link the dish to the gastronomic tradition. As for the allusion to truffles, it has in this case more to do with rural cooking habits than with refined cuisine. In the Maigret series, there are innumerable references to hearty homemade dishes with comparable connotations of simplicity, equality, and fraternity such as *blanquette de veau*, a traditional creamy veal stew (*Un échec de Maigret* 34), or *oeufs au lait*, a type of custard (*Maigret et le corps sans tête* 163). In no way could these preparations be evocative of culinary sophistication.

Not surprisingly, Maigret is particularly comfortable in kitchens, the main room in low-income homes, where he will readily chat with witnesses, far from bourgeois sitting rooms, to the amazement and delight of servants: "In the kitchen! At a table without a cloth. And yet it was true" (*Maigret se fâche* 59). That Maigret should not mind sitting at a table without a cloth is clearly revealing of his nonbourgeois upbringing, and symbolic of his truly "Republican" outlook. He is undoubtedly faithful to his sans-culotte forefathers. It is also known that the French *commissaire* has a weakness for beer and that, true to his rural origins, he occasionally relishes a glass of *prunelle* (sloe gin). Cognac would be too bourgeois and whisky too modern, or too exotic, and therefore alien to the peasant tradition. When absolutely needed, however, and in order to blend in, Maigret is known to make exceptions: "In keeping with the local color, Maigret ordered a whisky" (*Maigret, Lognon et les gangsters* 73).

It is true that beverage preferences are linked to regional customs, and one would logically assume that Simenon, being from a beer-drinking nation, would reflect his personal taste in his character. However, it is also true that the consumption of beer in France has increased greatly since World War II, while that of low-priced table wine has noticeably decreased.[6] It can be said that beer has by and large replaced ordinary red wine as the emblematic low-cost everyday national beverage. Furthermore, beer has much more of a democratic aura. It transcends class differences unlike wine, which cannot be as generic since its quality and price vary greatly.

Furthermore, beer is linked symbolically to the mythical as well as historical foundations of the nation. Under the Third Republic (and later the Fourth), elementary history books were reputed to start with the words "Nos ancêtres les Gaulois [Our ancestors, the Gauls]," and those national ancestors were known to drink *cervoise* (the Gallic word for beer).[7] Since it first appeared at the end of the 1950s, the highly successful comics series *Astérix*, set in 50 B.C., has reinforced the image of a utopian Gallic world of harmonious human relations where beer, well before the Republic came of age, was the beverage of *liberté, égalité, fraternité*. Wine, on the other hand, was left to the Romans, portrayed in *Astérix* as the decadent victims of progress and administrative tyranny.

The same mythical logic prevails in Anne de Leseleuc's historical detective stories, which are set in the Roman Empire during the first century. Her hero is a Gallo-Roman lawyer by the name of Marcus Aper.[8] Like the characters in *Astérix*, Marcus has a strong preference for his ancestors' *cervoise*, although he is not over-nationalistic and lives happily in Rome, where wine is naturally preferred. Once, when traveling in Gaul on a barge, where a meal has been served with red wine in accordance with the preference of the wealthy, he even bribes a mariner to obtain the man's lower-class beer (*Les Vacances de Marcus Aper* 135). Since *cervoise* is the beverage of the majority, Marcus's choice has a definite egalitarian overtone. It is also very telling that his personal servant, a slave whom he has freed, should spontaneously link beer to freedom. When asked whether he likes good beer, the former slave answers "Beer and freedom! [*La cervoise et la liberté*]" (*Le Trésor de Boudicca* 21). Beer is clearly an ideological metaphor.

Beer drinking is also indicative of a wholesome way of life. Its universal appeal is thus not only due to its democratic aura but to its healthful characteristics. In the Maigret series, in keeping with dominant French beliefs, it is defined as more refreshing and thirst quenching than alcoholic: "I am so thirsty! . . . A glass of cool beer, with a foamy head" (*Maigret et le clochard* 79). It is furthermore the beverage of well-balanced individuals like Marcus: "He felt good, his well-being encased by skin stretched taut over powerful muscles. He liked women, beer, and slowly simmered stews. He liked riding in the forest" (*Marcus Aper et Laureolus* 12).

Interestingly, these healthy and democratic culinary preferences (beer and stew) closely match Maigret's. Marcus, by the way, is also quite fond of *saucisson*, a type of hard salami emblematic of French working-class taste. In Leseleuc's novels, there are innumerable references to snacks composed essentially of *saucisson* and other hearty but unsophisticated meats, like *boudin* (blood sausage) (*Vacances* 181). From this perspective, Marcus has much in common with Bérurier, Frédéric Dard's well-known post-WWII Gargantuan character with a typically "Republican" and plebeian attitude.

Saucisson-loving investigators in the Republic's service are in culinary harmony with the common people, regardless of the historical context.

This preference that French investigators, as civil servants and official representatives of the State, display for good, nourishing, simple food is common enough to constitute a cultural pattern. Sauce-laden dishes, hearty stews, *blanquettes*, bean-based *cassoulets,* and other caloric delicacies thus constitute the pabulum of the Republican hero. Whereas the setting for British novels in the tradition of Conan Doyle, Agatha Christie, Dorothy Sayers, and P.D. James tends to be elegant and refined, implying also that characters have excellent table manners, the setting for *romans policiers* since World War II has typically featured common cooking and, occasionally, bad or even revolting table behavior. This is systematically the case in the San-Antonio series, whenever attention is focused on Bérurier and his total lack of breeding. Bérurier is a strong-minded commoner who will not change his ways and remains true to his milieu regardless of the situation. A short sentence suffices to describe him: "He holds a liter of red wine with one hand and a gigantic *rillettes* sandwich with the other, which he devours greedily" (*Viva Bertaga* 13). Or again, "He inhales two hundred yards of spaghetti, generously splashing tomato sauce on his shirt [*limouille*], his suit [*costard*], and a bit on mine" (*Champagne pour tout le monde* 80). Bérurier is a living caricature whose stubbornness, insatiable appetite, and physical strength make him comparable to the comics hero Obélix, Astérix's alter ego (Verdaguer "Héros"). However, more than Obélix, he exemplifies both a taste for popular food (he is, for example, fond of *saucisson*, rillettes, camembert, etc.) and the rebellious denial of upper-class manners. He is, in other words, a living Republican contradiction of aristocratic style.

Without any doubt, an antielitist stance prevails in French detective fiction. Significantly, the only famous French character who is close to the English tradition of gentility, Maurice Leblanc's turn-of-the-century Arsène Lupin, is known as *"le gentleman-cambrioleur* [the gentleman thief]," subtitle of the first book of these series, published in 1908, and followed by about fifty more. Lupin, who has the taste and manners of a nobleman, is by definition the exact opposite of the policeman in the Republic's service. In fact, in Lupin's adventures, the police force is systematically ridiculed and declared to be "eminently comical," as he writes in another 1908 story, *Arsène Lupin contre Herlock Sholmès* (19). It seems that in France, if the hero is to be aristocratic, he must live the life of an outlaw.

He will not, in other words, be allowed to represent the State and the nation's people.

Representativeness, linked to the official police status, has always played an important part in French detective fiction and explains to a great extent why, unlike in Anglo-Saxon countries, private eyes have never dominated the genre.[9] Whether they are civil servants or not, French investigators come as a rule from the same underprivileged socioeconomic milieu. This was true, from the 1920s to the 1960s, of Simenon's *commissaire* Maigret, Léo Malet's gumshoe Nestor Burma, and Frédéric Dard's *commissaire* San-Antonio and is still true of characters created much more recently by Jean Amila (Inspector "Géronimo"), Didier Daeninckx (Inspector Cadin), Christian Jacq (Judge Pazair), Thierry Jonquet (Inspector Dimeglio), Pierre Magnan (Commissaire Laviolette), and Daniel Pennac (Malaussène), to mention only a few.

A humble background may imply a lack of culinary sophistication but does not preclude the enjoyment of food. In fact, outside the *roman noir* tradition, French detective fiction has been characterized by simple table pleasures, which are often revealing of traditionalism. Commissaire San-Antonio, for example, has a weakness for *pieds et paquets* and *blanquette de veau* (like Maigret) cooked exclusively by his mother, and therefore linked to ancestry. Both dishes are the complete opposite of *cuisine minceur* (light cooking), particularly *pieds et paquets*, made of lambs' feet and tripe and cooked slowly for several hours. Culturally, these specialties belong in the same category as stews and macaroni au gratin. They are heavy, caloric foods indicative first of a strong attachment to home cooking and ancient lore and, consequently, suggestive of a strong past orientation. Magnan's Commissaire Laviolette is not unlike Maigret, but he is more of a sensualist and derives poetic enjoyment from aromatic emanations. As he strolls around a small Provence town, he inhales with great delight the smells that waft from neighborhood kitchens, which are described as "mixed smells of hare stew and wild boar casserole [*lièvres en civet et . . . marcassin en daube*] (*Le commissaire dans la truffière* 99). These delicious smells clearly have the ability to bring past and present together through a synesthetic process.

Stew lovers like Maigret and Laviolette are undoubtedly culturally conservative, and it is telling that Simenon and Magnan should describe in great detail settings (respectively Paris and small Provençal towns) that appear to have been frozen in time, although Simenon's stories span close to half a century and Magnan's, which supposedly take place today, give the impression of being set in pre-WWII France.

If stews and casseroles are on the one hand revealing of a democratic stance and on the other of a yearning for cultural permanence, they also require ravenous appetites characteristic of ancient mythical heroes, *bons géants* (gentle giants), who, according to Dontenville, are specifically French (15–16). These *bons géants* of French folklore are blessed with great virtues, they are not easily duped, and they are endowed with a cheerful personality. Gargantua, Obélix, and even Frédéric Dard's Bérurier are among their fictional avatars. In the French tradition, great appetites, which heavy stews and pasta casseroles are most likely to satisfy, are thus usually suggestive of moral strength as well as physical might. Upright investigators must display a genuine interest in heavy cuisine and eat impressive amounts of food. This in turn accounts for their equally impressive body weight.[10] Maigret is from this point of view prototypic. In Simenon's stories, there are numerous allusions to his heaviness. Once, for example, in order to physically defeat a criminal who is giving him trouble, Maigret throws himself on his opponent "with all his weight" (*La Pipe de Maigret* 181), and simply pins him down until reinforcements arrive. Bérurier is the closest in appearance to gentle giants, but the man under whose orders he operates, good-looking and male chauvinist Commissaire San-Antonio, is no weakling either, since he is supposed to weigh close to 200 pounds. As for Magnan's Commissaire Laviolette, he is described as "a nice big guy [*un bon gros*]" (*Les Secrets de Laviolette* 79). All these characters are as much faithful servants of the Republic and of the French people as they are enthusiastic eaters and drinkers.

In France, as a rule, fine policemen tend to be fleshy trenchermen. Anne de Leseleuc's Marcus Aper is another investigator who is typically ravenous as soon as he gets up and requires a substantial breakfast composed of various cold cuts, as is the case in *Marcus Aper chez les Rutènes* (44). In the same novel, a luncheon described as "frugal," although it features *saucisson*, blood sausage, and cheese, fails to satisfy him (36). The man's needs for nourishment are remarkable and, as is to be expected, are in keeping with his muscular strength and his uprightness. Incidentally, Arsène Lupin, as an aristocratic and therefore antithetical hero, is characterized by a total lack of interest in table pleasures. Like Sherlock Holmes, he even shows a propensity for asceticism. The following scene, which takes place in a restaurant, is in this respect revealing:

"What will the gentlemen have?"
"Whatever you wish," Arsène Lupin answered, in the manner of a man uninterested in food-related matters. . . . "Whatever you wish, as long as it contains neither meat nor spirits."
The waiter left with a disdainful look.
I exclaimed: "Don't tell me you are still a vegetarian!"
"More than ever," Lupin asserted. . . .
"And you never cheat?"
"Oh! I do . . . whenever I attend functions . . . not to stand out." (67)

Interestingly, Lupin relaxes his self-imposed dietary discipline in the same way that Maigret drinks whisky: when the situation requires it. It would be hard to imagine Simenon's character and his various epigones, such as Laviolette, as vegetarians. Such culinary self-denial would be perceived as both un-French and non-Republican with regard to the national mythological paradigm.

In keeping with a dominant cliché, food, and to a lesser extent cooking, often have a comforting effect. This is hardly unusual. For Montalbán's Pepe Carvalho, for example, culinary pursuits are a way to retreat into the past, and for the heroines of the American culinary whodunits already mentioned, cooking is akin to a revitalizing process. Each time, however, the banal compensational value of food may serve a different function and is linked to specific cultural priorities.

In France, most post-WWII investigators have in common a more or less misanthropic outlook: Simenon's Maigret, Dard's San-Antonio, Magnan's Laviolette, Leseleuc's Marcus, Pennac's Malaussène, Jacq's Pazair, to mention only a few representative characters, share a bleak perspective of human nature. By and large, it can be said that their interest in cuisine is proportional to their degree of pessimism. Commissaire Laviolette has thus a very logical explanation for his corpulence: "One day, in view of man's deeds, I started to overeat in search of solace" (*Les Secrets de Laviolette* 79). Eating is therefore not caused by personal disorders, which would be the conventional psychological explanation, but by a form of existential despair. However, in Laviolette's case, solace implies discriminating taste since the *commissaire* is more of a gastronome than most of his fellow pessimists. In France, misanthropes can be epicures, but on the whole, they have little interest in the act of cooking as a healing process.

Jean-Claude Izzo's inspector, Fabio Montale, is an exception. Not surprisingly for a French inspector, Montale has marked misanthropic tendencies, like his fictional predecessors and contemporaries. Mentally exhausted by his fellow men's baseness, he can only find inner peace in his kitchen, as if only culinary aroma could cleanse the effluvia of a rotten world: "Outside, there would always be the stench of rot" (279). The kitchen is therefore his ultimate sanctuary: "I could finally find peace. Cooking affected me that way. My mind stopped meandering in complex thought patterns. It devoted itself entirely to aromas, taste, and pleasure" (117).

Montale is not unlike Montalbán's Carvalho and may have been inspired by the famous Spanish character.[11] He has been raised in Marseille and is of Italian descent, as his name suggests, and he and Carvalho are culturally Mediterranean, which dictates their culinary preferences. Montale's favorite recipes, however, are not only a tribute to his ancestry but to his humble milieu, which is in keeping with the French Republican paradigm. His interest lies strictly in simple Italian dishes, not haute cuisine. Here is an example:

> I had started cooking early in the morning, while listening to old blues by Lightnin' Hopkins. Once I had gutted and cleaned the seabass, I stuffed it with fennel, then doused it with olive oil. Then I prepared the lasagna sauce. The rest of the fennel had cooked slowly in salted water with a bit of butter. In a well-oiled frying pan, I had sauteed minced onion together with garlic and finely chopped hot peppers. I added a spoonful of vinegar and tomatoes which had been placed briefly in boiling water, then diced. (116–17)

Izzo's *Total Khéops*, with its detailed recipes, has the characteristics of a culinary whodunit, but in this case, the Italian-Provençal cooking serves the purpose of reinforcing the character's ethnicity. In this respect, Izzo's inspector is very much an investigator of the 1980s and 1990s: he lives in a multicultural society.

In late-twentieth-century French detective fiction, culinary choices often reflect a preference for cultural eclecticism, which does not mean that ethnocentric perspectives are defunct. Daniel Pennac and Thierry Jonquet, two novelists who came to fame in the 1980s, are representative of this trend. Pennac's main character, Malaussène, who takes care of his numerous brothers and sisters, is a virtual orphan. What has become of his father it is not clear (there is a mere allusion to him in *Au bonheur des ogres* [32]). As for his mother, she is simply never at home. However, Malaussène is the de facto adoptive son of an Algerian family living in Paris—they are first mentioned in *Au bonheur des ogres* (52–53)—and the Ben Tayebs provide love and moral support instead of his real parents. They also provide vast amounts of food: the father, Amar, is a restaurateur "at whose place the Malaussène tribe has always eaten" (*La Petite Marchande de prose* 44). The Algerian parents thus play the role of the French absentees, with the ironic implication that Malaussène, whose generation must live with the shameful heritage of colonization, is now in the care of those who once were colonized. Symbolically, Malaussène has been orphaned by history, and it is now up to him, alone in a world where the colonizing generation no longer has a significant role to play, to atone for his nation's historical sins.

This being France, and Pennac being a humorist, Malaussène's atonement takes the form of food acculturation: the heirs of colonization spurn traditional *blanquette* and show a strong preference for couscous. When Clara, Malaussène younger sister, gets married, the feast is therefore logically in the Arab culinary tradition: "Mo le Mossi and Simon the Kabyle follow Clara in a van where seven lambs on the spit await the final mechouis. . . . Half a ton of couscous accompanies the mechouis (*La Petite Marchande de prose* 64). In Pennac's works, painful historical memories must be buried under mounds of couscous, although it is not clear whether the process of ingestion and digestion can neutralize them.

In Thierry Jonquet's books, the emphasis is on eclectic harmony, as is exemplified by his team of inspectors who work well together, although they are of diverse ethnic origins. These policemen are even characterized by their religious beliefs, which goes totally against the Republican tradition of laicism. Simenon or Dard, for example, would never have felt the need to specify their heroes' religious preferences: as long as one accepts the traditional Republican ideology, along with its areligious—or even antireligious—dictate, there is no reason to do so. The fact that policemen in the Republic's service should now be defined by their religion (one policeman is Jewish, another Protestant [19, 215] is a new cultural phenomenon, one that has an incidence upon the politics of food and therefore deserves attention.

Inspector Choukroun, clearly of North African descent, is described as being under the religious, and therefore culinary, influence of his brother-in-law, an orthodox Jew who owns a restaurant that specializes in kosher pizza. Elsewhere in *Moloch*, which in this respect contains better examples than *Les Orpailleurs*, another novel with the same cast of characters, references to Nazi atrocities and to kosher specialties are often complementary as Szaclman, a survivor of Buchenwald, typically reminisces about concentration camps while setting food on his table: "He unpacked the rest of the food: tarama with dill, a few slices of pastrami, kosher cold cuts, half-sour pickles, onion bread, chopped liver, cheese cake, and also two containers of creamy noodles" (*Moloch* 240–41). This feast, served to Nadia, a young woman whose parents shamefully profited from the Holocaust, has a symbolic function comparable to that of couscous in Pennac's books. It is incidentally telling that Szaclman should speak of "converting" people to good Jewish cooking (241), as if heightened awareness of past horrors could be induced by this form of culinary conversion. Both Nadia and Malaussène eat the food of the victimized to atone for historical injustices for which they feel indirectly responsible. There are other references in Jonquet's books to nontraditional or exotic foods. There is an allusion to a Thai restaurant, for example, where one can eat such delicacies as "chicken soup with lemon grass and steamed fish wrapped in banana leaves, among other specialties" (*Moloch* 113). Here again, these culinary details have little to do with exoticism and are mainly indicative of an ecumenical posture.

However, this multicultural trend has not replaced the more ethnocentric outlook. Both tendencies simply coexist in today's French detective fiction, and although culinary imports are numerous today, the national tradition is still quite strong. Interestingly, in some cases, haute cuisine has even replaced the democratic heavy stews, pasta casseroles, and *saucissons* favored by Maigret and his various avatars. Although this emphasis on gastronomic refinement is not on the same scale as in culinary whodunits, it is characteristic of recent years. Magnan's Laviolette, for example, may be a 1970s version of Maigret, but he is much more of a gastronome than his interwar model. This is in keeping with the evolution of the genre. Laviolette and his friend, Judge Chabrand, are in fact consummate epicures: "They settled comfortably in the eating and drinking delights of Digne. Thrush and wild boar pâté, quails and woodcocks for the select few came out of hiding. Superb discoveries were made in the wine cellars of two or three hotels" (*Le Sang des Atrides* 54). One might think one was reading Gault-Millau or Michelin.

Comparable examples can be found in Estelle Monbrun's *Meurtre chez Tante Léonie*, where a bourgeois and erudite atmosphere prevails, although in this case the tone is clearly humorous:

Professor Verdaillan, who held a national *agrégation* and a doctorate in literature, was finishing a delicious lunch in the privacy of the Petit Roi restaurant in Chartres. Pike quenelles, pheasant with currants, chocolate charlotte, accompanied by judiciously selected Bordeaux wines, had been impeccably served by attentive and experienced waiters. (60)

Christian Jacq's trilogy, *Le Juge d'Égypte*, contains passages that are in the same vein, although the story takes place under the reign of Ramses II. What matters in this case is the apparent cultural compatibility between modern French and ancient Egyptian gastronomy, with the implication that the greatness of civilizations can always be measured in terms of culinary refinement. Here is an example:

They sat down on curved chairs; on the low tables in front of each one of them, servants placed trays heaping with food. The chef had prepared delicious cubes of beef, which had been cooked in an earthenware pot with a rounded base as well as fowls roasted on the spit. The fresh bread came with butter made with fenugreek and caraway, without water or salt, which had been kept in a cool cellar to avoid discoloring; green peas and zucchini in sauce accompanied the meat.

A cupbearer filled the cups with red wine from the Delta area . . . (*La Justice du vizir* 132)

Although historical details abound (curved chairs, earthenware pot with a rounded base, fenugreek, etc.), the overall impression is that Egyptians under Ramses II had tastes comparable to those of today's French citizens. Moreover, this balanced ancient meal, by virtue of its lightness, is even in keeping with current *nouvelle cuisine* trends. As for the reference to red wine, of which there are many more in the trilogy, it naturally evokes cultural sophistication and greatness. Unfortunately, as is clear in Jacq's story, this greatness was threatened by the introduction of new values promoted by American-style capitalists. The correlation with today's France can hardly be missed.

New gastronomy and new culinary eclecticism are not necessarily typical of current detective fiction. As noted earlier, the dominant trend is in the tradition of the political *roman noir*, which characterizes itself by a concerted lack of references to good food and culinary pursuits. The *roman noir*, particularly since the so-called *néo-polar* of the 1970s, has been dominated by a sense of failure, disillusionment, and even despair and existential disgust or *nausée*, to use a Sartrian term. As one of Manchette's characters typically remarks in *L'Affaire N'Gustro*, "I suddenly feel that everything disgusts me" (177). Symbolically, nausea precludes interest in anything that might bring satisfaction, including food. Epicures, therefore, have no role to play in *romans noirs*, particularly in those written by novelists known for their formerly extreme left political inclinations such as Manchette, Daeninckx, Vilar, or Delteil. Such novels are typical of what is perceived as a postmodern era of lost revolutionary dreams, and political melancholia obviously precludes savoriness. In Manchette's *L'affaire N'Gustro*, for example, food references do not connote any form of enjoyment and serve essentially as temporal markers. Things simply happen before or after eating: "After the meal, java and liqueurs" (157). Nothing else is said about this meal. Eating is typically reduced to a mere necessity: "Having filled my stomach, I rush out to my appointment" (80).

Similarly, drinking is no longer pleasurable: characters do not relish their wine, and beer may even lose its essential refreshing quality. In one of Daeninckx's exemplary episodes, the hero is even denied his drinking pleasure when a waiter inadvertently sprays a cleaning product into his glass: "He had to clean the brass with an aerosol can while I was enjoying my beer. The smell of ammonia stung my nose. I held my glass away from my lips and ostentatiously emptied what was left into his rinsing water" (*Hors limites* 71).

"Flat Coke [*Coca éventé*]" is the equivalent of ammoniated water and complements "overly salty potato chips [*chips trop salées*]" (*Hors limites* 65). In Daeninckx's fictional universe, the hero will typically eat "a vile hotdog at a truck stop" instead of an appetizing *blanquette* in the privacy of his home or pheasant with currants in a cozy restaurant, and he quickly washes it down with some whisky instead of slowly relishing *prunelle* (*Le Facteur fatal* 166). Incidentally, in *romans noirs*, whisky commonly represents the negation of sapidity. In *La Nuit des grands chiens malades*, for example, Alain Fournier (better known under his pseudonym, A.D.G., and who is the other best-known writer of the *néo-polar* in the 1970s) even uses the hackneyed expression "squashed bedbug [*punaise écrasée*]" (19), which became associated with whisky after World War II, to describe its taste.

As a rule, lack of flavor is linked to the gloominess of the postindustrial landscape. In Delteil's *Mort d'un satrape rouge*, the hero is characteristically shown eating unappetizing lasagna in a pizzeria described as "a rather dismal establishment, which opened onto a desolate expanse, and which was stuck between two tall concrete buildings, where one constantly had to put up with vapid music" (30). There are numerous instances of such food and taste deprecation in today's *roman noir*.

Finally, as would be expected in this postindustrial context of tasteless-ness, the main function of alcoholic beverages, and particularly hard liquor, is to induce drunkenness. The offensive consequences of heavy drinking may even be mentioned since physiological nausea reflects exis-tential disgust: "We polish off two extra bottles. I barf massively into the drawers of my dad's desk" (*L'Affaire N'Gustro* 95). In keeping with this general trend, Daeninckx's suicidal inspector, Cadin, is portrayed just before his death as "a man destroyed by alcohol" (*Le Facteur fatal* 173), although at the onset of his career, he is known as a staunch teetotaler. In a world devoid of hope, drinking is essentially reduced to the banality of a self-destructive act.

It is therefore logical that characters' physical appearances should reflect indifference to culinary delights. Vilar's Victor Blainville, for example, a photographer with investigative talents, is eminently representative of this new family of heroes who are indifferent to cuisine. He weighs less than 170 pounds, although he is six feet four inches tall, and he is always in search of the strongest alcoholic beverages, never food (19). In an insipid world, he can only survive on psychotropic sustenance.

In various ways, the current *roman noir* is therefore characterized by its more or less radical denial of sapidity. This is not without interest from the point of view of the evolution of the genre. In fact, the degree of *noirceur* is by and large proportionate to the scarcity of satisfying gustatory experi-ences. Delteil's books, for example, are in this respect less extreme than Daeninckx's. In *Mort d'un satrape rouge*, even though culinary satisfaction is far from comparable to what it would normally be in a fictional setting in Simenon's tradition, not to mention a more recent gastronomic one, occa-sional allusions to simple treats such as Beaujolais wine, cooked ham, and cheese (122) suffice to counterbalance an otherwise dominant atmosphere of despair. In Delteil's books, there is still a glimmer of hope for the denizens of today's society. However, there is little, if any, sensuality. "Republican" heroes like Maigret, Bérurier and San-Antonio, Laviolette, or Marcus Aper may be avowed misanthropes, but they are not indifferent to pleasure, whether it be esthetic, gustatory, or, except for Maigret, carnal.

Izzo's cooking inspector and Dominique Sylvain's bisexual female private eye, who mixes champagne, exotic delicacies, and voluptuousness (50), are not different. They are sensualists, unlike *roman noir* heroes, who live in an insipid society. In today's French detective fiction, the author's philosophy of life can be defined with regard to the characters' appetites.

NOTES

1. The expression *polar gastronomique*, the French equivalent of "culinary whodunit," was used by P. Charbonneau in the review of Jean-Pierre Xiradakis's *Fricassée de meurtres à la bordelaise*, which appeared in the literary journal *Papilles*, a publication devoted to food in literature.

2. Within French detective fiction, the *roman noir*, which was introduced in France after World War II by such novelists as Léo Malet and Jean Amila, was at first a by-product of the American hard-boiled novel. Today, it dominates the genre, but it is now clearly associated with political *engagement*, more so in the 1990s than ever before. Didier Daeninckx's works are characteristic of current trends, and a collection such as "Le Poulpe" (Éditions Baleine), created by Jean-Bernard Pouy, is entirely devoted to the denunciation of social evils. Jean-Paul Schweighaeuser's *Le Roman noir français* constitutes a good introduction to this form of political fiction. Franz Blaha's chapter in Pierre Horn's *Handbook of French Popular Culture* (written in English) is also a useful survey of the genre.

3. "Il s'imbibe [he takes it all in]" is the verb typically used to refer to his approach (*Maigret et le clochard* 107). This and all other translations are mine.

4. There is a specific reference to Maigret's background in *Maigret se fâche*, for example, where reminiscence is triggered by an olfactory sensation: "It was warm in the house, where there hovered a pleasant smell of polishing wax, freshly cut hay, ripening fruit and slowly cooking food. It had been fifty years since he had last had that experience" (17).

5. For the connotation of the words *republican* and *democratic* in France, see Birnbaum (34–35).

6. According to the 1991 issue of Mermet's *Francoscopie*, for example, beer consumption increased by 360 percent between 1950 and 1990 (48). Consumption of ordinary wine, on the other hand, went from 95.6 liters (per year and per capita) in 1970 to 69.5 liters in 1982 and is still decreasing (*Francoscopie 1985* 147).

7. Anne-Marie Thiesse's *Ils apprenaient la France* is an excellent study on didacticism under the Third Republic.

8. The first book of the series (*Les Vacances de Marcus Aper*) was published in 1992. Other historical whodunits by Christian Jacq and Marc Paillet, set respectively in Ancient Egypt and Carolingian times, appeared in the following years, which suggests the emergence of a subgenre within French detective fiction.

9. There are exceptions, naturally. Léo Malet's Nestor Burma, a character who was created during World War II, is one of them (he made his first appearance in *120, rue de la Gare*, published in 1943). In today's France, private detectives are becoming more and more common, which is probably indicative of changing attitudes toward the role of the State.

10. It is true that Nero Wolfe's physique is even more impressive, but it does not mean that body weight has the same moral connotations in this country.

11. The Spanish detective is well-known in France. In Delteil's *Mort d'un satrape rouge*, for example, one of the less important characters is revealingly named Carvalho. This is no coincidence: it is a common practice among French detective fiction writers to encode their text with such references.

14. Film, Food, and "La Francité": From *le pain quotidien* to McDo

DANA STRAND

Every food habit plots a minuscule crossroads of (hi)stories.

Luce Giard

In 1991 the French Minister of Culture, Jack Lang, fearful that the nation's gastronomic supremacy was being threatened by societal changes that favored fast food over fine cuisine, launched a campaign to introduce cooking classes into the elementary school curriculum. This program of "awakening taste [*éveil au goût*]" undertaken in collaboration with the Institut français du goût and the Conseil national des arts culinaires, sought to reverse what some viewed as a disturbing trend in which the culinary arts (and the way of life in which they were rooted) seemed to be steadily losing ground in France. Seven years later, despite Minister Lang's efforts to restore the country to gastronomic preeminence, the trend appeared to continue unabated. Under the alarming headline, "Un patrimoine en danger," an article in the March 28, 1998 issue of *Le Monde* warned that "la grande cuisine française" was falling victim to urbanization, increased participation of women in the workforce, and the standardizing effects of globalization. In a story carried in the American press over the wire services recently the loss of French gastronomic glory was once again making news. The article reported that the French, eager to embrace a more modern, American-type lifestyle, are "turning away from serious food," willingly relinquishing their places around the tables at the nation's three-star restaurants to Michelin guide–toting foreign tourists (Kaplan).[1]

Official and unofficial expressions of concern over the devalued status of gastronomy in contemporary France underscore the important role cuisine has played in defining French culture. As Priscilla Clark has noted, "If every country has a culinary tradition, in France as nowhere else that tradition has become a national symbol of prestige, the incarnation of French civilization" (33). For Clark, the rules and regulations of French cuisine, established over a long history of internationally recognized dominance in the culinary field, have come to constitute a sort of *code civil*, transforming the preparation and consuming of food into an aesthetic and spiritual activity, a ritual whose meaning is closely tied to the French concept of national identity.

According to Roland Barthes, one of the most important functions of food in French society is to remind people that they are participating in a shared national past: "French food is never supposed to innovate except for rediscovering lost secrets; on the one hand, it implies an aristocratic tradition . . . and on the other, food is often charged with representing the savory survival of an old rural society (utopian besides)" ("Psycho-sociologie" 313). Whether reflecting real or invented memories of the aristocratic foundations of French culture, or the nationally shared nostalgia for an almost mythical "terroir," the historical grounding of French cuisine (what Barthes calls "that retro [*passéiste*] value of food") has certain undeniably conservative implications. For as Barthes notes, "French cuisine" allows the French citizen to experience "a certain continuity of the nation: food, through a thousand detours permits him or her to become implanted in his or her own past on a daily basis."

Within this highly charged field of signification, certain food products closely associated with "the art of living" are assigned a particularly imposing cultural value. Considered in France less as basic food staple than as a basic cultural symbol, bread has for years enjoyed such a status. The Littré devotes no fewer than six pages to the entry "pain," offering proof, if we needed it, of the important place this simple mixture of flour, salt, yeast, and water occupies in the French collective unconscious. While attitudes are certainly changing, the general consensus shared by people across the social spectrum has been that other components in a meal might reasonably be replaced, but bread (and wine) had to be thought of as "concrete *a priori* of all gastronomic practice" (Certeau 123). Until fairly recently, in fact, it was unlawful to discard unused bread in France, evidence of the sanctified position historically reserved for a food product strongly anchored in a set of nationally defined cultural beliefs that have traditionally served to provide a rallying point for imagining community in France (Apostolidès 294).

Given the important cultural significance of food in France, what do changes in the relationship the French have with food tell us about the current state of modern French culture? Or more specifically, what happens when the reassuring sense of continuity offered by allegiance to an imagined past traced through a revered culinary heritage ("one does not joke with bread") shows signs of breaking down? By taking a close look at two films that, in differing ways, highlight the sociological significance of bread and baking, at two distinct moments in recent French history, I hope to draw conclusions about the shifting ground of French national identity in the latter half of the twentieth century. Barthes maintains that "all food serves as a sign among the participants of a given population" (309). My analysis of these films, Marcel Pagnol's 1938 regional classic *La Femme du boulanger* and Claire Denis's *Nénette et Boni* (1996), will seek to read those signs as part of the complex and ever-evolving signifying system that produces changes in cultural meaning. Within the space separating the two bakers, the comic actor Raimu's prototypical provincial artisan and the laid-back expatriate American as portrayed by Vincent Gallo, lie traces of an important shift in the dominant image the films project of French society.

Released during the period between the wars, Pagnol's film is probably most frequently considered a representative work in the social realist tradition. Set in a small village in the south of France, the film explores popular, almost folkloric, themes through a set of characters whose strong regional accents, peasant attire, and rustic appearance seem to provide a window into rural life in the late thirties. The plot, borrowed from a 1942 short story of the same name by Jean Giono, is relatively straightforward: arriving in a village that has just lost its baker to suicide, the new baker, Aimable Castanier, and his wife, Aurélie, set out to fill the void left by the unexpected demise of their predecessor. But just when the community is settling into a pattern of normalcy, soothed by the reassuring aroma of freshly baked bread and the sight of smoke pouring forth from the bakery oven, the young, beautiful Aurélie runs off with Dominique, the darkly handsome Piemontese shepherd who has come to collect the daily supply of bread for the estate of his employer, the local marquis.

When Aurélie disappears, the baker is so distraught that he cannot bring himself to make bread, and the village must rally to restore order to the community. Despite their natural antipathy, the village priest and schoolteacher are dispatched to the marshland to retrieve the wayward

Aurélie. At first sight of the approaching duo (in a comic, bizarre scene, the schoolteacher carries the priest through the watery marsh on his back), Dominique flees, fearful of the consequences of his sinful act. Head bowed in a posture of contrite submission, Aurélie returns to Aimable, promising never again to stray. In a gesture heavy with symbolic meaning, she lights the bakery oven, signaling that the village, through the reaffirmation of the patriarchal order, will once again have its bread.

Given Marcel Pagnol's professed commitment to naturalism, critics have tended to see *La Femme du boulanger* as yet another of his films (e.g., the trilogy *Marius, Fanny, César*) designed to reproduce an authentic portrait of his beloved Provence, through on-location shooting of working-class or petit-bourgeois milieus. Yet, in a pertinent sociological reading of the film, Jean-Marie Apostolidès argues that realism is eclipsed in *La Femme du boulanger* by a studied reliance upon figures or types caught up in symbolic, mythological structures that reveal more about the dynamics of the collectivity than individual psychology. For Apostolidès, then, the personal story of seduction, adultery, and reconciliation is secondary to the one tracing the passage of the locality, an isolated community operating under its own laws and system of justice, away from feudal society toward a capitalist economy.[2]

At first glance, it would be difficult to claim that *Nénette et Boni*, which features characters whose quirky, unpredictable behavior resists easy categorization, provides a similar symbolic framework. Set in the teeming port city of Marseilles, the film seems to avoid representing any stable, recognizable collectivity at all, leaving the spectator with the impression that the characters lead their lives with very little reference to rules, even those defined in isolation from the larger society. *Nénette et Boni* has two intersecting story lines. The first tracks the erotic fascination with the neighborhood baker's wife of a nineteen-year-old man, Boni, who earns a living, when the spirit moves him ("I work when I want"), driving a pizza truck around the city.

The second follows Boni's fifteen-year-old sister, Nénette who, pregnant by someone whose identity she refuses to reveal, has run away from boarding school. In the course of the film, the spectator learns that the brother and sister, whose mother has recently died, are estranged from their father, who has unspecified connections to the underworld. In what appears to be a mob-related act of retribution, the father is eventually killed in a drive-by shooting. At the movie's end, Boni storms the hospital where Nénette has just given birth to her baby. Brandishing an air rifle usually reserved for taking potshots at neighborhood cats from the vantage point of his apartment rooftop, he abducts the infant to prevent his sister from putting him up for adoption.

If *La Femme du boulanger* seems to have ties to the realist tradition, *Nénette et Boni* is decidedly more impressionistic, blurring boundaries between dreams and reality, emphasizing visual and other sensory perceptions over the narrative line, and sketching complex, at times enigmatic, portraits of its lead characters. Yet, I want to suggest that, when considered in tandem, the Pagnol film and Claire Denis's modern update of the story featuring the seductive, disruptive powers of a baker's wife, offer commentary on such fundamental cultural issues as evolving definitions of national identity and the relationship of the individual to community. And at the heart of this commentary is food. In fact, when viewed together, both films highlight the symbolic resonances, evocative power, and changing cultural signifi-cance of bread (and such identifiably French baked goods as croissants and brioches), and in so doing, sketch a picture of French society in transition that is produced at the intersection of these issues.

The cultural and ideological implications of the Pagnol film are per-haps best understood through reference to the prevailing mood in France prior to World War II. Although the film's mythological structure and character types contribute to an impression of timelessness (there are few if any signs of the increasingly industrialized world beyond the tightly framed, visually claustrophobic confines of this Provençal village), its reaffirmation of certain values and community standards can be seen as a reaction to pressures in French society in the period between the two wars. Faced with the failures of the Popular Front to live up to its promises, the apparent resistance of a stagnant economy to modeniza-tion, and the threat of fascism, the French in the late 1930s were struggling with feelings of insecurity, fueled by growing uncertainty about the future. Released in the same year as Marcel Carné's troubling evocation of social degradation *Quai des brumes,* and Jean Renoir's darkly pessimistic *La Bête Humaine*, Pagnol's film might actually be considered as an alternative, retrospective, almost reactionary, cinematic response to the national malaise expressed in the two other films.

In assessing the success of another Pagnol film, *Regain* (1937), also based on a Giono work, Dudley Andrew explains the appeal of its celebra-tion of the return to a sense of stable community grounded in simple, enduring values: "Amid the calls and programs for social change that were heard from the Left and Right alike, the solid moral understanding evident both in Pagnol's characters and in the sure craft of his technique seemed a haven that attracted both the simple and the sophisticated" (Andrew 138). Championing the therapeutic possibilities of harmonious cooperation among villagers united against a threat to their commonly held goals, *La Femme du boulanger* shows that the divisive effects of competing political discourses can ultimately be overcome by a kind of locally defined common law firmly anchored in the comforting familiarity of the status quo.

Pagnol relies upon a shorthand version of cultural codes (what Andrew refers to as "charged icons"), defined by convention and tradition, to convey a sense of a shared "moral understanding."[3] In *La Femme du boulanger* these connotative codes intertwine to create a latent ideological effect as exemplary as any to be found in the "closed" nineteenth-century narratives Barthes uses as his models. For example, the film begins with a shot of the local school building bearing the words "École publique mixte" on its facade.[4] A reminder of the adamantly Jacobin agenda of the Third Republic, the image of the school cannot help but evoke the almost mythic link between public education and Republican values. Several sequences later, a confrontation between the village priest and the schoolteacher over whether Joan of Arc "heard" or "thought she heard" voices lays out schematically the ideological opposition so deeply implanted in the French mentality that, ironically, it has served until relatively recently as a unifying national trait (Mendras 167). Certainly the contemporary observer, recognizing the tug-of-war between the *instituteur* and the *curé du village* as quaintly and irreducibly "French," responds with a knowing smile to this and other scenes in which characters are almost endearingly true to type.

Early on in the film, the charged meaning of bread is made clear. The universal consternation provoked by the loss of the previous baker, the reverential tones used to express the villagers' shared anticipation of having the oven up and running once again are proof that bread has value that extends beyond its mere nutritive function. Furthermore, frequent invocations of the biblical phrase "daily bread" link bread to a utopian vision of a conservative Christian tradition that has been at the very core of French culture and society.

If bread has a synecdochal position in the film, neatly standing in for all those factors that signify the order and timeless simplicity of "La France profonde," the connection between the baker's wife and bread is far less straightforward. In his initial conversations with the village men, who have come to size him up, Aimable casts Aurélie in the role of muse, proclaiming that his primary goal is to make bread that is as beautiful as his wife. The cause and effect link between the woman and the bread she inspires explicitly spelled out in this scene is graphically illustrated in the following shot. As the villagers file into the bakery to view the first batch of bread, they cast sideways glances at Aurélie, who is filmed from behind. The camera then traces a smooth continuum from the faceless icon of female beauty to the oven from which will emerge the product of her powers of enchantment.[5]

In the scene establishing the sexual attraction between the baker's wife and Dominique, the sack of bread into which she slowly drops loaf after loaf, while staring into his longing eyes, visually unites the two future lovers, placing the bread at the center of the scene's exaggerated sensuality. Later on, during a dinner conversation between the curé and the marquis following the disappearance of the baker's wife, the topic shifts from adultery, sin, and forgiveness to the bread on the table between the two men. The marquis praises the baker's handiwork, remarking with a lascivious smile, "Yesterday I ate some so well that I may have to go to confession for it." Bread here is linked to human (and particularly male) passions and forbidden desire and seems, in some curious way, to occupy a place in the community's imagination that is interchangeable with that of the baker's wife.

After dining with the priest, the marquis calls a meeting in the village to decide on the appropriate course of action to combat the threat posed by the elopement, which he characterizes as an "an attack against our better judgment and our bellies [*attentat contre la morale et le ravitaillement*]." Urging the villagers to set aside their petty family quarrels and join forces to find the missing woman, he makes quite clear the metaphorical function served by the baker's wife when he says "she represents the daily bread." His comment, in conjunction with his final exhortation, "Let us thus begin tody our crusade for the beautiful baker," allies the female body with both the holy sacrament and the holy grail. The rather strange coupling of bread and the baker's wife with both the spiritual and the resolutely profane is in fact consistent with Pagnol's (and Giono's) project to propose a return to an emphasis on elemental forces as an antidote to the social upheaval facing France in the thirties. As the community's "god of libidinal religion" (Apostolides 299), Aurélie is the site of converging atavistic impuses structuring the narrative framework of the film.

If the baker's wife is the focal point for the village's erotic imaginary, the baker himself is defined in the film by the role he fulfills in the collectivity. When the villagers mobilize in order to put an end to his suffering, they do so less out of concern for his well-being than out of self interest. Despite his disheveled appearance and bumbling naïveté, he triumphs, not by dint of his own persuasive powers, but rather through a reaffirmation of group solidarity in the face of a threat from outside the community. Although at first glance, he does not appear to be a prime candidate for defender of the law of the father, Aimable nonetheless emerges as a representative of the patriarchal order. Like Aurélie, he is little more than a "narrative contrivance," to use Jeffords's term (87), occupying a position in this highly linear story designed to establish his legitimate claim to authority. As he assumes the power accorded him in the private space of the domestic circle, the tranquility of the communal public space is restored, and with it, the village's daily bread.

My choice of spatial metaphors here (I refer to Aurélie as a "site of converging impulses" and note the "position" occupied by the baker) is deliberate, for I mean to draw attention to the importance of the shape of the narrative in creating the grounds for the "solid moral understanding" Andrew has alluded to so perceptively. In discussing the operation of conventional narrative, Susan Jeffords underscores the link between narrative structure and gender. I cite her analysis at length, because I believe that a gendered reading of both *La Femme du boulanger* and *Nénette et Boni* can help elucidate the central questions at issue in this essay:

> Narrative is the mode of production of the interpretive strategies of
> patriarchy, as images are de-structured and then re-formulated to meet
> the needs of the constructions of externalized linear continuity. The
> female body, as the primary threat to the logic of patriarchal
> continuity, must be incorporated into these strategies through the nar-
> rative framework. The violence of dismemberment appears in/as
> narrative at the structural level, as plot begins by being dispersed into
> the elements of the tale and is resolved through the apparent
> reconciliation of these elements through the achieved coherence, a
> remembered whole. That coherence appears as the re-membered body
> of the female, now presented as what Stephen Heath has called the
> "narrative image," the remembered image left by the narrative's

passage. As de Lauretis phrases it for film, "the female position, produced as the end result of narrativization, is the figure of narrative
closure." As narrative "closes" on the re-created image of the woman,
the patriarchal narrator can see his own image re-structured and can
become "man." (Jeffords 91–92)

La Femme du boulanger offers a striking illustration of the collusion
between narrative and patriarchy outlined in the above paragraph.
Aurélie's body is at first dismembered through its eroticization and
fetishization, a process visually highlighted by the way in which she is
filmed: in a borrowing from Hollywood convention, we witness the spell
she casts written on the faces of the men who see her before we do. She is
then "remembered" as the appropriately chastened wife, pressured to
return to her role in the conjugal unit. In order for coherence to be maintained and for closure to be achieved, she (and the outsider, Dominique)
must submit to the unyielding demands of narrative, which are, not coin-
cidently, those of "patriarchal continuity." In the final scene of the film, the
violence of remembering and reconciliation is expressed through the
unsettling use of indirection. While Aimable remains true to his name,
welcoming his wife back with comforting words of forgiveness, he dis-
places his hostility onto the tabby cat, Pomponette, whose amorous
escapades conveniently parallel Aurélie's illicit adventure. With such vulgar insults as "garce," "salope", and "ordure," the baker chastises the errant
feline for abandoning her faithful partner, Pompon.[6]

As Aurélie, subdued by the complementary demands of narrative and
patriarchy, lights the oven in a ritualistic gesture marking the return to
equilibrium, the multilayered significance of bread is reaffirmed. Tied to
the archaic values the film champions, bread is sanctioned (if not sanctified) because allied with the satisfactions of the simple, uncomplicated
natural world (Barthes's "old rural society"). While I do not mean to imply
that *La Femme du boulanger* actually promotes a return to a pastoral way of
life (or that the film can be interpreted as an endorsement of Giono's isola-
tionist pacifism) the nostalgic showcasing of the Provençal village serves to
reinvent a common past.

In fact, through the extensive use of tight framing and highly structured
scenes, the film locates the contemporary spectator in a shared remembered
present that is quite overtly cinematic. As Chris Faulkner notes, Pagnol's
film making strategies have undeniable ideological consequences: "the

immobility of the image and the infrequency of shot/reverse shot structures preserve the integrity of Pagnol's diegetic world and draw attention to the thematic importance placed upon the relation of private to public space and private to public feeling" (Faulkner 162). Creating a familiar image of the ancestral "terroir" to which the French traditionally have laid claim, the story, narrative framework, and cinematographic techniques of *La Femme du boulanger* collude to provide a reminder of all those foundational myths of nationhood so disturbingly under seige in the troubled times of the thirties.

Released almost sixty years after Pagnol's film, Claire Denis's *Nénette et Boni* is also anchored in a distinctive place that colors both characters and events. Yet in contrast to Pagnol's village, the working-class neighborhoods of present-day Marseilles, with their racially diverse population and transient atmosphere, have a distinctly un-French feel to them. The film provides almost no sense of the larger community beyond the world of the adolescents who seem to improvise their lives, eating on the run, camping out wherever they can find a floor to sleep on. The few sequences that show what seems to be the stable family life of the baker, his wife, and their children consist of a series of extended, fairly static, close-ups backed up by nondiegetic music replacing dialogue. Compared to the cinéma vérité style of much of the rest of the film (especially the street scenes and the interior shots of Boni's apartment), these sequences have a dreamlike, unreal quality.

Despite the differences between Denis's film and Pagnol's, they do share some significant common ground, beyond the quite obvious choice of the baker's wife as a magnet for male desire, evoking the predictable link between gastronomic and sexual pleasure. For example, *Nénette et Boni* reworks some of Pagnol's "profoundly Marseillais" themes, such as illegitimate births ("filles-mères") and abandoned children (Riou, "Le masque et la plume"). As I have already noted, Pagnol's preoccupation with such themes reflects his nostalgia for a simpler way of life, one in which uncertainty over legitimacy, community, and identity is countered with a reaffirmation of traditional values. Glossing over conflicts, the film's linear narrative succeeds in overcoming the loss of patriarchal authority, by suppressing difference, whether in the form of the female (Aurélie) or the foreign (Dominique).

In contrast, Denis's approach to these themes springs from a radically different impulse, one that does not recognize the relevance of a French national continuity rooted in a past that, for reasons of race, ethnicity, gender, and class, is anything but shared. If Pagnol's films established a genre "metonymically representative of a 'sub'-culture (Marseilles), and metaphorically of a whole (French) culture" (Vincendeau 76), *Nénette et Boni* explodes the myth of both whole and sub-culture. It offers instead an image of characters groping clumsily toward a redefinition of their place in a society that seems to provide few if any "charged icons" to guide them. I would argue, furthermore, that one of the important signs the film provides of this cultural sea change is to be found in the role and treatment of food and eating.

Throughout the film, there are almost no scenes of characters engaging in what might even loosely be classified as dining. When he is hungry, Boni forages in his near-empty refrigerator for prepackaged food that he eats directly from the container as he stands in his cluttered kitchen. A pizzamaker, Boni sells to passersby from a mobile truck that sets up for business at random spots throughout the city. The impersonal, unplanned, and fundamentally informal nature of the exchange and consumption of food is about as far removed as one might imagine from the highly codified model of the typical French gastronomic experience. This model is, as we have seen, a throwback to an aristocratic tradition that has for years conditioned the stubborn identification of large segments of the French middle and upper classes with high culture in France.

In his study of the origins of aesthetic taste, Pierre Bourdieu locates the factors determining eating habits within a highly stratified social and economic matrix. Through detailed analysis of empirical research conducted in the 1960s, Bourdieu found that what the French ate (and how) was in large measure a function of class. Upper- and middle-class people interviewed for his study exhibited a tendency to shift the emphasis where food is concerned "from substance and function to form and manner," thus denying "the crudely material reality of the act of eating" (Bourdieu 196). The working classes, in contrast, displayed a tendency to stress the sheer pleasure of eating, while the upper classes expressed a preference for the more refined and less overtly physical satisfaction of an elegantly designed repast. Denis's characters seem to conform to neither class-related model, but rather reduce the act of eating to a mere necessity that stresses neither socially defined observation of a culinary "civil code" nor unmediated physical gratification. In a way, the film takes food (and the elaborate rules governing its preparation, presentation, and consumption) "off the table" as a marker of social status.

Furthermore, the narrative downplays the common assumption in French films and elsewhere that "breaking bread together" promotes familial or community understanding, healing emotional wounds and smoothing over differences. In *Nénette et Boni*, there is only one isolated shot in which food and the experience of eating might metaphorically suggest a psychological connection between characters. Toward the end of the movie Nénette spoon-feeds a mashed banana to her brother as he lies on his bed. Yet, because the short interlude is disconnected from the rest of the storyline and the actors remain silent and impassive, the film offers no clear message about how the scene should be interpreted, although Nénette's isolated nurturing gesture surely underscores the lack of the maternal presence in these adolescents' lives. In a failed attempt to reconcile with his children, their father brings them a peace offering of lobster bisque and steak, which Boni angrily rejects, chasing his father from the apartment. The grocery bag, still filled with uneaten food, remains as a sad reminder of the breakdown of the family: "Nourishing father whom Nénette and Boni do not want, food that they will probably not eat, hamburgers doing the job" (Strauss 65).

Perhaps no scene in the film so efficiently explodes the seamless mythos linking food, tradition, and fundamental Frenchness than the one in which Nénette, having just arrived by train in Marseilles, sits in front of a public fountain, eating a McDonald's hamburger. When she removes the meat from the bun, an offscreen voice asks, "You are not eating your bread?" As the camera pans to show a black man seated beside her, she responds, "You want it?" and gives it to him. Here, mass-produced, American-inspired fast food is passed between strangers, who consume the unappetizing fare with neither interest nor ceremony.

To my mind, this scene lends itself to different interpretations, depending on the perspective adopted by the cultural critic interested in negotiating meaning between the film and its context. From one point of view (one that might find favor with those who fear the debasement of French culture by the continual onslaught of American fast food, popular music, etc.), the scene appears to illustrate cultural rootlessness, particularly of the younger generation in contemporary French society. All notions of belonging, of distinguishing insider from outsider, are lost in this world of equivalence, where the word "pain" can signify both "baguette" and McDonald's hamburger roll, where culture becomes so homogenized that it no longer functions as a source of social cohesion.

On the other hand, the notable silence the film adopts in this and other segments toward differences of social class, race, ethnicity, in fact, toward otherness in general, suggests a more nuanced cultural reading of Denis's portrait of France might be in order. The camera's refusal to comment on the heterogeneity of Marseilles's population, its tacit acceptance of difference (Boni's friends are a medley of native French and North African; some characters speak with thick Southern accents, others have a more standard Parisian French) contribute to an image of a society whose cultural codes are fluidly defined.

As an American who barely speaks French, Vincent Gallo's baker stands in humorous contrast to his stereotypical counterpart, whose status in Pagnol's traditional community derives from the indispensable function he performs: "The king is on the level of social existence what the baker is on that of physical life, the being who assures the existence of the community" (Apostolides 295). Far from providing a rallying point for reaffirming the shared history of the collectivity, Denis's baker reveals his indifference to his "craft" when he responds to his wife's request for more croissants in mock annoyance (and in English!): "Croissants, always croissants. I'm sick of making them. 'Bring the croissants.' That's all she says." While Aimable's plight gave the villagers an opportunity to reinforce the line separating them from threatening outsiders, with her unabashedly American baker, Denis manages to install the Other at the very center of traditional French culture.

If in the milieu Denis depicts shared culinary experiences are not a source of social solidarity (as they certainly are in *La Femme du boulanger*), her film does exploit the conventional association between food and sexuality. Through a montage sequence of extreme close-ups, the mouth-watering pastries on display in the bakery announce the voluptuous body of the baker's wife. As Franck Garbarz puts it, "Claire Denis enjoys making the baker the temple of the young man's eroticism, slowing down for a close up on two or three sparkling [*chatoyant*] cakes overflowing with cream, then filming in counterpart the generous bust of the baker" (38). When the frustrated Boni cups each hand around a well-proportioned brioche, when he works himself into a preorgasmic frenzy kneading pizza dough, the sexual implications of the images are almost embarrassingly apparent.

While acknowledging the obvious sexual implications of Boni's erotic fantasies, some critics have quite perceptively considered them as part of a recognizable pattern in the film to foreground the senses. Thierry Jousse notes, for example, "the word 'sensual' has been used; I would rather use the word 'sensorial': the film depends a lot on correspondences (in the poetic sense of the word)—correspondences of forms, matter and place" ("Le masque et la plume"). Boni's wet dreams of the baker's wife are invaded by what becomes, through juxtaposition, the "erotic" gurgling of the automatic coffee maker. Close-ups of Boni's hands suggestively knead-ing dough and of the pastries in the bakery display cases emphasize the tactile quality of food: "eat the baker up with her eyes, taste the grain of his dewy flesh or the light passing over Boni's golden body, everything here makes one's eyes hungry. . . . And as everything eaten becomes food for the soul—the raw dough that Boni kneads frenetically, as well as flesh, the little cooked brioches he feels greedily—that appetite is never satis-fied" (Strauss 65).

The free-flowing current of desire set up by the film's reliance upon synesthesia in its most evocative scenes serves to disrupt the linear rela-tionship between subject and object of desire. Boni's erotic obsession with the baker's wife (and with the brioches and baguettes that function as visual metaphors for his erotic fantasies) becomes increasingly diffuse throughout the film. As he caresses his coffeepot, then his sister's swelling abdomen, and finally, her infant son, his desire seems to spill over, disturb-ing not only grounds on which traditional psychological analysis in film rests, but also the logical flow of the narrative. Where other filmmakers might develop the cause and effect connections between actions and psy-chological states through dialogue, Denis relies upon her images to create an atmosphere or evoke emotions with no clear source of origin in the nar-rative framework.

Some critics have called into question the filmmaker's storytelling tech-nique. Alain Riou has argued, for example, that "Claire Denis has a way of telling stories that is not very effective. . . . One feels the film is not mov-ing ahead" ("Le masque et la plume"). Although generally impressed by the film, an American reviewer was nevertheless also struck by Denis's departure from conventional plot development, writing that she "seems to have forsaken narrative structure for a particularly elliptical method of telling her story" (Karten). I would like to suggest that my earlier discus-sion of the relationship between patriarchy and conventional storytelling may offer some important insights into Denis's narrative strategies and, what is perhaps more important, their cultural implications.

As we have already seen, *La Femme du boulanger* conforms to the interpretive strategies of patriarchy, as defined by such feminist critics as Teresa de Lauretis and Laura Mulvey, who focus, among other things, on what they see as the unholy alliance between Freudian and narrative theories. With an emphasis on metaphorical relationships that lend themselves to coherence and closure, Pagnol's plot does advance, but only to repeat (reaffirm) the same old story—that of the triumph of patriarchy. Since the baker's wife is synonymous with the village's *nourriture de base*, she becomes the locus of community desire. Narrative closure is achieved by re-structuring the conventional male and female images, disrupted by the female disordering principal, and reestablishing the appropriate gendered positions.

Nénette et Boni, on the other hand, seems to take as a given the absence of the father, who has absconded with the ordering principle he represents. Adrift in a world that lacks the linearity achieved through a violent substitution of (paternal) logic for the (maternal) body, the title characters must also face the loss of the mother and all she stands for, "the disappearance of the maternal figure thrust the characters of *Nénette et Boni* into disarray and confusion. The whole film tries to remedy this disorder produced by the original abandonment" (Garbarz 38). The remedy proposed, however, does not entail imposing a rigidly defined narrative framework, structured by principles of metaphoric substitution, on human experience that clearly does not conform to that model. Instead, Denis offers an analogy that suggests an alternative model, replacing linear logic with the more erratic, less predictable principles of metonymic displacement. Boni's desire spreads out from the baker's wife, to his rabbit, from his automatic coffee maker to the visually suggestive brioches, and back again. As Thierry Jousse has so astutely observed, in commenting on the narrative structure of *Nénette et Boni*, "Denis turns in concentric circles around the story" ("Le masque et la plume").

The circular structure of the narrative is foregrounded through a seemingly insignificant plot element, but one whose importance may be signaled by the strategic location of its loosely related sequences. The film begins with a shot of a con man selling counterfeit telephone calling cards to an assembled group of immigrants. Later in the film, we see a random shot of an Asian woman in a phone booth, shouting in Vietnamese over the telephone. Finally, when Nénette is at the clinic talking to a social worker about her impending delivery, a phone call interrupts the interview. Telling an agent from the telephone company that she could not possibly have made all those calls to Ho Chi Minh City, because she knows no one in Vietnam, the social worker disputes the excessive charges on her bill. This humorous running anecdote provides a counterpoint to the central plot line involving Nénette's pregnancy and delivery, at the same time that it alludes to the unpredictable, but inescapable interconnectedness of strangers living in what is fashionably referred to as "the new global economy." As yet another barrier (the one separating respectable, law-abiding citizens from con men, or the line between indigenous French and immigrants) crumbles, it becomes increasingly clear that the relationship between spaces, whether they be public, private, gendered, national, or familial, will henceforth be under constant renegotiation.

Drawing upon images taken from both natural and culinary experiences, Denis herself has identified the breakdown of boundaries as an important theme in her film: "It is a story about the transformation of matter: like sperm becoming flesh. Like a tomato can become puree." Her reworking of this fundamental story of childbirth relies upon a kind of transformation that neatly sidesteps the cause and effect logic of paternity, a logic that, as we have seen, governs conventional narrative forms. The critic Franck Garbarz perceptively sums up the process at work in the film: "The making of bread and the working of the pizza dough illustrate physically the transformation of matter at the heart of the film: just as flour and water produce bread, the reunion of Nénette and Boni has reestablished the blood-line, constitute of the repair of the original abandonment."

Both in its narrative structure and its story line, then, the film undermines the legitimacy of paternal authority. Not only is Nénette and Boni's father denied by his offspring any claims to the role he abandoned when they were young, but the father of Nénette's child remains unidentified even at the film's end, opening the way for Boni to step in as both maternal and paternal figure. The manner in which he rescues the infant from parental abandonment draws attention to his dual role. Concealing his air rifle in a bouquet of gladioli, he kidnaps the child from a frightened nurse at gunpoint. In this scene, which is a clear intertextual reference to the male action movie genre, Boni converts what most contemporary spectators would immediately interpret as a violent, antisocial act into a compassionate, nurturing one, when he is shown, in the final scene, cradling the newborn in his arms.[7]

In bypassing the "cinematic recipes" of past French films (Strauss 65), Claire Denis has fashioned a portrait of a present-day France that resolutely refuses to present itself as even a partial filmic construction of nation. Avoiding the use of iconographic codes and conventions tied to notions of Frenchness ("la francité"), or at the very least to representations of the subculture of the Marseilles region, *Nénette et Boni* all but ignores the cultural patrimony that has been and remains a distinguishing characteristic of much mainstream cinema. A comparison of Denis's film with Robert Guediguian's *Marius et Jeannette* (1997), set in L'Estaque, a working class neighborhood of Marseille, in this regard is revelatory. While *Marius et Jeannette* features a "feel-good" community-wide aioli party as well as a food fight at a local bar during which innumerable varieties of fish (including eels and squid) are launched into the air, *Nénette et Boni* includes no reference to the region's culinary heritage.

In the place of images preserving homogenizing myths of national and regional identity, the film offers a vision of French society that continually confounds expectations. When the local baker is a blue-eyed American named Vincenzo, with less than the expected reverence for his artistry, when lobster bisque gives way to burgers and pizza, when she "has a bun in the oven [*avoir emprunté un pain sur la fournée*]" (Nénette's illegitimate child) ends up in the arms of a sex-crazed nineteen-year-old, and all bets are off. In the new France Denis dishes up for her spectators, attachment to a shared past, culinary or otherwise, no longer promises to offer a reassuring answer to the nagging question of national identity. Instead, her film implies that a working definition of "la francité" will have to be invented and reinvented from an ever-evolving list of ingredients—a task to be undertaken in earnest by those who "know how to eat their bread."

NOTES

1. I would like to express my gratitude to the students in the Media Studies 241 class I taught in the winter of 1999. Their insights have contributed greatly to my understanding of the questions addressed in this essay.

2. Lynn A. Higgins finds signs of national growing pains (although of a

different sort) in other Pagnol works, particularly his cinematic novelization, *L'Eau des collines* (1963). See her essay "Pagnol and the Paradoxes of Frenchness."

3. Although I find Andrew's terminology particularly well-suited to my analysis, I should nevertheless acknowledge that his "charged icons" call to mind Roland Barthes's theory of semiotic codes that provides a useful approach to reading films culturally. Julia Lesage has, in fact, undertaken a fascinating study of Renoir's *The Rules of the Game*, based on the five codes Barthes applies to his reading of Balzac's novella *Sarrasine*. See her summary of the exercise in "*S/Z* and *The Rules of the Game*."

4. That is to say, a public school for both boys and girls.

5. Pagnol's first choice of an actress to play the role of Aurélie was Joan Crawford, who alas was not available. Pagnol felt that as a Hollywood icon who spoke no French, Crawford would project an alluring, yet at the same time negative image (Beylie 78).

6. Roughly: bitch, whore, and trash.

7. Two films representative of the male action genre with similar scenes are James Cameron's *Terminator II: Judgment Day* (1991) and John Woo's *Hard Boiled* (1992), which even features a maternity ward. I am indebted to Raul Ruiz and Mieke Strand for bringing these examples to my attention.

15. Screening Food:
French Cuisine and the Television Palate

TOBY MILLER

In the early 1960's, National Educational Television (NET) initially rejected a Boston-based culinary program hosted by a woman named Julia Child. The rationale was that the cooking show was an outdated format from the '50s. Child was picked up by a regional outfit called the Eastern Educational Network, which was her eventual platform for international fame and fortune.

James Ledbetter

People lined up at 6 a.m. to get seats—on a Saturday morning, no less. Inside, the 2,000-person crowd jumped to its feet, cheering and clapping in unison as the music keyed up and an announcer shouted, "Let's get ready to rumble." . . . [W]hooping fans were assembled for the taping of a show by Emeril Legasse, a gourmet master chef with blue-collar appeal who has turned the Food Network into "Must See TV." Once a 24-hour outlet for Julia Child reruns, the cable channel has become eye-candy for food voyeurs who watch more for entertainment than cooking advice.

Jennifer Brown

Assumptions about subjectivity based on food are extreme and common: research on public opinion in the United States shows vegetarians—who are thought to eat broccoli, quiche, brown rice, bean sprouts, and avocado sandwiches—are assumed to be antiwar and prodrugs and to drive imported cars (the nineteenth-century belief was that vegetarianism quelled masturbation). Gourmets, by contrast, are expected to favor caviar, oysters, and French-roast coffee. They are regarded as liberal, drug-taking sophisticates. Fast–or synthetic–food eaters are found to be religious, conservative, and liable to wear polyester (Fine and Leopold 169, 187; Falk 68–70). Now *you* know, too.

Pierre Bourdieu lists two "paradoxes of the taste of necessity" that capture this dynamic nicely:

> Some simply sweep it aside, making practice a direct product of economic necessity (workers eat beans because they cannot afford anything else), failing to realize that necessity can only be fulfilled . . . because the agents are inclined to fulfil it. . . . Others turn it into a taste of freedom, forgetting the conditionings of which it is the product. . . . Taste is *amor fati*, the choice of destiny, but a forced choice. (*Distinction* 178)

The clear class distinction between an apparently functional diet and a more aesthetic one may be not so neat, however, as when Bourdieu studied quotidian French tastes three decades ago. Since that time, cooking has become a daily part of television fare, nowadays with its own networks. Being on television means democratization as surely as it means commodification—the lifeworld may be compromised, but its pleasures are spread around a little, too. Raymond Oliver made this point three decades ago in his celebration of modern transportation and technology as articulators of cuisine across classes (7)—he might have added commodification to the list.

The trend is accelerating away now. Nineteen ninety-three brought the TV Food Network to U.S. cable as the idea of CNN's creator ("The Week"). Later in the decade we were treated to Carlton's satellite food network on British television. One of its globally exported game shows addresses women audiences (the commercials are mainly for women's health and beauty culture) stressing that the presentational norms promoted apply to professional chefs, hosts entertaining, or the solitary but discriminating home cook. The common *theme* was that food could be fun. (The common *requirement* for programs to be included on the channel was that they be paid for in full by food companies.) By the late nineties, this premium on fun saw the U.S. Food Network featuring Al Roker and other personality segments, paid for by an annual programming budget of over $40 million ("Food Network Switches"; "Food Network Gets").

This legacy of needing to prove that preparing food can be pleasurable clearly has two antecedents. The first, and most important, is a sexual division of labor that has required women to undertake unpaid domestic tasks on behalf of others. The second is the unattainability of fine food, the sense that one can never "get it right." Distinctions between ordinary fare and "fine" cuisine are central to this second antecedent. Buried within that issue lies the popularization of French cooking. Has this led to a democratization, or to even stronger senses of cultural capital? There is a powerful liberal lineage to French food as well as an elitist one: restaurants were named as such in France in 1825 and rapidly became sites for democratizing knowledge of different foodstuffs and preparations as well as spreading notions of correct conduct across societies, beyond the ruling classes (Finkelstein 34–36, 46).

Resolving such issues goes beyond the purview of this chapter. But I hope to address the issue by asking: what role has television played in the popularization of French cuisine? This is impossible to consider in a thoroughly international, comprehensive manner without a major research project. In the absence of such an enterprise, this chapter endeavors to give some contour to the spread of French cuisine on TV. It examines the roles of Julia Child, on U.S. public television from the 1960s to the 1980s, and the two main food TV networks of the 1990s: the U.S. Food Network and the global UK-based Carlton Food Network. Throughout, my argument will be that Anglo-speaking countries have negotiated a cosmic ambivalence about French culture, an oscillation between contempt and admiration that has found televisual form in popularization. In the process, French food is demystified.

In the 1960s, this means a scion of the U.S. gentry rolling up her jolly-hockey-mistress sleeves and being ordinary on nonprofit TV. In the 1990s, it means multicultural chefs blending world cuisines on a money-hungry, quasi-infotainment cable system.

BEGINNINGS

Television and food had a totally functional start: frozen dinners were first marketed in the United States in 1953 as a meal to be had in front of the TV or in an emergency. Preparation of food was minimized at times of leisure and crisis (Beardsworth and Keil, "Putting" 142; Mintz, "Feeding" 51). But this changed a decade later via Julia Child.

Julia Child was the broker of French cuisine to the North American WASP population. The A&E Cable network's video *Biography* of her, "An Appetite for Life," describes her as "a national icon" and her show as "a new French Revolution . . . televised." Before the start of public TV across the country, her *French Chef* series was syndicated by Boston's WGBH in 1963 through National Educational Television (starting at almost the same moment as Raymond Oliver's recipe show began in France). From the first, Child was also central to public television's commodification—noted San Francisco station KQED sold her cooking knives that year as its first membership "gifts." The series itself was underwritten by Polaroid. Like her book that was also on sale (*Mastering the Art of French Cooking*), Child's avowed intent was to illustrate that "cooking was not a chore but an art." In fact, commercialism was at the heart of this—her first appearance was an attempt to promote sales of the book, and producers then decided she was the person to build a program around. Starting in 1962 with pilot programs, she made 119 episodes of *The French Chef*. With national distribution in 1964, the coming of (putatively) noncommercial TV to the American scene was signaled by Julia Child as much as anyone else. In recognition of the fact, she won a Peabody Award in 1965 and made the cover of *Time* the following year. *Newsweek* said she was "helping to turn Boston, the home of the bean and the cod, into the home of the brie and the coq." By the mid-sixties, KQED was receiving twenty thousand letters a week about the show. It went into color in 1970, when PBS distributed it nationally. Other series followed across the next three decades, such as *Julia Child and Company*, *Julia Child and More Company*, *Dinner at Julia's*, *Cooking with Master Chefs*, *In Julia's Kitchen with Master Chefs*, *Baking with Julia*, *Cooking in Concert* pledge-drive specials, and *Julia Child & Jacques Pépin: Cooking at Home* (Stewart 42, 61, 130–31, 133, 138–39). Child remains part of PBS branding today, a key signifier of the network and its alleged superiority to and separateness from commercial TV (Baker and Dessart 243).

The ontology of immediacy that live TV can offer was clearly in evidence on the first shows. At that time, programs were rehearsed then shot in a single take onto kinescopes. Editing was virtually impossible. Child's manifold errors on camera, such as flipping an omelet or pancake onto the stove then putting it back into the pan, served to make a virtue of low production values, adding a dollop of authenticity and approachability to television. These mistakes hid the fact that she spent nineteen hours preparing for each program and relied on a large team of unpaid workers behind the scenes. Even though the wine bottles on display were generally filled with nonalcoholic beverages, her jolly attitude to drink was a staple (Stewart 131). This stood in some contrast to the Puritanism of much U.S. society and became a winning point with many viewers, along with the casual air that mystified the Tayloristic managerial devices underpinning her performances. She also offered tips on hosting a party as well as preparing the food, so that viewers could become accomplished hostesses. At the same time, the cosmic American ambivalence toward France (a loathing of supposed Gallic national indolence blended with a paradoxical admiration for the French lifestyle, a hatred of big government mixed with inferiority alongside national cultural institutions) was apparent in the fetishized attitude toward French food. Something odd, foreign, but somehow better, needed an introduction from an adopted Brahmin such as Child, suitably ensconced in the allegedly Anglo-Celtic Boston, to be acceptable. French food was brokered into ordinariness by the white ruling class—so ordinary that she eventually qualified for parody on *Saturday Night Live*.

Child fitted the bill of what ethnomethodologists refer to as the "personalized stranger," a figure known through media coverage of the details of his or her private life rather than through direct human interaction, but taken by the public to be someone they "know" at quite an intimate level—not as far as secrets are concerned, but in the sense of a person with whom diurnal interaction is taken for granted (Watson 16, 19 n. 19). In Child's case, this served to humanize her and cloud the commercial imperatives underpinning the program-book sales and commercial underwriting.

None if this critique serves to deny the importance of her symbolism to many viewers. Consider this, from one of my informants:

> There were times, as a desperate young mother living in a provincial town, when I felt that all that stood between me and insanity was hearty Julia Child—cooing at that pink pig in her arms—ready for roasting, demonstrating the art of cooking with dry vermouth, assuring me that there were places fragrant with herbs and full of deep and pleasurable knowledge, and that anyone who wanted to could participate. Me—at the ironing board at 10:00 p.m.—imagining myself in those better places (I guess she was like a bedtime story!).

This is evocative prose indeed. It speaks to the paucity of credibly "real" women on TV at the time (the 1960s), the medium's minimal address of women's concerns, and the sense of access that Child offered. This was an access to secular transcendence, and it predated the advent of second-wave feminisms.

The PBS archives hold her recipes from those days, plainly typed lists and instructions that were mailed out on demand. Her braised salmon offering from program number 302 promises that this is "not nearly the tour de force that it sounds." The syntagmatic arrangement of words is telling—the sentence ends with French-language bravura, a high note of achievement. But it begins with a careful Anglo adverbial qualifier, a "sensible" prefix to Gallic style. In the famous program number 261—"The Omelette Show"—she avows that viewers require "a devil-may-care attitude for those that may fall on the stove or onto the floor."

This blend of the high and low promised a meeting, of course, at a place called midcult. Which is where we greet the new technologies and deregulatory possibilities of the last two decades.

CABLE AND SATELLITE

Child's equivalent and collaborator in the nineties is Jacques Pépin, but the notion of the TV chef as a role model for women is passé. Pépin, French himself, uses his daughter, a Franco-American, to be the naive inquirer, the viewer brought onto the set for participant observation. As their book for PBS puts it: "On the set, Claudine sees her role as that of the voice of the people." His terpsichories and flights are domesticated by her asking, "Can I freeze it?" The book concludes with a paean to the "generous corporate citizens" that underwrite the show. Or rather it does not quite end there: on the reverse page there are color advertisements for the products sold by these "citizens" (Pépin xviii, 267–68). He is also a United Airlines "Celebrity Chef," complete with the corporation's ringing endorsement as a "classically trained native of France" fit to design meals (for First and Business Class) (Porterfield).

On the avowedly commercial Food Network, Pépin's rough-and-ready Fall River equivalent is Emeril Lagasse, complete with his doctorate from the Johnson and Wales University culinary program specializing in French food and his network promos at the Super Bowl ("New"; Food Network). Working-class credentials displace a blue blood's slapdash amateur excellence.

Lagasse provides the station's top-rated show. When the network offered free tickets to a live taping in the fall of 1997, 50,000 people telephoned in twenty-two minutes (Brown; Brooker). As of late 1999, the Food Network was available in 43 million U.S. households (up from 30 million in 1998), as well as in Japan, Canada, and Australia. Despite some multiculturalism and increasingly broad programming, French cuisine is one of its default settings ("Scripps Networks"; "Scripps October"). U.S. audience growth has been steady. From the 1997–98 to 1998–99 seasons, numbers increased from 170,000 to 230,000 among 18–34 year-olds and from 450,000 to 670,000 among 18–49 year-olds. The overall numbers were up 50 percent and advertising revenue had grown by 80 percent to $36 million, while regional web sites across the United States were planned ("Univision"; "Food Network Gets"; "Cable's"). Popularization was underway, way beyond the ghetto of PBS.

The United States's cosmic ambivalence toward the French and their food is just as evident in Britain. The key 1970s TV chef in the United Kingdom, Delia Smith, would customize French dishes, renationing them for her audience by substituting ingredients to make the food more accessible to Anglo viewers. This was also a speciality of Graham Kerr, a queer-acting ex–New Zealand air force officer (originally from the United Kingdom) whose fey and seemingly drunk rushes around the set were famous in the United States, Australia, and Britain from the early 1970's. Many of my informants recalled him as the first "flamboyant" man they saw live on TV, a sort of culinary Paul Lynde. Another key figure was Paul Bocuse, whose French cuisine went onto Australia's multicultural station SBS in the 1980s and into the Federal Republic of Germany alongside Max Enzinger's *Trimm Dich* ("Get Fit"), which introduced *nouvelle cuisine* there.

This ambiguity in the British reaction to French food is nicely exemplified in two TV anecdotes. A 1990 episode of the British talk show *That's Life* saw the studio audience fed some snails, unaware of what they were eating. Once told, their faces distorted into English versions of barnyard animals and they sought to vomit the remains. Consider also this 1989 commercial for precooked sausages ready for microwave "preparation." A yuppie white man is taking advantage of his health-conscious wife's temporary absence to eat some "bangers." His conspiratorial gaze at the viewer concludes with a satisfied, "Now that's what I call nouvelle cuisine" (Fiddes 33, 97).

In the mid-1990s there was some controversy on British television over white presenters Keith Floyd and Robert Carrier fronting *Floyd on Africa* and *Carrier's Caribbean* respectively, programs that touched on Francophone and Anglophone colonial traditions insensitively (Beattie et al. 153). With the establishment of Britain's Carlton Food Network on cable and digital satellite (the only such service in Europe) and its 1999 expansion to 300,000 multichoice cable homes in sub-Saharan Africa, this cross-cultural component became all the more significant. Unlike earlier broadcast television in Britain, which had privileged French and some South Asian cuisine, the new genre network had to be all-encompassing. French recipes were far from dominant in the programming philosophy of the station, although Bruno Loubet hosts *Chez Bruno* and we also see *Antony's Morocco* featuring Francophone foods (Carlton). Channel Four offers *TV Dinners*, including tales of a twelve-year-old Irish scout troop leader who prepares French sauces for her colleagues, all cooked outdoors.

In 1999, the new Philippines Lifestyle Network began on cable, with four hours of programming each day coming from the U.S. Food Network ("Scripps"). In such places as Hong Kong, French food in 1999 remained an exoticism from travel programs, not yet a genre on cooking shows. But hold hard. The old colonial empires stand ready to send out correct forms of cuisine to the very areas they had come to govern a century earlier. They have even managed an article in *Rolling Stone* magazine (Bozza). A multicultural, but very French-inflected Food Network show has also emerged, Ming Tsai's *East Meets West with Ming Tsai*. Looking "like a self-improvement infomercial, or maybe a Visa ad," it quickly won a daytime Emmy (Schillinger 60). In November 1999, the network opened a window in Manhattan's Chelsea district where passers-by could watch programs in production. The Brahmin and her corporate underwriters have been displaced by multicultural, commodified hosts. Julia Child, farewell.

ACKNOWLEDGMENTS

Thanks for their aid as informants to Barbara Abrash, Manuel Alvarado, Rebecca Barden, Sarah Berry, William Boddy, Ed Buscombe, Robyn Donahue, Liz Ferrier, Sara Gwenllian-Jones, John Hartley, Heather Hendershott, Mariana Johnson, Anna McCarthy, Alec McHoul, Eric Kit-Wai Ma, Rick Maxwell, Silke Morgenroth, Laurie Oullette, Dana Polan, Christie Slade, Marita Sturken, Allen Weiss, George Yúdice, Barbie Zelizer, and Vera Zolberg.

16. Tractatus Logico-Gastronomicus

ALLEN S. WEISS

> Our taste is no longer our own, we no longer command
> it, it changes without our consent.
>
> *La Rochefoucauld*

Taste (culinary and otherwise) constitutes a sign of individual style, a mode of constituting the self, a mark of social position, an aesthetic gesture. While inaugurating the most intimate pleasure, cuisine simultaneously offers an incontrovertible aspect of social facade. Against the *solipsism*, *narcissism*, and *phantasms* of what would be the incommunicable idiosyncracy of pure subjective taste must be counterbalanced the *communality*, *seduction*, and *mythology* of gastronomy. Regardless of the mode of cuisine in question—ancient, peasant, familial, bourgeois, haute, international, *nouvelle*, exotic—this essay will continually fluctuate between these two limits, subjective and objective, personal and interpersonal.

If every dish is a symbol, then every cuisine implies a metaphysics, all too often doomed to remain implicit. The social and aesthetic significance of a dish is most often dissimulated by the vagaries of personal "taste," buried in the dense dialectic between forgetting and anamnesis that forms and informs our senses, sensitivity, sensibility. Taste is a dynamic principle, not a static qualification or attribute, the origins of which are lost in pure contingency, and escape the essentialism which haunts the other arts. Ultimately, the only manner to estimate gastronomic values and origins, to consider the question of taste, is through a "Proustian" digression: lengthy, sensual, detailed, eloquent, seductive, and most especially, contingent. For our earliest culinary memories, the most archaic ones, are more ancient than paleolithic cooking, and as intimate as love.

The preference for any flavor is a function of the transmigrations, transfigurations, and reincarnations of childhood taste as it enters the public realm of culinary production and consumption, followed by transformations that continue throughout one's lifetime, sometimes conscious, often not. Here, the daily habits of culinary routine simultaneously and paradoxically establish provisional limits to future gastronomic experimentation and appreciation. Taste never exists in a vacuum: it is a style like any other, organized by a selective code linking the work of farmer, merchant, chef, and gourmet, and vacillating between tradition and creation. This social "liaison" forms a hermeneutic gastronomic circle within which there always exist vestigial indications of ethics, theology, psychology, aesthetics, etiquette, and magic. Thus the question of taste is of a dense ambiguity, though not unfathomable.

The difficulty in discussing "taste" is not only due to the radical subjectiveness inherent in the cliché *de gustibus non est disputandum* (there is no disputing taste), but also in the lexical and epistemological equivocation of the word. Taste is simultaneously subjective, objective, and qualificative. According to context, *taste* means: (1) the sense by which we distinguish flavors; (2) the flavors themselves; (3) an appetite for such preferred flavors; (4) the discriminative activity according to which an individual likes or dislikes certain sensations; (5) the sublimation of such value judgments as they pertain to art, and ultimately to all experience; (6) and, by extension and ellipsis, taste implies *good* taste and style, established by means of an intuitive faculty of judgment. Yet it is precisely the figurative definition of taste, *goût*, that holds sway in quotidian discourse, defined by the *Littré* as: "An entirely spontaneous faculty preceding reflection, possessed by everybody, but which is different in each person, permitting us to appreciate the beauties and the defects in works of the spirit and in artistic productions, as taste permits us to appreciate good and bad flavors" (*Littré* 2814).

In the *Critique of Judgment*, Kant proposes a solution to the problematic of taste, (that is, the antinomy of the judgment of taste), an axiomatic ostensibly useful in attempting to answer the commonplaces posed by the tasteless: "everyone has his own taste" and "there is no disputing taste," or "I don't know if it's good, but I know what I like," and "it pleases me, therefore it is good." This theory is based on the notion of a *subjective universality*: the claim that beauty functions in a rhetorical mode as a demand, establishing a universal validity which is nevertheless without any regulating concept. Taste thus becomes a universal voice speaking in the imperative mode, implying the possibility of communicating private sensations, representations and judgments; it proffers the seemingly paradoxical universality of a singular judgment. Yet Kant's examination of judgments of taste, while being logically subtle, is rhetorically and lexically impoverished: the question of taste is in fact considerably more complex, admitting the intricacies of monologue and dialogue, theory and poetry, explication and seduction, obscurity and contradiction. The Kantian metaphysics must be supplemented by a historicized rhetoric, in order to integrate the singularities of enunciation and situation into aesthetic judgment, all the while weighing the structures of the aesthetic (culinary) object and its variegated history. *Subjective universality* must be counterbalanced by an *existential historicity*; taste must indeed be discussed and disputed, as it is a profoundly dialogical form of experience.

In both Kantian metaphysics and everyday discourse, the ellipsis "taste" always implies "good taste," never "bad taste." The question of taste therefore entails the existence of a discursive community motivated by an aesthetic imperative, and not the sheer negation of value (couched in a naive relativism) so often imposed by the tasteless. Taste demands engagement, not disengagement. Thus the argument of the fast food lover who claims that taste cannot be disputed is amiss: the question of "McDonald's" is primarily of sociological, not gastronomic, interest. While fast food offers minor gastronomic interest, its cultural effects, to the contrary, are enormous, and pose a distinct threat to the formation of taste. While numerous cultural historians and practitioners of the varied arts have argued for the culinary interest of fast food, I have yet to see a great chef admit to being inspired by such alimentation. And it must be stressed that this is in no way a matter of elitist suppression of the popular arts, since the entire modern history of European and American cuisine has admitted a profound interchange between haute cuisine and both bourgeois and peasant cooking.

Given the broadness of the meaning of "taste," the spontaneity and individuality of such judgments are but a small part of the total constituent features of taste. Subjective judgment is a phantom haunting culture and criticism. The personal, contingent, seemingly irrational origins of taste are inextricably intertwined with the social, collective, and rational structures of culture. Even as the infant struggles to speak its first words, it is always already born into a linguistic system, fully formed yet mutable, infinite yet intimate, formal yet flexible. Likewise, the origins of taste in our infancy (beneath and beyond all physiological thresholds) is but the adaptation and eventual transformation of the "tastes" of our parents and ancestors, of our region and country—perennially classic and bizarre, traditional and idiosyncratic.

Thus our gastronomic points of reference—those tastes which provide the *existential a priori*, the examples, paradigms, and emblems, for the development of our culinary judgment—originate in our childhood world. This is described nowhere so well as in Proust's *Du côté de chez Swann*:

> For, to a permanent background of eggs, cutlets, potatoes, jam and biscuits that she no longer even bothered to announce, Françoise added—according to the labors of the fields and the orchards, the fruits of the sea, the hazards of commerce, the kindness of neighbors and her own genius, all this done so well that our menus, like those quatrefoils sculpted on the portals of thirteenth century cathedrals, reflected somewhat the rhythms of the seasons and the stages of life: a brill because the merchant guaranteed its freshness, a turkey because she saw a beautiful one at the market of Roussainville-le-Pin, cardoons with marrow because she had never made it that way for us, a roast leg of lamb because the outdoors whetted the appetite and there was enough time to return for it in seven hours, spinach for a change, apricots because they were still rare, currants because in two weeks there would be no more, raspberries because Monsieur Swann specially brought them, cherries, the first from the cherry tree in two years, cottage cheese and cream because I used to like it, an almond cake because she ordered it the night before, a brioche because it was our turn to offer one. (70) (See Fischler and Thorne; also Desbiolles)

The narrator's taste literally depends upon the talents and taste of Françoise, as she transforms the world's caprices into her own. Curiously, mentioned here is only one choice specifically intended to please the narrator. Before one's individual taste becomes a matter of self-conscious thematization, choice, and development, it exists as a semiconscious selection and differentiation within the culinary field. There is a profoundly nostalgic dimension to taste; this is just as true for disgust. Yet like the deepest meanings of dreams, which always escape the dreamer, this culinary dimension is but a vague aura of ineffable pleasure and mystery for the eater.

Separating the abundance, ostentation, opulence, and aesthetic weightiness of medieval and Renaissance cuisine from the lightness, delicacy,

elegance, and near translucency of our contemporary versions is the aristocratic and bourgeois haute cuisine of the eighteenth and nineteenth
centuries, epitomized by great dishes from Carême through Escoffier,
where increasing technical complexity reigned. The precise modality of
this complexity is based on the invention, in the mid-eighteenth century,
of modern *liaisons* for sauces, that combination of cream, butter, and flour
that would be the basis of French cooking for the following two hundred
years. It is precisely at this point that cuisine surpassed what Philippe
Gillot speaks of as a *mise-en-présence* of foodstuffs and tastes, to achieve a
modern, intrinsically culinary *mise-en-oeuvre* (104). Thus all the major
cooking techniques—roasting, boiling, stewing, frying, grilling, sautee-
ing, steaming—are now utilized to reveal and harmonize, rather than
juxtapose and distort, the original and unique flavors of the main ingredients. It is as if the taste for Renaissance *vanitas* were superceded by a desire
for the *natures mortes* of Chardin, Cézanne, and the masters of Zen calligra-
phy. That any flavor may exist in its own glory is precisely the summit of
contemporary cooking; as Jean-François Revel explains, ". . . the summits
of the art are attained precisely in those periods where the refinement of
recipes associates a complexity of conception with the lightness of results"
(*Sensibilité* 21). Complexity of conception provides the range of variations
on a theme that permit continual inventiveness; the lightness of realization
assures the presentation of the essential, primal qualities of foodstuffs,
always harkening back to the nostalgia for simple flavors raised to their
quintessential powers. Essence dominates appearance.

Modernist art and modern cuisine have a central trope in common:
invention. Indeed, even simplification is a mode of invention. If there were
to be a theorization of cuisine, it would constitute a theory of exceptions,
nuances, refinements. Culinary taste would transform aesthetics by
redefining the limits of art within the human sensorium, and in doing so
transform all previous relationships between the arts, and between the aes-
theticization of the senses. The gastronomic must no longer serve as mere
metaphor for the arts, but must take its place with the muses.

The modernist conditions of cuisine must be placed in a historical context, insofar as they reveal a startling coincidence between the *nouvelle
cuisine* and the discourse of postmodernism in the arts, both of which
share several central tenets: self-conscious reflexivity (experimentation to
reveal the primary qualities of the component materials of a work); ques-
tioning of origins (the realization that all inventions are but variations,

transmutations, or inspirations based on previous works); regionalism (the decentralization and relativization of techniques, materials, and styles); exoticism (the juxtaposition and incorporation of foreign elements on equal footing with native material). Indeed, if we consider postmodernism to have chronologically followed the late-1960s movements of minimalism and conceptualism, then we may consider the French *nouvelle cuisine*, originating at approximately the same moment, as a true aesthetic avant-garde. We cannot be blind to such stylistic innovations and conceptual complications, to these coincidences and intersections, if we are to enhance our appreciation of contemporary cuisine in relation to the other arts.

As contemporary cuisine tends to highlight and accentuate the natural flavors of the isolated main aliment, subsidiary flavorings tend to become more and more subtle, consisting of just what is needed to heighten, rather than transform or dissimulate, the central flavor. Thus the operative terms for the use of condiments are often referred to as *un rien, un soupçon, une touche, une idée* (a nothing, a suspicion, a touch, an idea). Curiously, these are all philosophical notions that, if juxtaposed in a somewhat surreal manner, would entail not mimesis but countermimesis, not the sublime but a sensual countersublime. For what would the touch of an idea or *a suspicion of nothingness* be if not specific forms of *subjective universality*? Here, in a rhetorical gesture intended to give rise to discourse, taste would be constituted simultaneously by: (1) recognition of typicality, (2) judgment of quality, (3) choice of style—recognitions, judgments, and choices often operative at infinitesimal levels of determination.

Taste as discrimination must be differentiated from taste as appreciation, even though the former is a necessary precondition of the latter. It might thus be fruitful to consider the question of taste according to a structural analysis, so as to contextualize the possibilities of choice without eliminating the problematic of idiosyncrasy. In this way, the issue of taste may be explained in terms of the constitution of pertinent factors in a differential system. An appropriate model might be the semiotic analysis of colors, which, mutatis mutandis, offers valuable insights concerning the confluence of subjective, objective, and cultural values that constitutes perception (Eco). The differences between identification and discrimination, appreciation and preference, must be considered. The eye can discriminate many more colors (nearly ten million!) than can be named; taste too is exceedingly complex, where the five basic gustatory qualities of which all flavors are constituted (bitter, sour, salty, sweet, neutral) appear in infinite variation. The manner in which the naming of the visible spectrum (schematized as red, orange, yellow, green, blue, indigo, violet) groups and limits these differences is not only the discursive foundation of all chromatic symbolism, but is also a factor in the effective reduction of color discrimination. The extremes of describing color would be either the subjective literary recollection of contingent appearance, or an objective statement of wavelength; while the latter would be incapable of taking into account all of the subsidiary (and often synaesthetic) aspects of the lived context that codetermines the appreciation of color, the former always entails imprecision and ambiguity, permitting a certain range of interpretation.

The need for precise description or nomination is well known to wine tasters; the creation of a specialized vocabulary is necessary for both the communication and discrimination of flavors: aggressive, sharp, amorous, ample, amusing, aqueous, ardent, aristocratic, austere, balsamic, brilliant, brusque, coaxing, caressing, solid, charged, structured, delicate, discreet, distinguished, elegant, worn, blooming, bland, feminine, fine, melting, foxy, gay, heavy, herbaceous, formless, liquorous, long, thin, soft, rounded, nervous, clean, noble, unctuous, open, closed, perfidious, little, pinching, powerful, pure, round, rough, severe, solid, supple, suave, tender, tranquil, sad, velvety, old (Chatelain-Courtois). This highly abbreviated, and vastly heterogeneous, list is only a sample; furthermore, such qualifications shift in significance for each type of wine described. The palate—of colors, of tastes—is always circumscribed by the limits of description. When Toulouse-Lautrec claimed that a good wine should be "like a peacock's tail in the mouth," he meant it both in qualitative terms, as a beautiful burst of color-flavor, and in quantitative terms, an all-encompassing, complex coloration, containing the entire spectrum. Hyperbole helps us escape the limitations of language! Jean Dubuffet explains this phenomenon in a particularly Nietzschean mode:

> And yet we also have the feeling that the repertory of words utilized in each of our languages is extremely narrow in relation to the innumerable apprehensions of thought, and that each of these words suffers a great poverty in their abstract status, in order to translate the particular situations of each designated thing and the associations that link thought to it. It is said that there are fifteen different ways of saying "camel" in Arab, and there are without a doubt as many ways of saying "seal" or "snow" in Eskimo. But do only fifteen suffice? A

hundred times a hundred thousand are needed. And in this regard, we
still wouldn't have enough. For thought is in motion, while words are
inert bodies. What we need is words in motion. (Dubuffet 231)

The matter is reduced to its simplest terms in the joke about the man
who claims that he can, without fail, identify any wine in the world.
Blindfolded, he is put to the test by his friends. Offered a glass, he takes
a sip and proudly proclaims: "Red!" Certainly, the more differential
qualities one looks for, the better one may judge, and the higher the level
of connoisseurship. Though the nature of quotidian discourse on wine
rarely takes on the specialization of professional tastings, judgments nevertheless vary according to the level of competency regarding
complexity. The more specific the categorization, the more subtle need
be the qualifications: red/white; Bordeaux/Burgundy; Médoc/Graves;
Haut-Médoc/Médoc; Pauillac/St.-Julien; Mouton-Rothschild/Lafite-
Rothschild;   Mouton-Rothschild   1966/Mouton-Rothschild   1970;
Mouton-Rothschild 1966 tasted in 1979/Mouton-Rothschild 1966 tasted
in 1999. The narrower the range of objects, the greater the need for qualification, description, differentiation. It happens that in contemporary
appreciation of wine, complexity is highly valued (notwithstanding the
phenomenon of the *vins nouveaux*). Yet it should be apparent that every type
of wine (though hardly every bottle) has its own virtue, as well as its place
in a respective cuisine.

It is precisely in wine tasting (where the sheer numerical and "stylistic"
possibilities of invention are relatively circumscribed in relation to those of
cooking) that we may establish a combinatory grid that permits the sort of
subtle and precise determinations that may inform connoisseurship. For to
combine the results of horizontal tastings (several vintages of a single
wine; a diachronic analysis) and vertical tastings (several wines of a single
vintage, usually limited to one town or region; a synchronic analysis)
would be to taste wines not against personal preferences, nor against
appropriate foods, but rather within a range of related wines, such that
typicality may be delimited. Yet it must be stressed that this grid is unsta-
ble, as wine ages to a point of perfection, and then declines in quality; the
palate is transformed with age and disease; preferences change with knowledge and experience; and culinary aesthetics, regarding both wine and
food, shifts with styles and epochs. Whence the crucial role of memory in
taste: one need not only be able to differentiate according to increasingly
subtle criteria, but also to remember and mentally contrast those typical

gustatory characteristics that make such differentiation possible. Yet the selectiveness of memory creates both identities and differences: for the chef, what is crucial is how a recipe is transformed into one's own. Culinary idiosyncrasy is the vanguard of progress; the recipe is not a canon, code, or regulation, and the typicality or "authenticity" of a dish is but a range of possibilities, an indeterminate ideal, a pole of transformations.

Qualifications of taste (as sensual discrimination, aesthetic judgment, and critical appreciation) are not simply physiological, psychological, or aesthetic: they are also symbolic, insofar as the discriminations of taste are filtered through language. Appreciation demands discrimination; discrimination presupposes appreciation. This does not imply that only those tastes that are named are experienced, but rather more broadly that language establishes and foregrounds gustatory relations, kinships, limits, determinations, specifications, nuances. Nominalism is both a trap and a guide. As the common name of a single species of plant or animal changes from region to region, its taste also changes—due to both terrestrial and linguistic shifts. Differences in taste may be dissimulated as well as revealed by language and culture: such determinations are made according to the manner in which the global system of taste relations (in a given culture and cuisine) are established by a continual sedimentation of gustatory references and cross-references. As is the case of phonemes in a given language, all sounds and combinations are possible, though relatively few make sense.

The lexical imprint on the semantic field may be the cause of regional and even national blind spots regarding taste, as well as of the creation of false discriminations and determinations. These complications may be caused by *inadequacy of word to taste* (which is the case for the vast majority of unnamed nuances); *inadequacy of taste to word* (for example, my own blind spot regarding truffles, the much vaunted taste of which remains a mystery to me, even after repeated efforts); or *lexical ambiguity* (which entails, or reveals, confusions of taste). A case in point might be useful. I continuously have arguments in France about the relationship between two related though distinct herbs, what in English are differentiated as *dill* (normally, in French, *aneth*) and *fennel* (*fenouil*). These are botanically differentiated respectively as *Anethum graveolus* and *Foeniculum vulgare*, both of the family *Umbelliferae*. While many people in France argue that they are either the same thing or else minor variations of the same herb, I, with Polish and Hungarian origins—cultures where dill is widely used, and fennel relatively unappreciated—can not only differentiate between the two, but have as great an aversion to fennel and anis as I have a taste for aneth. The cause of this gallic equivocation is complex. Visually nearly identical, *aneth* and *fenouil* are defined in a confusing manner by the major French dictionaries:

(1) *Le Petit Robert* defines *fenouil* (*fenouil doux* [sweet fennel]) as *feniculum* of the family *Ombelliféracées*, referring in the same entry to *aneth* (*fenouil amer* [bitter fennel]) without any further botanical specification; the entry for *aneth*, in turn, simply refers the reader to *fenouil*. Thus the two appear to be synonymous, with a minor unarticulated variation specifically marked in terms of a major variation of taste (sweet/bitter).

(2) *Littré* is somewhat more precise, yet also ambiguous: *fenouil* is defined as *anethum foeniculum* of the family *Ombellifères*, while *fenouil bâtard* (bastard fennel) is defined as *anethum graveolens*; all the while, *aneth* is given no more precision than that of being a *plante ombellifère*. According to these definitions, the two may be different, though not necessarily.

(3) *Harrap's New Standard French and English Dictionary* translates *fenouil* as *fennel*, *fenouil officinal* as *sweet fennel*, and *fenouil bâtard* as *dill*; in turn, *aneth* is translated as *anethum*, *aneth odorant* as *dill*, and *aneth doux* as *fennel*. In the other direction, *fennel* is translated as both *fenouil* and *aneth doux*, while *dill* is translated as both *aneth odorant* and *fenouil bâtard*. Here, perhaps thanks to the non-French origin of the text, at least the two are differentiated, albeit with a certain confusion. The continual association, indeed confusion, between the two plants is based on botanical family resemblance, not on species differentiation, whereas the latter, more precise determination is obviously of greater culinary import. As would be said in linguistics, a disambiguification is needed.

Clearly, the extremely limited culinary use value of these herbs in France hardly motivates a well-defined linguistic differentiation; *dill* is not a pertinent feature of contemporary French cuisine, as is the case in the Baltic countries. But this situation is fated to change, as the culinary lexicon is being pressured from two sides: first, the increased internationalism of gastronomy demands more precise vocabulary and translations; second, research into ancient, medieval, and Renaissance cuisine (where variants of these plants were abundantly used), demands equal precision—a precision already inherent in the Latin distinctions between species, genus, and family, but one that is but slowly passing into everyday French usage. (Indeed, one notes the increasing presence of dill on French tables linked precisely to the widespread popularity of smoked, marinated, and raw fish.)

Taste (as discrimination of flavor) is a function of refinement: empirical tastes (flavors) are determined and organized according to cultural meanings and usages. Gastronomic tradition is a symbolic system dependent upon the pertinence of specific objects within the system; conversely, gastronomic creativity establishes new pertinent features, and thus transforms the system. The determination of what constitutes pertinent factors within any given gastronomic discourse is precisely at the origin of the gastronomic symbolic: by transgressing prescribed thresholds between flavor determinations and their use values, a culinary allusion may be transformed into a gastronomic essence. To refine differentiation and to make categories more subtle is to improve taste, and thus to consequently elaborate the codes of taste. This is precisely the role of the specialist, both chef and gastronome, since polemic—whether between chef and chef, chef and gourmet, or gourmet and critic—is necessary for the advancement of cuisine as a fine art. To escape the limits of the given gastronomic rules of an epoch is to enrich the field of taste (flavor and quality). As new pertinent features are foregrounded (the possibility of differentiating fennel and dill, for example), there evolves a discovery of dishes based on these acquired tastes, such as the Russian beef Stroganoff (slices of beef in a sauce of cream and mustard with dill). Though the addition of dill in this dish is not always called for in Russian recipes, its use establishes the dish as all the more distinctive. Indeed, one of my favorite Paris restaurants, Le Hangar, emblematizes this situation by making an excellent beef Stroganoff, though, perhaps as a concession to French taste, the dill is eliminated; needless to say, I resist the temptation, for this particular variation poses a definite gustatory lack for my palate. Nevertheless, the possibility of the intrusion of dill upon the French palate redefines certain affinities between herbs, sauces, and meats, such that the nature of the entire system changes by the expansion and reorientation of acceptable relationships between terms. Here, the art of gastronomy is to reveal and name hitherto unknown nuances, indeed to discover entirely unknown dishes and cuisines.

Yet it is one thing to create such complex taste grids and structural gastronomic combinatories; it is another to form a taste, a culinary style (whether as chef, gourmet, or writer). Style is a function of what the philosopher Maurice Merleau-Ponty referred to as "coherent deformation," which implies the existence of a series of transfigurations within a normative system: not creativity versus tradition, but creativity *informed* by tradition, and tradition *transformed* by creativity. I always wonder, when reading a restaurant review or a recipe, precisely what motivated the writer to order and write about any given dish. One evening, while dining at Léon de Lyon with Jean-Claude Bonnet, renowned specialist on Antonin Carême and Grimod de la Reynière, we both ordered, for different reasons but with equal pleasure, *Choux farcis aux truffes fraîches (ris de veau, crêtes de coq, dés de foie gras)* (stuffed cabbage with fresh truffles [sweetbreads, cockscombs, diced foie gras]). He chose the dish out of literary and historic curiosity, because the ingredients were those of the famed libertine suppers of the eighteenth century; I, with nostalgic glee incited by the imp of the perverse, chose the dish with the desire to compare it to one of my mother's specialties, stuffed cabbage (the national dish of my father's birthplace). Both of us were thrilled, though, as may well be imagined, each of us formed quite different evaluations and nearly antithetical narratives. A third dinner companion, who ordered a pot-au-feu, considered our choice incredulously (Weiss 1997, 99–110)!

In terms of culinary creativity, each epoch has its paradigmatic realm of invention. In this regard, the salad may be considered a veritable ontological transformer in the nouvelle cuisine. As Claude Fischler explains in *L'Homnivore*, "The salad will impose itself as a territory of superlative freedom, of a more or less considered madness. It is by definition the domain of melange and organized disorder. It therefore escapes from traditional culinary grammars, and henceforth permits unhindered transgression and innovation" (264). It is generally considered that this freedom-in-salads was inaugurated, in its *nouvelle cuisine* version, by Michel Guérard; Jacques Manière even named his own a *salade folle*. However, before 1975 no starred Michelin restaurant listed a salad among its specialities; the first to do so, in that year, were Alain Chapel with a *salade de homard*, and Pic with a *salade de pêcheurs au xérès* (263). The dialectic between the indigenous and the exotic is a key factor in both modernist and postmodernist art, cuisine included; as in poetry, the constant tension between the limits of the familiar and the effects of creative defamiliarization mark the boundaries of the culinary possibilities of an epoch. Consider one of the creations of Alain Senderens, who was instrumental in helping establish the *nouvelle cuisine* by integrating foreign techniques and recipes into French cooking, as well as by rediscovering long lost recipes from ancient, medieval and Renaissance sources. At his former Parisian restaurant, L'Archestrate, one of his masterpieces was a particularly luscious salad: *Salade de homard aux mangues et basilic* (lobster and mango salad with basil). The question as to whether this dish was inspired by or merely homologous to the traditional Vietnamese papaya and shrimp salad with lemongrass is a moot point. Senderens's salad is rendered de luxe by substituting lobster for shrimp, and it is gallicized (via Provence) by substituting basil and vinaigrette for lemongrass and the fermented fish sauce *nuoc mam*. Crucial is both the manner in which such salads stretch the limits of what constitutes a "salad" in France, as well as the inspiration that such an influx of exotic flavors offers for other creations, such as Senderens's *Homard à la vanille* (vanilla lobster).

In counterdistinction to the domestication of the exotic, we may also consider the question of typicality in terms of the renovation of the indigenous. Formerly, at the Restaurant Chantecler of the Hôtel Negresco in Nice, the then head chef Dominique Le Stanc foreshadowed his brilliant transformations of regional cuisine—such as the *Risotto aux artichauts, parmesan et râpée de truffes noires* (risotto with artichokes, parmesan and black truffles) or the *Fricassée de St-Jacques et langoustines au basilic* (fricassee of sea scallops and crayfish with basil)—with the offering of a fanciful appetizer: a lilliputian *pan bagnat*. This sandwich, typically niçois but for its size, small as the tip of one's thumb, offered all the archetypical flavors (tuna, crudités, olives, oil) condensed into one bite—all the more amusing because once a year, on the beach opposite the hotel, one of the popular, if grotesque, attractions of this city is the creation of a gargantuan *pan bagnat* one kilometer long!

I have met a person—cultivated, equilibrious, sane, aesthete—who often quite simply cannot decide what to eat. His indecision is such that it almost paralyzes him. To resolve the situation, he enters a supermarket, chooses a customer at random, and follows that person, placing into his shopping cart all the same things chosen by the other. Like a "man without qualities" living according to the surrealist ideal of objective chance, he instantiates the depressing contemporary commonplace of conditioned, stereotyped, limited taste. In a consumer society of the spectacle, his comportment reveals precisely why for many, *taste is the discourse of the other*. It is only through a combination of knowledge and pleasure, of connoisseurship and discovery, that we can make it our own.

This essay is based on an earlier version, published in Allen S. Weiss, *Flamme et festin : Une poétique de la cuisine*. Paris: Éditions Java, 1994.

BIBLIOGRAPHY

A. D. G. (pseudonym of Alain Fournier). *La Nuit des grands chiens malades*. Paris: Gallimard (Folio), 1972.

Almanach perpétuel des Gourmands contenant Le Code Gourmand, et des applications, règles et méditations de gastronomie transcendante. Paris: Barba, 1830.

Amila, Jean. *Contest-flic*. Paris: Gallimard, Série noire, 1972.

Andrew, Dudley. *Mists of Regret: Culture and Sensibility in Classic French Film*. Princeton, NJ: Princeton University Press, 1995.

Apostolidès, Jean-Marie. "Figures populaires, figures mythiques dans *La Femme du boulanger*." In *Popular Traditions and Learned Culture in France: From the Sixteenth to the Twentieth Century*. Ed. Marc Bertrand. Saratoga, CA: Anma Libri, 1985. 287–304.

Appadurai, Arjun. "How to Make a National Cuisine: Cookbooks in Contemporary India," *Comparative Studies in Society and History* 30 (1988): 3–24.

Aragon, Louis. *Le Paysan de Paris*. Paris: Gallimard, 1961.

Aron, Jean-Paul. *Le Mangeur du XIXe siècle*. Paris: Robert Laffont, 1973.

———. *The Art of Eating in France: Manners and Menus in the Nineteenth Century*. Trans. N. Rootes. London: Owen, 1975 [1973].

Astruc, Alexandre, and Michel Contat. *Sartre par lui-même*. (Film) 1972.

Athenaeus. *The Deipnosophists of Athenaeus of Naucratis*. 7 vols. Trans. C.B. Gulick. Cambridge, MA: Harvard University Press [Loeb Classical Library], 1969.

Baker, William F. and George Dessart. *Down the Tube: An Inside Account of the Failure of American Television*. New York: Basic, 1998.

Bakhtin, Mikhaïl. *L'Oeuvre de François Rabelais et la culture populaire au Moyen Âge et sous la Renaissance*. Paris: Gallimard, 1970.

Balzac, Honoré de. *Oeuvres diverses*. Ed. M. Bouteron and H. Longnon. Paris: Conard, 1938. 2 vols.

———. *La Comédie humaine*. 12 vols. Paris: Gallimard [Pléiade], 1976–81.

Barthes, Roland. *Mythologies*. Paris: Seuil, 1957.

———. "Pour une psycho-sociologie de l'alimentation contemporaine." In *Pour une histoire de l'alimentation*. Ed. J.-J. Hémardinquer. Paris: Armand Colin, 1970.

————. "Steak and chips." In *Mythologies*. Trans. A. Lavers. New York: Hill and Wang, 1972.

Baudelaire, Charles. *Oeuvres complètes*. Paris: Gallimard [Pléiade], 1976.

Beard, James. *Menus for Entertaining*. New York: Delacorte Press, 1965.

Beardsworth, Alan, and Teresa Keil. "Putting the Menu on the Agenda." *Sociology* 24:1 (1990).

Beattie, Liza, Furzana Khan, and Greg Philo. "Race, Advertising and the Public Face of Television." In *Message Received: Glasgow Media Group Research 1993–1998*. Ed. Greg Philo. Harlow: Longman, 1999.

Beauvoir, Simone de. *Mémoires d'une jeune fille rangée*. Paris: Gallimard, 1958.

————. *La Force de l'âge*. Paris: Gallimard, 1960.

————. *La Cérémonie des adieux*. Paris: Gallimard, 1981.Becker, Howard. *Art Worlds*. Berkeley: University of California Press, 1982.

Beecher, Jonathan. *Fourier—The Visionary and his World*. Berkeley: University of California Press, 1986.

Belasco, Warren J. "Ethnic Fast Foods: The Corporate Melting Pot." *Food and Foodways* 2:1 (1987): 1–30.

Bell, David F. *Models of Power: Politics and Economics in Zola's* Rougon-Macquart. Lincoln: University of Nebraska Press, 1988.

————. "Statistical Thinking in Balzac: Le Cousin Pons." *SubStance* 23:2 (1994), 22–37.

Benjamin, Walter. "Paris, Capital of the Nineteenth Century." Trans. Edmund Jephcott. In *Reflections: Essays, Aphorisms, Autobiographical Writings*. New York: Harcourt Brace Jovanovich, 1978. 146–62.

Berg, Christian. "Huysmans et l'Antiphysis." *Revue des Sciences Humaines* (1978): 170–71.

Bersani, Leo, and Ulysse Dutoit. "Beauty's Light." *October* 82 (1997): 17–29.

Beylie, Claude. *Marcel Pagnol ou le cinéma en liberté*. Paris: Atlos L'Herminier, 1986.

Birnbaum, Pierre. *La France imaginée*. Paris: Fayard, 1998.

Blaha, Franz G. "Detective/Mystery/Spy Fiction." In *Handbook of French Popular Culture*. Ed. Pierre L. Horn. New York: Greenwood Press, 1991. 39–57.

Boisard, Pierre. *Le Camembert—Mythe national*. Paris: Calmann-Lévy, 1992.

Bonnain-Merdyck, Rolande. "Fourier, gastrosophe." In Henri Lefebvre et al., *Actualité de Fourier*. Paris: Anthropos, 1975, 145–80.

Bonnet, Jean-Claude. "Présentation." In Grimod de la Reynière, *Écrits gastronomiques*. Ed. Jean-Claude Bonnet. Paris: UGE/10–18, 1978. 7–92.

Bordes, Elie. *Le Drame spirituel dans l'œuvre de Maxence Van der Meersch*. Tourcoing: Georges Frère, 1944.

Bourdieu, Pierre. "Intellectual Field and Creative Project" [1966]. *Social Science Information* 8:2 (1969), 89–119.

————. *Distinction: A Social Critique of the Judgement of Taste*. Trans. Richard Nice. Cambridge, MA: Harvard University Press, 1984.

————. *Homo academicus*. Trans. P. Collier. Cambridge: Polity Press, 1988 [1984].

————. *The Field of Cultural Production*. New York: Columbia University Press, 1993.

————. *Méditations pascaliennes*. Paris: Le Seuil, 1997.

————. *The Rules of Art. Genesis and Structure of the Literary Field*. Trans. S. Emanuel. Stanford, CA: Stanford University Press, 1996 [1992].

————. *On Television*. Trans. P. Ferguson. New York: The New Press, 1998 [1996].

Bozza, Anthony. "The TV Program 'Pressure Cooker' on the Food Network." *Rolling Stone*. 18 February 1999: 67.

Briffault, Eugène. *Paris à table*. Paris: J. Hetzel, 1846.

Brillat-Savarin, Anthelme. *Physiologie du goût*. Paris: Charpentier, 1839 [1826].

————. *The Physiology of Taste*. Trans. M.F.K. Fisher. New York: Harcourt Brace Jovanovich, 1978.

————. *Physiologie du goût*. Paris: Flammarion, 1982.

Brooker, Katrina. "On the Food Network: Lust, Weirdos, Saturated Fat." *Fortune*. 6 July 1998: 34.

Brown, Jennifer. "Food Network Audience Increases." *Associated Press Online* 26 March 1999.

Bruno, G. *Le Tour de la France par Deux Enfants*. Paris: Eugène Belin, 1994.

Buvik, Per. "L'Amour et le manger. Autour de *Sainte Lydwine de Schiedam*." In *Huysmans, entre grâce et péché*. Ed. Alain Vircondelet. Paris: Beauchesne, 1995. 33–49.

"Cable's Food Network to Launch Regional Web Sites." *Media Daily* 4:5 (1997): n. p.

Camporesi, Piero. *L'Enfer et le fantasme de l'hostie*. Paris: Hachette, 1989.

————. *The Magic Harvest. Food, Folklore and Society*. Trans. J. K. Hall. Cambridge, MA: Polity Press, 1993 [1989].

Carême, Antonin [Marie-Antoine]. *Le Maître d'hôtel français*. 2 vols. Paris, 1832–33.

————. *L'Art de la cuisine française au dix-neuvième siècle. Traité Élémentaire et Pratique suivi de dissertations culinaires et gastronomiques utiles aux progrès de cet art*. 2 vols. Paris: chez l'auteur, 1833.

————. *L'Art de la cuisine française au dix-neuvième siècle*. Paris, 1833–35. Rpt. Paris (1847), Kerangué et Pollès (1981), with vols. 3 and 4 by Plumerey.

————. *Le Pâtissier royal parisien*. 2 vols. 3d. ed. Paris, 1841 (1815).

————. *Le Maître d'hôtel français ou Parallèle de la Cuisine ancienne et moderne selon les quatre saisons*. 2 vols. Paris: J. Renouard et Cie., 1842 [1822].

————. *Le Cuisinier parisien, ou L'Art de la cuisine française au dix-neuvième siècle*. Paris: Firmin-Didot, 1896 [1828].

Carlton Food Network. <http://www.cfn.co.uk>.

Certeau, Michel de, Luce Giard, and Pierre Mayol. *L'Invention du quotidien 2. Habiter, cuisiner*. Paris: Gallimard, 1994.

Chalon, Jean. *Portrait d'une séductrice*. Paris: Stock, 1976.

————. *Colette, l'éternelle apprentie*. Paris: Flammarion, 1998.

Chang, K.C., ed. *Food in Chinese Culture. Anthropological and Historical Perspectives*. New Haven, CT: Yale University Press, 1977.

Charbonneau, Pascale. Rev. of *Fricassée de meurtres à la bordelaise*, by Jean-Pierre Xiradakis and Pierre Leterrier. *Papilles* October 1994: 56.

Chatelain-Courtois, Martine. *Les Mots du vin et de l'ivresse*. Paris: Belin, 1984.

Clark, Priscilla. "Thoughts for Food, I: French Cuisine and French Culture." *French Review* 49 (1975): 32–41.

————. "Literary Culture in France and the United States." *The American Journal of Sociology* 84 (1979): 1057–77.

————. *Literary France: The Making of a Culture*. Berkeley: University of California Press, 1987.

Clément, Marie-Christine, and Didier Clément. *Colette gourmande*. Paris: Albin Michel, 1990.

Code Gourmand. Manuel complet de Gastronomie. Paris: Ambroise Dupont, 1827.

Colette. "Récriminations." In *Oeuvres*. Paris: Éditions Gallimard [Pléiade].

————."La Cire verte." In *Le Képi*. In *Oeuvres complètes*. Paris: Le Fleuron, 1950. 237–51.

————. "A Moroccan Luncheon." In *Places*. Trans. David Le Vay. London: Peter Owen, 1970. 91–94.

————. *Looking Backwards*. Trans. David Le Vay. Bloomington and London: Indiana University Press, 1975.

————. *The Claudine Novels*. Trans. Antonia White. London: Penguin, 1987.

Compagnon, Antoine. "La dernière victime du narrateur." *Critique* 598 (1997): 131–46.

Cooper, Ann. *"A Woman's Place Is in the Kitchen"—The Evolution of Women Chefs*. New York: Van Nostrand Reinhold, 1998.

Corbet, (Abbé) Jules. *Histoire dogmatique, liturgique et archéologique du sacrement de l'eucharistie*. Paris: Société générale de librairie catholique, 1885–86. Vol. XI.

Cornwell, Patricia. *Postmortem*. New York: Charles Scribner's Sons, 1990.

Crosland, Margaret. *Colette: The Difficulty of Loving*. New York: Bobbs-Merrill, 1973.

Curnonsky and Marcel Rouff. *La France gastronomique. Guide des merveilles culinaires et des bonnes auberges françaises. La Savoie*. Paris: F. Rouff, 1923.

Daeninckx, Didier. *Le Géant inachevé*. Paris: Gallimard [Folio], 1984.

————. *Le Facteur fatal*. Paris: Denoël [Folio], 1990.

————. *Hors limites*. Paris: Julliard, Pocket, 1992.

Del Castillo, Michel. *Colette, une certaine France*. Paris: Stock, 1999.

Delteil, Gérard. *Mort d'un satrape rouge*. Paris: Éditions Métaillé, 1995.

Derenne, Jean-Philippe. *L'Amateur de cuisine*. Paris: Editions Stock, 1996.

Desbiolles, Maryline. *La Seiche*. Paris: Le Seuil, 1998.

Desnoiresterres, Gustave. *Grimod de La Reynière et son groupe; d'après des documents entièrement inédits*. Paris: Didier et cie, 1877.

D'Hollander, Paul. *Ses apprentissages*. Paris: Klincksieck, 1979.

Dontenville, Henri. *Mythologie française*. Paris: Payot, 1973.

Dorenburg, Andrew, and Karen Page. *Becoming a Chef*. New York: Van Nostrand Reinhold, 1995.

Dormann, Geneviève. *Amoureuse Colette*. Poitiers: Ed. Hersher, 1984.

Dubuffet, Jean. "Un grand salut très différent au Martelandre." In *Écrits bruts*. Ed. Michel Thévoz. Paris: Presses Universitares de France, 1979.

Dupont, Jacques. *Colette*. Paris: Hachette, 1995.

Duras, Marguerite. *Les Petits Chevaux de Tarquinia*. Paris: Gallimard, 1973.

Eco, Umberto. "How Culture Conditions the Colours We See." In *On Signs*. Marshall Blonsky, ed. Baltimore: Johns Hopkins University Press, 1985.

Elias, Norbert. *The Court Society*. Trans. E. Jephcott. Oxford: Blackwell, 1983.

———. "The History of Manners." In *The Civilizing Process*. Trans. E. Jephcott. Oxford and Cambridge, MA: Blackwell, 1994 [1939].

Encyclopédie ou Dictionnaire raisonné des sciences des arts et des métiers. Stuttgart: F. Frommann Verlag, 1966 [1751–80].

Ennès, Pierre. "1789–1848—Naissance de la table moderne." In *Histoire de la table*. Ed. Pierre Ennés, Gérard Mabille, and Philippe Thiébaut. Paris: Flammarion, 1995.

Escoffier, Auguste. *Souvenirs inédits. 75 ans au service de l'art culinaire*. Marseille: Éditions Jeanne Laffitte, 1985.

Falk, Pasi. *The Consuming Body*. London: Sage, 1994.

Fantasia, Rick. "Fast Food in France." *Theory and Society* 24 (1995): 201–43.

Faulkner, Christopher. "René Clair, Marcel Pagnol and the Social Dimension of Speech." *Screen* 35 (Summer 1994): 157–70.

Ferguson, Priscilla Parkhurst. *Paris as Revolution. Reading the 19th-Century City*. Berkeley: University of California Press, 1994.

———. "Cuisine! Cuisine! The Memory Machine." Paper presented at the meetings of the Social Science History Association. New Orleans, November, 1996.

———. "The Careers of Chefs: 'French' and 'American' Models of Cuisine." In *Eating Culture*. Ed. Ron Scapp and Bryan Seitz. Albany: State University Press of New York, 1998.

———. "Paysages culinaires." In *Paysage et Identité régionale*. Université de Grenoble-Valence (2000).

———, and Sharon Zukin. "What's cooking." *Theory and Society* 24 (1995): 193–99.

Ferrier-Caverivière, Nicole. *Colette l'authentique*. Paris: PUF, 1997.

Fiddes, Nick. *Meat: A Natural Symbol*. London: Routledge, 1991.

Fine, Ben and Ellen Leopold. *The World of Consumption*. London: Routledge, 1993.

Fine, Gary Alan. *Kitchens: The Culture of Restaurant Work*. Berkeley: University of California Press, 1996.

———. "Justifying Work: Occupational Rhetorics as Resources in Restaurant Kitchens." *Administration Science Quarterly* 41 (1996): 90–115.

Finkelstein, Joanne. *Dining Out: A Sociology of Modern Manners*. New York: New York University Press, 1989.

Fisher, M.F.K. *The Art of Eating*. New York: Macmillan, 1954.

———. *With Bold Knife and Fork*. New York: Perigee Books, 1969.

Fischler, Claude. *L'homnivore*. Paris: Odile Jacob, 1990.

Flandrin, Jean-Louis. "La diversité des goûts et des pratiques alimentaires en Europe du XIVe au XVIIIe siècle." *Revue d'histoire moderne et contemporaine* 330 (1983), 66–83.

———, and Philip and Mary Hyman. "La Cuisine dans la littérature de colportage." In *Le Cuisinier François*. Ed. Jean-Louis Flandrin, Mary Hyman, and Philip Hyman. Paris: Éditions Montabla, 1983.

———, and Massimo Montanari, eds. *Histoire de l'alimentation*. Paris: Fayard, 1997.

Food Network. <http://www.foodtv.com>.

"Food Network Gets its Show on the Road." *Electronic Media* 5 April 1999: 4.

"Food Network Switches Menu." *Chicago Sun-Times* 31 March 1999: section 2 5XS.

Fourier, Charles. *Oeuvres complètes*. 12 vols. Paris: Anthropos, 1966–68.

Francis, Claude, and Fernande Gautier. *Colette*. Paris: Perrin, 1997.

Freud, Sigmund. *Totem and Taboo. Some Points of Agreement Between the Mental Lives of Savages and Neurotics*. Trans. James Strachey. New York: Norton, 1952.

———. *Introductory Lectures in Psychoanalysis*. New York: W.W. Norton & Company, 1977.

Gaillard, Françoise. "*A Rebours* ou l'inversion des signes." In *L'Esprit de Décadence I*. Colloque de Nantes (1976). Paris: Minard, 1980.

Garbarz, Franck. "*Nénette et Boni* : mère, pourquoi nous as-tu abandonnés." *Positif* (February 1997): 38–39.

Gide, André. *Voyage au Congo*. Paris: Gallimard, 1927.

Gillet, Philippe. *Le Goût et les mots: Littérature et gastronomie (XIVe–XXe siècles)*. Paris: Payot, 1993.

Girard, Alain. "Le Triomphe de La Cuisinière bourgeoise: Livres culinaires, cuisine et société en France aux XVIIe et XVIIIe siècles." *Revue d'histoire moderne et contemporaine* 24 (October–December 1977), 497–523.

Girard, René. *Violence and the Sacred*. Trans. Patrick Gregory. Baltimore: Johns Hopkins University, 1977.

Giraudoux, Jean. *La Guerre de Troie n'aura pas lieu*. Paris: Livre de Poche, 1964.

Goblot, Edmond. *La Barrière et le niveau—Essai sur la bourgeoisie française moderne*. Paris: Presses Universitaires de France, 1967 [1927].

Grimod de la Reynière, Alexandre-Balthazar-Laurent. *Almanach des Gourmands*. Paris: Maradan (vols. 1–6) and Chaumerot (vols. 7–8), 1803–12.

————. *Journal des Gourmands et des Belles, ou l'Épicurien français*. Paris: Capelle et Renand, 1806.

————. *Écrits gastronomiques*. Ed. Jean-Claude Bonnet. Paris: Union générale d'éditions (10/18), 1978.

————. *Almanach des Gourmands servant de guide dans lesmoyens de faire excellente chère par un vieil amateur*. 8 vols.Paris: Valmer, 1984 [1803–1812].

————. *Manuel des Amphitryons—Contenant Un Traité de la Dissection des viandes à table, la Nomenclature des Menus les plus nouveaux pour chaque saison, et des Élémens de Politesse gourmande*. Paris: Éditions A.M. Métailié. 1984 [1808].

Gringoire, Th. and L. Saulnier. *Le Répertoire de la cuisine*. Paris: Flammarion, 1982.

Guy, Christian. *Une Histoire de la cuisine française*. Paris: Les Productions de Paris, 1962.

Haining, Peter, ed. *Murder on the Menu: Cordon Bleu Stories of Crime and Mystery*. London: Souvenir, 1991.

Hegel, G.W.F. *The Phenomenology of Spirit*. New York: Oxford University Press, 1977.

Higgins, Lynn A. "Pagnol and the Paradoxes of Frenchness." In *Identity Papers: Contested Nationhood in Twentieth-Century France*. Ed. Steven Ungar and Tom Conley. Minneapolis: University of Minnesota Press, 1996. 91–112.

Hobsbawm, Eric. "Inventing Traditions," and "Mass-Producing Traditions: Europe, 1870–1914." In *The Invention of Tradition*. Ed. Eric Hobsbawm and Terence Ranger. Cambridge: Cambridge University Press, 1983.

Hochschild, Adam. *King Leopold's Ghost*. New York: Houghton Mifflin Company, 1998.

Huetz de Lemps, Alain, and Jean-Robert Pitte, eds. *Les Restaurants dans le monde et à travers les âges*. Grenoble: Glenat, 1990.

Huysmans, Joris-Karl. *Against Nature*, London, Penguin Books, 1959.

————. *A Rebours*. Paris: Gallimard [Folio], 1977.

Sainte-Lydwine de Schiedam. Paris: Maren Sell, 1989.

Istendael, Geert van. "Ô Belgique." In *Belgique toujours grande et belle, Revue de l'Université de Bruxelles*. Ed. Antoine Pickels and Jacques Sojcher. Bruxelles: Editions Complexe, 1998. Vol. 1–2: 431–32.

Izzo, Jean-Claude. *Total Khéops*. Paris: Gallimard, Série noire, 1995.

Jacq, Christian. *Le Juge d'Égypte (III): La Justice du vizir*. Paris: Plon, Pocket, 1994.

Jans, Adrien. *A la rencontre de Maxence Van der Meersch, romancier de la pitié et de l'amour*. Liège: La Sixaine, 1946.

Jeffords, Susan. "Narrative as Violence, Violence as Patriarchy, Patriarchy as Story-Telling." In *Gender: Literary and Cinematic Representation*. Ed. Jeanne Ruppert. Gainesville: University Press of Florida, 1994. 83–95.

Jonquet, Thierry. *Les Orpailleurs*. Paris: Gallimard [Folio policier], 1993.

———. *Moloch*. Paris: Gallimard, Série noire, 1998.

Kaplan, Bernard D. "As the French Turn Away from Serious Food, Tourists Come to the Rescue of Restaurants." *Minneapolis Star-Tribune* 12 July 1998: G7.

Karten, Harvey S. *Nénette et Boni*. *Internet Movie Database*. Online. 1997. Available FTP: rec.arts.movies.reviews.

Koestenbaum, Wayne. "Angelina Jolie, The Indiscreet Object of Desire." *The New York Times Magazine, The "Me" Millennium* (October 17, 1999).

La Chapelle, Vincent. *Le Cuisinier Moderne*. The Hague, 1735.

Lacrosse, Jean-Marie. "La Belgique telle qu'elle s'ignore." *Le Débat* 94 (mars-avril 1997): 12–41.

Ladenson, Elisabeth. "Colette For Export Only." *Yale French Studies* 90 (1996), 25–46.

Larousse, Pierre. "Gastronomie," *Grand Dictionnaire Universel du XIXe siècle*. Geneva and Paris: Slatkine Reprints, 1982 [1866–79].

Leblanc, Maurice. *Arsène Lupin contre Herlock Sholmès*. Paris: Le Livre de poche, 1963.

Ledbetter, James. *Made Possible By …: The Death of Public Broadcasting in the United States*. London: Verso, 1998.

Léliaert, Bernardin. *Un Grand Romancier de "chez nous," Maxence Van der Meersch*. Arcachon: Edmond Dujardin, n.d.

"Le masque et la plume." Transcription: Jean-François Houben. France Inter. Online. February 1997. Available FTP: chez.com/chtrain/nenette.html.

Lesage, Julia. "*S/Z* and *The Rules of the Game*." In *Movies and Methods*. Ed. Bill Nichols. Berkeley: University of California Press, 1985. 2:476–99.

Leseleuc, Anne de. *Les Vacances de Marcus Aper*. Paris: 10/18, 1992.

———. *Marcus Aper chez les Rutènes*. Paris: 10/18, 1993.

———. *Marcus Aper et Laureolus*. Paris: 10/18, 1994.

———. *Le Trésor de Boudicca*. Paris: 10/18, 1996.

Lévi-Bruhl, Lucien. *La Mentalité primitive*. Paris: Presses Universitaires de France, 1960.

Lévi-Strauss, Claude. *Le Cru et le cuit*. Paris: Librairie Plon, 1964.

Littré, Émile. *Dictionnaire de la langue française*, vol. 2. Monte-Carlo: Éditions du Cap, 1974.

L.S.R. *L'Art de bien traiter*. Paris, 1674. [Rpt. Daniel Morcrette, Luzarches, 1978.]

MacDonogh, Giles. *A Palate in Revolution: Grimod de La Reynière and the Almanach des Gourmands*. London: Robin Clark Limited, 1987.

Magnan, Pierre. *Le Sang des Atrides*. Paris: Fayard, [Folio], 1977.

———. *Le Commissaire dans la truffière*. Paris: Gallimard, [Folio], 1978.

———. *Les Secrets de Laviolette*. Paris: Denoël, [Folio], 1992.

Manchette, Jean-Patrick. *L'Affaire N'Gustro*. Paris: Gallimard [Folio], 1971.

Manson, Cynthia, ed. *Crime à la Carte*. New York: Penguin, 1994.

Marin. *Les Dons de Comus*. Paris, 1740.

Marks, Elaine. *Colette*. New Brunswick, NJ: Rutgers University Press, 1960.

Martens, Francis. "La Begique en chantant." In *Belgique toujours grande et belle, Revue de l'Université de Bruxelles*. Ed. Antoine Pickels and Jacques Sojcher. Bruxelles: Editions Complexe, 1998. Vol. 1–2: 19–40.

Mauss, Marcel. *The Gift*. Trans. I. Cunnison. New York: Norton, 1967.

Mendras, Henri. "What is Left of 1789?" In *Unfinished Revolutions: Legacies of Upheaval in Modern French Culture*. Ed. Robert T. Denommé and Roland H. Simon. University Park: Pennsylvania State University Press, 1998. 165–73.

Mennell, Stephen. *All Manners of Food. Eating and Taste in England and France from the Middle Ages to the Present*. Oxford: Basil Blackwell, 1985.

Mercier, Louis Sébastien. *Tableau de Paris*. Amsterdam, 1783.

———. *Tableau de Paris*. Ed. Jean-Claude Bonnet. 2 vols. Paris: Mercure de France, 1994 [1788].

Mermet, Gérard. *Francoscopie*. Paris: Larousse, 1985, 1991.

Michelet. *La Mer*. Ed. Jean Borie. Paris: Gallimard [Folio], 1983.

Mintz, Sidney W. "Feeding, Eating, and Grazing: Some Speculations on Modern Food Habits." *Journal of Gastronomy* 7:1 (1993): 46–57.

———. *Tasting Food, Tasting Freedom—Excursions into Eating, Culture, and the Past*. Boston: Beacon Press, 1996.

Mitchell, Yvonne. *Colette: A Taste for Life*. New York: Harcourt, Brace, Jovanovich, 1975.

Monbrun, Estelle. *Meurtre chez Tante Léonie*. Paris: Viviane Hamy, 1994.

Monnier, Adrienne. *The Very Rich Hours of Adrienne Monnier*. Trans. Richard McDougall. New York: Charles Scribner's Sons, 1976.

Montaigne, Michel de. *Oeuvres complètes*. Paris: Éditions Gallimard [Pléiade], 1962.

Montalbán, Manuel Vázquez. *Les Recettes de Carvalho*. Paris: Bourgois, 1996.

Morgan, Lady (Sydney). *France in 1829–30*. 2 vols. 2nd edition. London: Saunders and Otley, 1831.

Muel-Dreyfus, Francine. *Vichy et l'éternel féminin. Contribution à une sociologie politique de l'ordre des corps*. Paris: Seuil, 1996.

"New York-Food Network's." *Multichannel News* 12 July 1999: 66.

Nora, Pierre. *Realms of Memory*. 3 vols. New York: Columbia University Press, 1996–98.

Oliver, Raymond. *La Cuisine: Secrets of Modern French Cooking*. Trans. and Ed. Nika Standen Hazelton with Jack van Bibber. New York: Tudor, 1969.

Ory, Pascal. *1889, L'Expo Universelle*. Paris: Complexe, 1989.

———. "Gastronomie." In *Les Lieux de Mémoire*. Ed. Pierre Nora. Paris: Gallimard [Quarto], 1992. 3: 3743–69.

———. Oyono, Ferdinand. *Le Vieux Nègre et la médaille*. Paris: Editions 10/18, 1956.

Ozouf, Mona. *Women's Words: Essay on French Singularity*. Trans. Jane Marie Todd. Chicago: University of Chicago Press, 1997.

Parinaud, André. *Colette: Mes vérités Archives Sonores*. Institut National de l'Audio-visuel. Cassettes Radio France. 1991.

Pennac, Daniel. *Au bonheur des ogres*. Paris: Gallimard, [Folio], 1985.

———. *La petite marchande de prose*. Paris: Gallimard, [Folio], 1989.

Pépin, Jacques. *Jacques Pépin's Kitchen: Cooking with Claudine*. San Francisco: KQED Books & Tapes, 1996.

Périgord, A.B. de [Horace Raisson]. *Nouvel Almanach des Gourmands servant de guide dans les moyens de faire excellente chère*. Paris: Baudoin Frères, 1825.

Pfirsch, Jean-Vincent. *La Saveur des sociétés. Sociologie des goûts alimentaires en France et en Allemagne*. Rennes: Presses Universitaires de Rennes, 1977.

Phelps, Philip. *Colette's Earthly Paradises: An Autobiography Drawn from Her Lifetime Writings*. New York: Farrar, Strauss, and Giroux, 1966.

Pichois, Claude, and Alain Brunet. *Colette*. Paris: Editions de Fallois, 1999.

Pirenne, Henri. *Histoire de Belgique*. Bruxelles: H. Lamertin, 1973.

Pitte, Jean-Robert. *Gastronomie française: Histoire et géographie d'une passion*. Paris: Fayard, 1991.

———. "Naissance et expansion des restaurants." In *Histoire de l'alimentation*. Ed. Jean-Louis Flandrin and Massimo Montanari. Paris: Fayard, 1997. 765–78.

Ponge, Francis. *Le Parti pris des choses*. Paris: Gallimard, 1942.

Porterfield, Jim. "Pépin's Hands-On Cuisine." *Hemispheres* October 1999: 149.

Proust, Marcel. *By Way of Sainte-Beuve*. Trans. Sylvia Townsend Warner. London: Chatto & Windus, 1958.

———. *Contre Sainte-Beuve*. Paris: Gallimard [Pléiade], 1971.

———. *Du côté de chez Swann*. Paris: Gallimard [Folio], 1987 [1913].

———. *A la recherche du temps perdu*. 4 volumes. Ed. Jean-Yves Tadié. Paris: Gallimard [Pléiade], 1987–.

———. *In Search of Lost Time*. Trans. C.K. Scott Moncrieff and Terence Kilmartin. Revised by D. J. Enright. London: Chatto & Windus and Random House, 1992.

Rabelais, François. *Gargantua*. Paris: Editions Garnier Frères, 1962.

Rearick, Charles. *Pleasures of the Belle Epoque*. New Haven, CT: Yale University Press, 1985.

Revel, Jean-François. *La Sensibilité gastronomique de l'Antiquité à nos jours*. Paris: Éditions Suger, 1985.

————. *Un Festin en paroles: histoire littéraire de la sensibilité gastronomique de l'Antiquité à nos jours*. Paris: Plon, 1995.

Richard, Jean-Pierre. *Proust et le monde sensible*. Paris: Seuil [Points], 1974.

Richardson, Joanna. *Colette*. New York: Franklin Watts, 1984.

Richman, Phyllis C. *The Butter Did it: A Gastronomic Tale of Love and Murder*. New York: Harper Collins, 1997.

Rival, Ned. *Grimod de La Reynière, Le Gourmand Gentilhomme*. Paris: Le Pié Clercs, 1983.

Rouff, Marcel. *Les Devoirs de l'amitié*. Paris: Les Cahiers de Paris, 1926.

————. *Sur le quai Wilson*. Paris: Éditions Émile-Paul Frères, 1926.

————. *La Vie de Chateaubriand*. Paris: Gallimard, 1929.

————. *La Vie et la passion de Dodin-Bouffant gourmet*. Paris: Stock, 1984.

————. *La Vie et la passion de Dodin-Bouffaut gourmet*. Paris: Le Serpent à Plumes, 1994.

San-Antonio (pseudonym of Frédéric Dard). *L'Histoire de France vue par San-Antonio*. Paris: Presses Pocket, 1964.

————. *Viva Bertaga*. Paris: Fleuve noir, 1968.

————. *Champagne pour tout le monde*. Paris: Fleuve noir, 1981.

Sand, George. *Le Compagnon du Tour de France*. Paris: JCM, 1979.

————. *Le Péche de Monsieur Antoine*. Meylan: Aurore, 1982.

Sarde, Michèle. *Colette libre et entravée*. Paris: Stock, 1984

Sartre, Jean-Paul. *L'Être et le néant*. Paris: Gallimard, 1949.

Schehr, Lawrence R. *The Shock of Men: Homosexual Hermeneutics in French Writing*. Stanford, CA: Stanford University Press, 1995.

Schillinger, Liesl. "Ming's Thing: How to Become a Celebrity Chef." *New Yorker* 15 November 1999: 60–67.

Schweighaeuser, Jean-Paul. *Le Roman noir français*. Paris: PUF [Que sais-je?], 1984.

"Scripps Networks Programming to Air in Philippines." *Business Wire* 21 July 1999.

"Scripps October Revenues Increase 8.7 Percent." *PR Newswire* 8 November 1999.

Simenon, Georges. *Maigret se fâche, La pipe de Maigret*. Paris: Presses de la cité, 1949.

————. *Maigret, Lognon et les gangsters*. Paris: Presses de la cité, 1952.

————. *Maigret et le corps sans tête*. Paris: Presses de la cité, 1955.

————. *Un Échec de Maigret*. Paris: Presses de la cité, 1956.

————. *Maigret et le clochard*. Paris: Presses de la cité, 1963.

Simmel, Georg. "The Sociology of the Meal" [1910]. Trans. M. Symons. *Food and Foodways* 5 (1994): 345–50.

Spang, Rebecca. *The Invention of the Restaurant: Paris and Modern Gastronomic Culture*. Cambridge, MA: Harvard University Press, 2000.

Stern, Jane, and Michael Stern. *American Gourmet: Classic Recipes, Deluxe Delights*,

Flamboyant Favorites, and Swank "Company" Food from the '50's and '60's. New York: Harper Collins, 1991.

Stewart, David. *The PBS Companion: A History of Public Television*. New York: TV Books, 1999.

Stout, Rex. *Murder is Corny*. In *Trio for Blunt Instruments*. New York: Viking Press, 1964.

Strauss, Frédéric. "Miam, miam." *Cahiers du cinéma* (February 1997): 64–65.

Suddaly, E., and P. J. Yarrow. *Lady Morgan in France*. London: 1979.

Sue, Eugène. *Les Sept Péchés capitaux—La Gourmandise*, in *Oeuvres complètes*, vol. LII. Geneva and Paris: Slatkine Reprints, 1992.

Sylvain, Dominique. *Baka!* Paris: Viviane Hamy, 1995.

Teuteberg, Hans-Jurgen, and Jean-Louis Flandrin. "Transformations de la consommation alimentaire." In *Histoire de l'alimentation*. Ed. Jean-Louis Flandrin and Massimo Montanari. Paris: Fayard, 1997. 725–46.

Thiesse, Anne-Marie. *Ils apprenaient la France*. Paris: Éditions des sciences de l'homme, 1997.

Thorne, John (with Matt Lewis Thorne). *Outlaw Cook*. New York: Farrar, Straus, Giroux, 1992.

Thurman, Judith. *Secrets of the Flesh: A Life of Colette*. New York: Alfred A. Knopf, 1999.

Todd, Christopher. *A Century of French Best-Sellers (1890–1990)*. Lewiston, NY: Edwin Mellen Press, 1994.

"Univision Announces Record 1998–1999 Season and May Sweeps." *Business Wire* 21 July 1999.

Van der Meersch, Maxence. *Corps et âmes*. 2 vols. Paris: Albin Michel, 1943.

———. *Pourquoi j'ai écrit* Corps et âmes. Paris: Albin Michel, 1956.

Vandersypen, Ch. *Les Chasseurs-Chasteler et La Brabançonne, 1830–1880*. Bruxelles: Bruylant-Christophe & Cie, Éditeurs, 1880.

Van Dormael, Jaco. "'Nous, on est *brol*.'" In *Belgique toujours grande et belle, Revue de l'Université de Bruxelles*. Ed. Antoine Pickels and Jacques Sojcher. Bruxelles: Editions Complexe, 1998. Vol. 1–2: 491–93.

Van Waerebeek, Ruth (with Maria Robbins). *Everybody Eats Well in Belgium Cookbook*. New York: Workman Publishing, 1996.

Verdaguer, Pierre. "Le héros national et ses dédoublements dans *San-Antonio* et *Astérix*." *French Review* 61 (1988): 605–14.

———. *La Séduction policière: signes de croissance d'un genre réputé mineur*. Birmingham: Summa, 1999.

Viala, Alain. *Naissance de l'écrivain*. Paris: Minuit, 1984.

Vilar, Jean-François. *Les exagérés*. Paris: Seuil, Points, 1989.

Vincendeau, Ginette. "In the Name of the Father: Marcel Pagnol's 'Trilogy': *Marius* (1931), *Fanny* (1932), *César* (1936)." In *French Film: Texts and Contexts*. Ed. Susan Hayward and Ginette Vincendeau. London: Routledge, 1990. 67–75.

Waller, Margaret. "Disembodiment as a Masquerade: Fashion Journalists and Other 'Realist' Observers in Directory Paris." *L'Esprit Créateur* 37:1 (1997): 44–54.

Watson, Rod. "The Public Announcement of Fatality." *Working Papers in Cultural Studies* 4 (1973): 5–20.

Weber, Eugen. *From Peasants into Frenchmen*. Stanford, CA: Stanford University Press, 1976.

"The Week United States: Are We at 500 Channels Yet?" *Time International* 17 May 1993: 15.

Weiss, Allen S. *Flamme et festin: Une poétique de la cuisine*. Paris: Java, 1994.

—————. "The Ideology of the Pot-au-feu." In *Taste, Nostalgia*. Ed. Allen S. Weiss. New York: Lusitania Press, 1997.

Wenfu, Lu. *Vie et passion d'un gastronome chinois*. Trans. A. Curien and Feng Chen. Arles: Éditions Philippe Picquier-Unesco, 1988.

Wheaton, Barbara. *Savoring the Past. The French Kitchen and Table from 1300 to 1789*. Philadelphia: University of Pennsylvania Press, 1983.

Wolfe, Tom. *The Painted Word*. New York: Farrar, Straus and Giroux, 1975.

Xiradakis, Jean-Pierre, and Pierre Leterrier. *Fricassée de meurtres à la bordelaise*. Paris: La Table Ronde, 1994.

Zukin, Sharon. *Landscapes of Power: From Detroit to Disney World*. Berkeley: University of California Press, 1991.

—————. *The Cultures of Cities*. Oxford and Cambridge, MA: Blackwell, 1995.

CONTRIBUTORS

George Bauer was Professor of French at the University of Southern California. He published on Sartre (*Sartre and the Artist*), Duras, and gender studies, and was one of the first to write about connections between food and French literature.

Priscilla Parkhurst Ferguson is Professor of French and Sociology at Columbia University. She has published extensively on food, French culture, revolutionary Paris, and nineteenth-century French literature.

Michael Garval is Assistant Professor of French at North Carolina State University. He has published articles on Balzac and has finished a book on French authors and public monuments.

Francis "Pim" Higginson is Assistant Professor of French at Bryn Mawr College. He works on African Francophone literature and the interrelations among the arts.

Philip Hyman is an internationally known food writer who contributed the historic sections to the recent twenty-two-volume series on French food *L'Inventaire du patrimoine culinaire de la France.*

Brigitte Mahuzier is Associate Professor of French at Bryn Mawr College. She has published articles on Colette, Proust, and gay and lesbian studies, and has been working on the interrelationship between food and literary writing.

Toby Miller is Professor of Cultural Studies and Cultural Policy at New York University. He has published extensively on film and film theory, radio, and other media.

Gerald Prince is Professor of French at the University of Pennsylvania and has published extensively on nineteenth- and twentieth-century French literature. His work includes studies of narratology, Maupassant, Sartre, and stylistics.

Lawrence R. Schehr is Professor of French at the University of Illinois at Urbana-Champaign. He has published numerous books on nineteenth- and twentieth-century French literature and on gay studies.

Naomi Schor is Professor of French at Yale University, and has published numerous books and articles on nineteenth-century French literature, including *Zola's Crowds* and *Reading in Detail*.

Franc Schuerewegen is Professor of French at the University of Antwerp. He has published numerous books and articles on Balzac, Proust, Claude Simon, Verne, and French culture, including *Balzac contre Balzac*.

Marc Smeets is a graduate student at the University of Nijmegen finishing his dissertation on the figuration of food in French decadent literature.

Stéphane Spoiden is Assistant Professor of French at the University of Michigan (Dearborn). He has published on twentieth-century French culture, decadence, and the image of Belgium as a cultural entity.

Dana Strand is Professor of French at Carleton College. She has published on contemporary French literature and culture, with articles on Butor, Colette, and Leila Sebbar.

Pierre Verdaguer is Associate Professor of French at the University of Maryland. He has published books and articles on twentieth-century French literature and culture, and works on French detective fiction.

Allen S. Weiss is the author and editor of over twenty-five volumes. He teaches in the Departments of Performance Studies and Cinema Studies at New York University.

INDEX OF NAMES

INDEX OF CUISINE